Practical Ruby Projects

Ideas for the Eclectic Programmer

Topher Cyll

Practical Ruby Projects: Ideas for the Eclectic Programmer

Copyright © 2008 by Topher Cyll

ISBN-13 (pbk): 978-1-59059-911-2

ISBN-10 (pbk): 1-59059-911-X

ISBN-13 (electronic): 978-1-4302-0470-1

ISBN-10 (electronic): 1-4302-0470-2

Printed and bound in the United States of America 9 8 7 6 5 4 3 2 1

Lead Editors: Chris Mills and Tom Welsh
Technical Reviewer: Ben Matasar
Editorial Board: Steve Anglin, Ewan Buckingham, Tony Campbell, Gary Cornell, Jonathan Gennick, Jason Gilmore, Kevin Goff, Jonathan Hassell, Matthew Moodie, Joseph Ottinger, Jeffrey Pepper, Ben Renow-Clarke, Dominic Shakeshaft, Matt Wade, Tom Welsh
Project Manager: Candace English
Copy Editor: Kim Benbow
Associate Production Director: Kari Brooks-Copony
Production Editor: Laura Esterman
Compositor: Molly Sharp, ContentWorks
Proofreader: Martha Whitt
Indexer: Carol Burbo
Cover Designer: Kurt Krames
Manufacturing Director: Tom Debolski

Distributed to the book trade worldwide by Springer-Verlag New York, Inc., 233 Spring Street, 6th Floor, New York, NY 10013. Phone 1-800-SPRINGER, fax 201-348-4505, e-mail orders-ny@springer-sbm.com, or visit http://www.springeronline.com.

For information on translations, please contact Apress directly at 2855 Telegraph Avenue, Suite 600, Berkeley, CA 94705. Phone 510-549-5930, fax 510-549-5939, e-mail info@apress.com, or visit http://www.apress.com.

The source code for this book is available to readers at http://www.apress.com.

Dedicated to the Author and the Engineer, for all they taught me.

Contents at a Glance

About the Author xv

About the Technical Reviewer xvii

Acknowledgments xix

CHAPTER 1   Introduction 1

CHAPTER 2   Making Music with Ruby 7

CHAPTER 3   Animating Ruby 51

CHAPTER 4   Pocket Change: Simulating Coin Systems with Ruby 93

CHAPTER 5   Turn-Based Strategy in Ruby 119

CHAPTER 6   RubyCocoa 153

CHAPTER 7   Genetic Algorithms in Ruby 197

CHAPTER 8   Implementing Lisp in Ruby 223

CHAPTER 9   Parsing in Ruby 261

INDEX 293

Contents

About the Author xv

About the Technical Reviewer xvii

Acknowledgments xix

■CHAPTER 1   **Introduction** 1

Why Ruby? 1

      The Language. 1

      The Community 2

Why This Book? 2

Getting Set Up 3

Source Code in This Book 4

Your Projects. 5

■CHAPTER 2   **Making Music with Ruby** 7

MIDI: Giving Yourself a Vocabulary 7

Talking C and Making Noise 9

      Sharing Code 10

      Interfacing with Windows Multimedia 12

      Interfacing with CoreMIDI. 16

      Interfacing with ALSA 19

Building a Metronome 22

      Keeping Time 23

      A Working Metronome. 25

      Fixing Your Timer Drift. 26

      Writing the Play Method 26

      Avoiding Too Many Timers 28

Composing 29

      Notation. 29

      Patterns 29

      Playing Songs 33

Tempo Tap 34

Taking Patterns Further 35

Saving Your Music 36

Live Coding 39

Interfaces for Live Coding 40

Improvements for Live Coding 45

Summary 49

■CHAPTER 3 Animating Ruby 51

Scalable Vector Graphics 51

SVG Basics 52

SVG Shapes 52

The Animator 55

Rendering the Animation 57

Registering and Running Callbacks 58

Embedded Ruby Templating 60

Rendering the Frames 61

Binding Objects 62

Wrapping SVG with Objects 64

Drawing One Cube 65

Drawing Many Cubes 67

Domain-Specific Languages 67

Implementing GridDrawer 69

Metaprogramming 71

The Draw Method 73

Deferring Execution 74

Adding Deferred Execution to GridDrawer 76

A Few More Helper Methods 77

Your First Animation 78

Putting the Animations Together 83

ImageMagick 83

iMovie 83

JPGVideo 85

Don't Give Up 86

Spicing It Up 86

Summary 91

■**CHAPTER 4**   **Pocket Change: Simulating Coin Systems with Ruby** 93

Going Shopping 93
How to Make Change 95
  The Greedy Algorithm 95
  Problems with the Greedy Algorithm 96
  Brute Force 96
  Adding the min_by Method 97
  Putting It All Together 98
Dynamic Programming. 99
The Customer. 100
  Memoization 106
  Hash Problems 107
  Paying 109
The ChangeSimulator 110
So How Heavy Are Your Pockets? 111
Replacing a Coin 111
Adding a Coin. 112
Optimal Coins. 113
  Two Coins 114
  Three Coins. 114
  Four Coins. 114
  Beyond. 115
Wizard Money 116
In the Literature 117
Summary 118

■**CHAPTER 5**   **Turn-Based Strategy in Ruby**. 119

A Strategy. 119
An Implementation 121
Building the World Around Us 121
  Starting with Terrain 122
  Implementing Maps with Matrices 122
  Cartography 101 124
  Where Does Terrain Come From? 125
  Representing a Map 128

Meeting Your Heroes 129

The Universal Skeleton 129

Stubbing Out Undefined Classes 132

Representing Units 133

Making Choices 133

Finding Possible Moves 135

Choosing Among Actions 135

Taking Action 136

The Players 139

The Artificial Intelligence Doesn't Seem So Intelligent 142

Writing a Command-Line Player 143

The Game 144

Putting It All Together 150

Summary 152

■CHAPTER 6   **RubyCocoa** 153

The Very Basics 153

Opening a Window 154

Learning Objective-C Basics 155

Calling Objective-C from Ruby 156

Applications and Windows 157

Building a Turn-Based Strategy Game 158

Building a Player Using Cocoa 158

An Odd Way to Do Things 161

Understanding Views, Controls, and Cells 162

Adding a View 163

Displaying Messages 166

Creating a Row of NSButtonCells 167

The Choice Bar 169

Drawing the Map 172

Making Choices 177

Selecting Units from the Map 180

Highlighting Map Locations 180

Handling Clicks 181

Using Image Tiles 184

    PlanetCute to the Rescue 184

    Switching from Colors to Images 185

    Adding Image-Based Tilesets to DinoCocoaPlayer 186

    Fixing the Weirdness 187

Packaging It Up 192

Summary 195

CHAPTER 7   **Genetic Algorithms in Ruby** 197

Simulating Evolution 198

    Implementing the Algorithm 199

    Running the Iterations 200

    What's Required to Be a Genome? 201

    Remembering Winning Solutions 202

Thinking About Encodings 203

    Using Integers As Bit Strings 203

    Playing with Crossover 204

    Modeling Crossover 205

    Uniform Crossover 206

    Point Crossovers 207

Using Mutation 208

    Subclassing Integer 208

    Subclassing BitInt 209

    Wrapping BitInt Return Values 210

Making Change . . . Again! 211

    Choosing an Encoding 212

    Running the Simulation 214

    Looking at the Results 215

Adding Further Improvements 216

    Dealing with Invalid Genomes 216

    Letting Parents Live On 216

    Experimenting with Gray Code 217

    Roulette Selection 219

Summary 221

■CHAPTER 8   **Implementing Lisp in Ruby** 223

Learning Lisp 224
Choosing Your Lisp Data Types 224
Building Cons Cells 224
Saving Values in the Environment 226
Understanding eval and apply 230
  eval 230
  apply 232
  Talking About Special Forms 233
  Finishing eval 233
  Using the Helper Functions Arrayify and Consify 234
Making It Look Like Lisp 235
Choosing Your Primitive Functions 236
Creating an Interpreter Object 238
But What About Special Forms? 240
  Adding quote 240
  Adding define and set! 241
  Adding Conditional Expressions 241
  Adding lambda 242
Implementing Macros 247
  Implementing the let Macro 248
It Just Ain't Lisp Without eval 250
Adding Lexical Macros 251
Interoperating with Ruby 253
  Opening a Window to Ruby 254
  Sending Messages 254
  Making Lisp Lambda Work in Ruby 255
Summary 256

■CHAPTER 9   **Parsing in Ruby** 261

Parsing with Ruby 262
  Understanding Grammars 262
  Recursive Descent Parsing 263
  RParsec 263

Parsing S-Expressions 265

Revisiting S-Expressions 265

Parsing Integers 265

Unit Test Everything 266

Parsing Floats 267

Deciding Between Different Number Types 268

Parsing Symbols with Regular Expressions 268

Parsing Values 270

Parsing Lists and Discarding Return Values 271

Using the Lazy Combinator 272

Parsing Your First S-Expressions to the End of File Marker 273

Quoting in Lisp 274

Parsing String Literals 274

Abstracting String Parsing 276

Putting It to Work 277

Parsing List Comprehensions 278

Making a Plan 278

Creating Abstract Syntax Tree Nodes 279

Reusing Combinators from the Last Parser 280

Parsing the List Comprehension Syntax 281

Testing Your Partial Implementation 282

Parsing Method Calls with Dot 282

Eliminating Left Recursion 283

Method Calls in List Comprehensions 285

Running the Comprehensions 286

Adding Some Convenience 288

Abusing Ruby Bindings 289

Summary 290

■INDEX 293

About the Author

TOPHER CYLL is a software engineer and writer living in Cambridge, Massachusetts. He received his bachelor's degree in computer science from Williams College and works for a small Boston-area startup.

In reverse alphabetical order, he finds programming languages, music, Free Software, education, bioengineering, and beer terribly exciting.

Topher loves Ruby not only for the language itself, but also for the light-hearted and intellectually curious community that surrounds it.

About the Technical Reviewer

 **BEN MATASAR** is a developer at Smallthought Systems, where he works on Dabble DB, an online database written from scratch in Squeak Smalltalk. He considers himself lucky because he is able to make a living writing mostly Smalltalk and Ruby. He earned a B.S. in Electrical Engineering and Computer Science from the University of California at Berkeley, and is a political activist in his home state of Oregon. He bounces between Portland, Oregon, and Vancouver, British Columbia.

Acknowledgments

Thanks go to the wonderful Apress team and all my editors.

I'm grateful to Ben Matasar and Adam Bouhengal for brainstorming and listening to my ideas with a critical ear. Thanks to the hackers on the Intel Oregon CPU Architecture Team and to the sharp minds at Adverplex for their support and enthusiasm. Special thanks to the eclectic programmers of the Portland Ruby Brigade for showing me the curious excitement of Ruby.

Additional thanks to my family, friends, and roommates for cutting me a year's worth of slack. I owe you!

■ ■ ■

CHAPTER 1

Introduction

This book is titled *Practical Ruby Projects*. And let me start by saying that the projects *are* practical. But they might not be quite what you're used to. Flip through the book. You won't find any references to enterprise deployment. Not a word about business logic. In fact, hard as it is to believe, there's no web programming! But if you exclude those things, what's left? Why, everything else, of course!

Each chapter in this book turns Ruby loose on a new interesting problem or project. They range from creative endeavors to investigative simulations to the exploration of computer programming languages themselves. Ruby is a programming language, but it's also a tool to create, understand, and entertain. This book is all about Ruby.

Why Ruby?

Since this book was written with the assumption that you have a basic knowledge of Ruby, odds are you already know about Ruby's strengths.

The Language

You know that Ruby's blocks are a joy to use. You know how Ruby's programmer-oriented core API can make programming feel effortless. Despite what the popular press some-times says, Ruby isn't the final word in programming languages. But Ruby holds a unique position in the current landscape.

Borrowing from the Smalltalk tradition, Ruby brings a new level of purity to the world of contemporary object-oriented languages that includes Java and Python. It has also brought the concision and utility of Perl to the world of structured development. Finally, it's captured some of the dynamism of Smalltalk and introduced it to the current pro-gramming landscape.

It's a wonderful language for hacking, design, and programming, not to mention an excellent tool for scripting, text-processing, and system administration. Combined with the Ruby on Rails web development buzz, Ruby's future is promising, particularly with progress toward a faster runtime environment.

The Community

I first encountered Ruby in 2004 while working at Intel in Hillsboro, Oregon. The approved higher-level languages were Perl and Ruby. I was a Python programmer at the time and felt a little bit threatened by Ruby's supposed elegance. But I knew Perl well enough to know I was going to want to learn Ruby.

It was an exhilarating experience. In between maintaining legacy Perl modules, I started plowing through the pickaxe book (*Programming Ruby: The Pragmatic Programmer's Guide* by Dave Thomas with Chad Fowler and Andy Hunt [Pragmatic Bookshelf, 2004, 2nd Edition]). And, at some point, I stopped reaching for Python in my personal projects and started turning to Ruby.

That's when I went to my first Portland Ruby Brigade (PDX.rb) meeting. Which brings me to Ruby's second strength: its community. Now, every language community has its own flavor and culture. Maybe it is just because it's a fresh language with the right set of features, but the programmers you meet in the Ruby track at conferences, the hackers at your local Ruby Brigade, and the guy down the hall at work sneaking Ruby into the system all seem to have something in common. They're curious, reflective, and lighthearted, but they're also highly effective programmers. And they're all working on some kind of project. It'll be born of personal interest, but odds are it will be shared—and adopted. That's just the community standard around here!

Why do Rubyists choose Ruby? Probably because it gets their work done. But I suspect that the project culture is part of it. This book was inspired by the amazing Rubyists out there hacking on their own projects and sharing them with the world.

Why This Book?

Whether you maintain a host of Ruby libraries, simply tinker on your own code at night, or are just getting started with Ruby and looking for new ideas, you're part of this select and curious project culture. This book is a collection of ideas that excite me, which are interesting to code and understand on their own. They're also great stepping stones for deeper work or even potential sources of ideas to mine for your projects, not to mention that most of the chapters touch on the strange and interesting corner cases of the Ruby programming language.

Unlike an introductory book, this is a project book, and the chapters are designed to be mostly independent (although a few are complementary). So if a chapter looks good to you, skip right to it! Here's what to expect.

In Chapter 2, you'll use Ruby to play and compose music and briefly discuss live coding music as a performance art. In the process, you'll use Ruby's dynamic linking interface to call directly into C code, letting you build a cross-platform MIDI library that works on Windows, Mac, and Linux.

Chapter 3 focuses on using Ruby to build animations programmatically. You'll use scalable vector graphics (SVG) to describe shapes and pictures that will be rendered into frames and ultimately combined into movies. By the end you'll have a distinctly pro-Ruby animation.

Chapter 4 uses simulation to explore the world of pocket change. Ever wondered if we could make better change and carry fewer coins if we had a different system of denominations? You'll use Ruby to build a simulator to answer that question. In the process, you'll look at how Ruby can help you learn about the world.

Chapter 5 is all about games, turn-based strategy games to be specific. You'll experiment using a very loosely coupled system to model the complex rules of a strategy game and build the core game engine.

In Chapter 6, you'll take the game engine from Chapter 5 and put a beautiful interface on it using RubyCocoa for Mac OS X. You'll learn about Objective-C, Cocoa, runtime bridges, and, of course, do a lot of GUI programming.

Chapter 7 focuses on genetic algorithms. Inspired by the process of evolution, genetic algorithms are an interesting technique for exploring large search spaces when solving problems. You'll cook up an implementation in Ruby and then turn it loose on the coin problem from Chapter 4. It will let you tackle much larger problems than you could previously.

Chapter 8 explores what it is that makes a programming language, while also delving into Lisp. By the end of the chapter, not only will you have your own Lisp interpreter (written in Ruby), but also an improved understanding of both languages! And, of course, you'll have insight into how to build your very own programming language.

Chapter 9 looks at the art of parsing text. This often overlooked skill is an indispensible part of any programmer's toolbox. You'll address it in the context of programming languages (building on Chapter 8) as well as exploring new syntactic ground, but the tricks learned will be applicable to a wide range of everyday text-processing problems.

And as I mentioned, each chapter is designed to be explored on its own, extended for future work, or even mined for ideas related to other original, independent concepts.

Getting Set Up

You're obviously going to need Ruby installed! This book was written using the Ruby 1.8 series. The code was tested on Ruby 1.8.5, but it should work on any 1.8 release. Time will tell how well it bridges the gap to 2.0. (I'm optimistic.)

Ruby is available for most major operating systems from its web site: www.ruby-lang.org/. There are detailed instructions for each platform, but the basic idea is that Windows users should use the installer bundle, Linux users should use their distribution's package manager, and Mac users can choose between an installer or a package manager like MacPorts.

You'll also want RubyGems installed. RubyGems is the convenient system for managing Ruby libraries. Depending on how you installed Ruby, you may or may not have RubyGems already installed. You can easily check by typing the following into irb:

```
require 'rubygems'
```

■**Tip** *irb* is the interactive Ruby environment. Type some Ruby in and see the result. You'll probably need to open a terminal or command prompt, and then type **irb** to launch it.

If you get a LoadError, you'll need to install RubyGems. There are excellent directions available at www.rubygems.org/read/chapter/3.

Once you've installed RubyGems, installing any of the gems mentioned in the following chapters is as simple as typing (at the terminal or command prompt):

```
gem install GEMNAME
```

If you'd like to install all the gems before you start, you can install the midilib, sexp, rparsec, and extensions gems.

Source Code in This Book

Most computer books have some source code kicking around inside their covers. This book has a lot of it. Source code is presented throughout the book in monospaced font. Method definitions are usually written in open class style, so they can be cumulatively executed in an irb session or sequentially added to a file (most of the projects only require a single file for code).

The bundled versions of the source code for each chapter are available online. Each chapter is provided in a separate directory containing multiple versions of the source files moving through time. Each new section of code is successively integrated into each new source file. So while the chapters provide a walk through the code, you can also look at how it all fits together at each step in the process.

While following along in the text, there are a few helpful conventions to be aware of. In most cases, each line of Ruby code fits on a printable line. However, in a few cases, I have been forced to break lines on the page. You'll recognize this by the ↪ symbol.

This is not to be confused with the transformation symbol ➤. This symbol is used in various sections of imperative code (for demonstration purposes) to show the return value of an evaluated expression. For example:

```
1 + 1 ➤ 2
```

Your Projects

While the ideas in this book are useful and exciting concepts, the best projects always come from your own interests. I hope these projects are engaging and fun, but I also hope they're a place from which to explore.

I'm looking forward to seeing your projects in the Ruby community. Blog, publish, speak—whatever works best. I can't wait to see what you're working on!

CHAPTER 2

■ ■ ■

Making Music with Ruby

In his book *Hackers: Heroes of the Computer Revolution* (Doubleday, 1984), Stephen Levy describes Peter Samson's struggles to get the TX0 to play music. This was in the early days of computing at MIT, and to the right sort of person, the results were astonishing.

In my own life, it wasn't a game that first riveted me to that 286. It wasn't even a programming language. It was the sound of 12 tinny, hard-coded songs bleeping out of a PC speaker.

It can be frustrating to programmers that many modern computer music systems are designed either as full applications or as complete programming languages or environments. There's a shortage of good libraries to get you started making music in your favorite programming languages. Of course, you could do much worse than to learn one of the specialized environments. They're immensely powerful. If you like this chapter, you should definitely have a look at systems like SuperCollider, Impromptu, ChucK, and cmusic.

```
http://supercollider.sourceforge.net/
http://impromptu.moso.com.au/
http://chuck.cs.princeton.edu/
www.crca.ucsd.edu/cmusic/
```

In this chapter, you're going to build a music system from the ground up in Ruby. The goals are (of course) to use Ruby, make getting started easy, and keep it simple enough for users to extend. Music theory is, alas, beyond the scope of this chapter (and I'm not the guy to teach it anyway). But hopefully this will be enough to make you dangerous. You can always learn the rest later.

MIDI: Giving Yourself a Vocabulary

Music is just sound waves, and computer music is no different. But the vocabulary of sounds isn't necessarily the best vocabulary with which to describe or compose music. Directly controlling sound wave synthesis does unlock the full range of musically possibility, but most of the time it's just overwhelming.

Luckily computer music has evolved a vocabulary that closely parallels traditional music notation. Well, sort of. The standard is called Musical Instrument Digital Interface, usually shortened to MIDI. MIDI is a lot of things, including a device specification, a wire protocol, and an abstract software API. It's this abstract API I'll be targeting; in fact, a very small subset of this API is all you need.

I'll use these three basic operations: note on, note off, and program change. Note on starts playing a note, and note off stops playing a note. These operations require a channel number (used to distinguish between instruments), a note number, and a velocity. Each of the 16 MIDI channels belongs to an instrument. The velocity represents how hard a note has been pressed or released and is expressed between 0 and 127.

The note number identifies a specific note and is also expressed between 0 and 127. Although initially, note numbers can be confusing compared to conventional musical notation (A, B, C, D, E, F, and G), they make your job as a programmer much easier. Middle C is note number 60. Each increase in the note number represents a half step up the scale. A difference of 12 represents a whole octave. You can see this relationship visually in Figure 2-1 (make sure to count the black notes as well when measuring the distance).

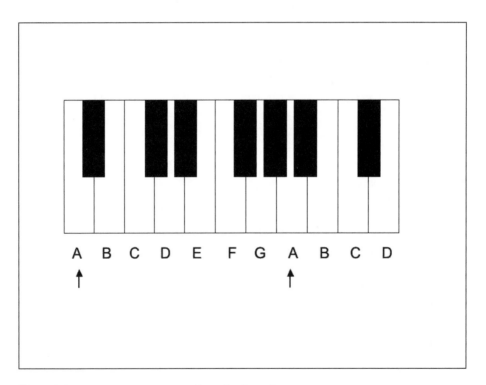

Figure 2-1. *An octave range on a piano keyboard*

To play middle C on your first instrument as hard as possible, you would send a note on message to channel 0, with a note number of 60 and a velocity of 127. Then a short time later, you would send a note off message to channel 0, with a note number of 60 and a velocity of 127. The note off velocity can differ from the note on velocity, of course. Some synthesizers ignore the note off velocity, but to those that use it, it represents how quickly the note has been released.

The other important operation is program change. Most synthesizers support a wide selection of instruments. However, since MIDI only supports 16 channels, not all of these can be active at once. The program change command takes a number for an instrument preset and a number for the channel and binds the instrument to that channel (in fact, 127 turned out to be too few instruments, so an additional mechanism was added, but you can ignore that).

Of course, don't get too attached to MIDI. There are some powerful and impressive sound synthesis systems out there that allow you to take music beyond simple note on, note off instructions. I'll talk a briefly about these systems in the "Summary" section at the end of the chapter, but in the meantime, try not to get too locked in to one way of looking at digital music.

Talking C and Making Noise

Since MIDI is so convenient, let's use it to make some noise. All of the big operating systems provide MIDI support, but you'll need to interface with those system libraries from Ruby. These libraries are typically written in C, and getting Ruby to talk to them can be tricky. Traditionally, the "bindings" between a high-level language like Ruby (which is implemented in C) and lower-level C libraries are written in C.

Using this strategy, you'd write a C file that interfaced and linked with the MIDI libraries. This C file would also use the Ruby C API to expose this functionality to Ruby as objects. This approach is very flexible because you can use the full power of C to interface with the library exactly as it was designed. Unfortunately, it also means dealing with the hassles of writing and compiling C code. Distribution also becomes harder because users of your bindings may need to compile them as well.

Luckily, Ruby provides a *dynamic linking* library to interface directly into C libraries from Ruby! The library is called Ruby DL, and it comes with Ruby right out of the box.

Caution There is a new version of Ruby DL in progress. Version 2 will fix some of the problems associated with the original. However, the code in this chapter is written for version 1 (the version that is bundled with the Ruby 1.8 series).

You're now going to build Ruby MIDI bindings for all three major operating systems (via the Multimedia API for Windows, CoreMIDI for OS X, and the Advanced Linux Sound Architecture [ALSA] for Linux). Each section in the chapter will contain more information about Ruby DL, so you'll probably want to read about all three, not just the section for your particular operating system. All the code in this chapter should go in a file named `music.rb` right up until the end, when you'll add an additional file as well.

Sharing Code

All of these platform-specific MIDI interfaces will share some code. In addition to providing code for its own setup and tear down, you'll require each operating system–specific interface to implement a `message` method. The method will take up to three integers to be turned into a valid MIDI message. Not all MIDI messages can fit in just three bytes. However, the three types of messages you're concerned with do. Note on and note off both require three bytes, while program change only requires two.

The specification of these messages is actually pretty interesting. There are two kinds of MIDI bytes. *Status* bytes always have a 1 in their most significant bit, while *data* bytes always have a 0 in their most significant bit. If you think about a byte as a number (from 0 to 255) instead of simply a set of bits, then numbers 0–127 are interpreted as data bytes and numbers 128–255 are interpreted as status bytes. In turn, status bytes are basically commands.

Every type of status byte takes a corresponding number of data bytes as parameters. You can actually avoid resending the status bytes when repeating messages by simply sending more data bytes, but there's no need to use the feature. Therefore, every message you send will start with a status byte and contain only the data bytes it requires as parameters.

In order to conserve wire bandwidth, the designers of MIDI used another interesting trick (for many commands)—part of the status byte is also used to encode the MIDI channel the command affects! For example, picture this:

```
1001****
```

The four most significant bytes encode the status type (note on). The four least significant bytes (marked in the preceding code snippet with asterisks) encode which of the 16 channels will be affected.

Another way to think about this is that the status byte 144 means "note on channel 0," the status byte 145 means "note on channel 1," and so on! Meanwhile "note off channel 0" is represented by 128.

■Caution Being marketed to musicians, MIDI uses terminology that often begins counting at one. Channels and instruments are therefore numbered 1–16 and 1–128, instead of the more natural representations 0–15 and 0–127, which closely match their binary representations. Since we're computer programmers, we'll stick to the latter version. If you ever find yourself with a sound that doesn't seem quite right, check to make sure you're not off by one because of the conversion.

Both note on and note off are then followed by two data bytes. The first encodes the note to play (between 0–127), and the second encodes the velocity. Note on messages with velocities of 0 are also sometimes used to mean note off.

Program change is even simpler because it takes one data byte. However, just like note on and note off, program change encodes a channel in its status byte. Thus the data byte specifies which of the 128 instruments to map to the specified channel.

Given the preceding information, here's the common code all the MIDI interfaces will share.

fiddle

```ruby
require 'dl/import'

class LiveMIDI
  ON  = 0x90
  OFF = 0x80
  PC  = 0xC0

  def initialize
    open
  end

  def note_on(channel, note, velocity=64)
    message(ON | channel, note, velocity)
  end

  def note_off(channel, note, velocity=64)
    message(OFF | channel, note, velocity)
  end

  def program_change(channel, preset)
    message(PC | channel, preset)
  end
end
```

You start by requiring the dl/import module. I'll talk about that more in the next section, "Interfacing with Windows Multimedia." In the meantime, what else do you see? The constants 0x90, 0x80, and 0xC0 are hexadecimal numbers that represent the magic values for note on, note off, and program change for channel 0. You can then use the bitwise or operator to combine them with the channel on the low bits to produce the complete status byte. Note and velocity are passed straight on to message. As you can see, I've also specified a default velocity of 64.

■**Tip** Hexadecimal numbers are in base 16. They use the characters 0, 1, 2, 3, 4, 5, 6, 7, 8 , 9, A, B, C, D, E, and F to represent digits 0 through 15. If you want to see the decimal value of a hex number, type it into `irb` prefixed with a `0x` to let Ruby know it's in hex.

Now you need `open` and `message` methods for each operating system (a `close` method would be nice as well). Because the code for one platform will fail on a different platform, only the code for the current operating system will be loaded. I could have used subclasses here, but because the three sets of code are incompatible, I'll simply use open classes to load them directly into the main `LiveMIDI` class, depending on the operating system.

```ruby
if RUBY_PLATFORM.include?('mswin')
  class LiveMIDI
    # Windows code here
  end
elsif RUBY_PLATFORM.include?('darwin')
  class LiveMIDI
    # Mac code here
  end
elsif RUBY_PLATFORM.include?('linux')
  class LiveMIDI
    # Linux code here
  end
else
  raise "Couldn't find a LiveMIDI implementation for your platform"
end
```

The code throws an exception if it can't find a good match.

Interfacing with Windows Multimedia

You'll start with Windows. The code begins with this unusual piece of Ruby:

```ruby
class LiveMIDI
  module C
    extend DL::Importable
    dlload 'winmm'
  end
end
```

Here's what you're doing. You've reopened the LiveMIDI class using Ruby's open classes. But then you define a module named C inside the class! You usually see this the other way around (classes inside of modules). But this is legal Ruby. In fact, classes can contain both modules and other classes. Not only is this useful from time to time, it makes sense, since Class is a subclass of Module. Once you've opened up this inner module, you extend DL::Importable.

Now is a great time to talk about two of Ruby's weirder keywords: extend and include. Both inject the contents of one module (or class) into another module (or class). extend injects a module's class methods into the target, while include injects a module's instance methods into the target. In this case, you want easy access to DL::Importable's class methods, so you'll use extend to put them in your namespace.

Here's an example of how you call the extern method that you gained access to when you extended DL::Importable.

```
class LiveMIDI
  module C
    extend DL::Importable
    dlload 'winmm'

    extern "int midiOutOpen(HMIDIOUT*, int, int, int, int)"
    extern "int midiOutClose(int)"
    extern "int midiOutShortMsg(int, int)"
  end
end
```

Each call to the extern method is passed a string containing a C function signature. If you've coded C before, these should look familiar. If not, here's the key to deciphering them. The second word is the name of the function. So your first extern call declares the C function midiOutOpen. The first word is the return type of the function. As you can see, midiOutOpen returns an integer. The types of the function's parameters are written inside the parentheses.

The preceding types are not the exact types used in the API. The actual definition uses a variety of custom-defined C types. However, because you'll be ignoring most of the parameters, there's no harm in just pretending they're all int types. You can also ignore the fact that the parameters are technically of the type unsigned int because they will never need to be converted back into Ruby types. Of course, do try to be careful when working with return values.

For the experienced C programmers who know about pointers, let me mention that Ruby DL doesn't really care what type of pointer you are declaring, only that it is a pointer. I've left this definition using the custom type HMIDIOUT, but in most of the rest of the code in this chapter, I've simply written void* for efficiency. If that didn't make any sense, don't worry! You don't need to understand C pointers to get this code working.

So now you have a class that contains a module that's had the extern class method called repeatedly inside it. It turns out that every call has been defining methods in the C module. This lets you write the following:

```ruby
class LiveMIDI
  def open
    @device = DL.malloc(DL.sizeof('I'))
    C.midiOutOpen(@device, -1, 0, 0, 0)
  end
end
```

The cool thing about using a module this way is that not only are the C functions neatly tucked out of the way in the C module inside the class, it's also easy to call them and easy to tell that they are invocations of C functions.

C programmers out there will also recognize the familiar call to malloc in the preceding code. The memory allocate (malloc) function returns the address of a block of memory of the requested size. The programmer can then use the memory however he or she wants.

Notice how you use the DL.sizeof method to get the size of an integer and used that in your request to malloc for memory. Since malloc returns a pointer, and midiOutOpen also takes a pointer (to what is essentially an integer), you can pass @device right into midiOutOpen. The -1 parameter instructs the system to choose the default MIDI device. The other parameters can safely be ignored and passed in 0 values. To be rigorous, you'd need to check the return code of C.midiOutOpen to see if the function succeeded. But I think we should play it fast and loose here in order to keep the code short.

You'll also define a close method that will end the class's connection to the MIDI subsystem. If your code is just exiting, there's no need to call the close method because the operating system will handle that situation itself. But having close around means you can shut down and open our MIDI connections as you please.

```ruby
class LiveMIDI
  def close
    C.midiOutClose(@device.ptr.to_i)
  end
end
```

C programmers are probably wondering at this point if you're going to call the free function on the memory you requested to return it to the operating system. The good news is you don't have to! When the Ruby object that represents your allocated memory is garbage collected, the memory will automatically be released. (If you'd like to prevent this happening, use the `free=` accessor to set the clean-up function for that allocation to `nil`.)

All that's left is the `message` method. The API method you'll be using takes a MIDI message as an unsigned four-byte integer. You'll use default arguments to accept up to three, then cram them all into that integer, and Windows will do the work of sending them on to the synthesizer correctly.

```ruby
class LiveMIDI
  def message(one, two=0, three=0)
    message = one + (two << 8) + (three << 16)
    C.midiOutShortMsg(@device.ptr.to_i, message)
  end
end
```

You use the shift operator `<<` to move the two and three bytes over into their appropriate locations inside the 32-bit number, and then add all three together (you could also have used `bitwise or`). Care to try it out all you Windows developers?

```ruby
midi = LiveMIDI.new
midi.note_on(0, 60, 100)
sleep(1)
midi.note_off(0, 60)
sleep(1)
midi.program_change(1, 40)
midi.note_on(1, 60, 100)
sleep(1)
midi.note_off(1, 60)
```

You should hear a nice middle C played on a piano. Then you should hear another middle C on the violin after the code executes a program change to set the second channel's instrument.

■**Note** There are no rules about which instrument numbers correspond to which instrument. There is, however, a standard called General MIDI. When a synthesizer uses the General MIDI instrument layout, you can count on piano being instrument 0 and violin being instrument 40, as well as many other fixed placements.

Now, how would you go about doing the same thing on a Mac?

Interfacing with CoreMIDI

Apple's CoreMIDI subsystem is a little different from the Windows Multimedia API.
For one, while the Multimedia API functions are primarily intended for playing music,
CoreMIDI is intended mostly as a MIDI routing system. Your code will attempt to auto-
connect to a MIDI output, but unless you have a program that accepts and plays MIDI
streams open, you won't hear a sound, no matter what MIDI messages you're sending.
Which is not to say you couldn't use Apple's built-in audio libraries to do things the way
you did in Windows. It's possible to instantiate a Downloadable Sounds (DLS) synthesizer
and send MIDI messages to it directly. In the interest of keeping the code simple, though,
you'll rely on a third-party application to turn our MIDI messages into sounds.

Pete Yandell's excellent SimpleSynth is a free application built upon the DLS synthesizer. You can download it from his web site at http://pete.yandell.com/software/. Run
SimpleSynth now. Your Ruby code will connect automatically and use it to play.

You're going to end up importing more functions than you did in the Windows
example. This is because you have to do a little extra work to auto-connect to an available
MIDI destination (in this case, provided by SimpleSynth).

Don't forget that, although this code is also injected in the LiveMIDI class, because
of the if statement, only one operating system's implementation code will be loaded
and used.

```
class LiveMIDI
  module C
    extend DL::Importable
    dlload '/System/Library/Frameworks/CoreMIDI.framework/Versions/Current/CoreMIDI'

    extern "int MIDIClientCreate(void *, void *, void *, void *)"
    extern "int MIDIClientDispose(void *)"
    extern "int MIDIGetNumberOfDestinations()"
    extern "void * MIDIGetDestination(int)"
    extern "int MIDIOutputPortCreate(void *, void *, void *)"
    extern "void * MIDIPacketListInit(void *)"
    extern "void * MIDIPacketListAdd(void *, int, void *, int, int, int, void *)"
    extern "int MIDISend(void *, void *, void *)"
  end
end
```

Much as in previous code, you have methods to connect and disconnect from the
MIDI subsystem. You also have methods to choose a destination port, as well as create an
output port, build MIDI packet structures, and send MIDI messages.

However, this isn't enough! The MIDIClientCreate function takes a name parameter
but, unfortunately, not a regular C string. Instead, it takes a special CoreFoundation string.

Note Apple's `CoreFoundation` provides a set of data structures and functions for C. They are used by many of Apple's lower-level systems.

So you'll add a second module to your `LiveMIDI` class to contain the required `CoreFoundation` function. You'll call it `CF` for obvious reasons!

```ruby
class LiveMIDI
  module CF
    extend DL::Importable
    dlload '/System/Library/Frameworks/CoreFoundation.framework/Versions/Current/➥
CoreFoundation'

    extern "void * CFStringCreateWithCString (void *, char *, int)"
  end
end
```

This function takes a `CoreFoundation` allocator as its first parameter (thankfully, if you pass in null, it'll just use the default allocator). The `C` string comes next. And, finally, you pass in an integer to describe the encoding of the string (you'll just use 0).

With that out of the way, you can write the `initialize` method:

```ruby
class NoMIDIDestinations < Exception; end

class LiveMIDI
  def open
    client_name = CF.cFStringCreateWithCString(nil, "RubyMIDI", 0)
    @client = DL::PtrData.new(nil)
    C.mIDIClientCreate(client_name, nil, nil, @client.ref);

    port_name = CF.cFStringCreateWithCString(nil, "Output", 0)
    @outport = DL::PtrData.new(nil)
    C.mIDIOutputPortCreate(@client, port_name, @outport.ref);

    num = C.mIDIGetNumberOfDestinations()
    raise NoMIDIDestinations if num < 1
    @destination = C.mIDIGetDestination(0)
  end
end
```

Those function names look pretty funny. It turns out that Ruby DL lowercases the first character of each function in order to make them proper Ruby methods. So `MIDIClientCreate` becomes `mIDIClientCreate`. It looks weird but it's harmless.

The method names the MIDI client, and then creates it. It also names the output port, and then creates it. Finally, it searches for an output destination. If it can't find one, it raises a `NoMIDIDestinations` exception.

In the process, however, it created several instances of the `PtrData` class. These Ruby objects represent pointers. Using the `ref` method, you can pass pointers to these pointers into CoreMIDI functions, and CoreMIDI will set them to point at the appropriate structures.

Because CoreMIDI automatically closes ports when a client closes, the `close` method is a one-liner.

```ruby
class LiveMIDI
  def close
    C.mIDIClientDispose(@client)
  end
end
```

Which brings us to the `message` method. Unfortunately, the `MIDISend` function is more complicated than the function you used on Windows. It takes a *packet list* structure that you'll allocate with `malloc`. You'll allocate a full 256 bytes (an unnecessarily large value, but one that you won't ever overflow with your single message packet lists). The packet can then be initialized with a call to `C.mIDIPacketListInit`.

Once initialized, you can add packets to the list using `C.mIDIPacketListAdd`. That function takes the packet list and size and a pointer to know where to put the next packet. It also takes an optional time value (if you would like the message delivered at a later time). It's fine to pass in `0`, meaning now, but the time is represented as a 64-bit data type. As long as you're on a 32-bit platform, you can get around this using two integer values. You then pass in the number of MIDI bytes you're adding and a pointer to the bytes themselves.

```ruby
class LiveMIDI
  def message(*args)
    format = "C" * args.size
    bytes = args.pack(format).to_ptr
    packet_list = DL.malloc(256)
    packet_ptr  = C.mIDIPacketListInit(packet_list)
    # Pass in two 32 bit 0s for the 64 bit time
    packet_ptr  = C.mIDIPacketListAdd(packet_list, 256, packet_ptr, 0, 0, ➥
args.size, bytes)
    C.mIDISend(@outport, @destination, packet_list)
  end
end
```

The trickiest step here is the usage of pack. The pack method is a standard Ruby Array method. The method contains a list of values that will be encoded into a byte string using the format supplied as an argument. In this case, the format will contain a letter C for each argument passed in.

Tip In Ruby, if you multiply a string by a positive integer, you'll get a new string containing that many repetitions of the original string. A similar trick works on arrays as well!

Since the letter C tells pack to encode the data as an 8-bit character, your arguments will each be encoded into an 8-bit value. The addition here, of course, is that Ruby DL has provided a to_ptr method that returns a DL pointer to allocated memory containing the byte string. You can then use it as you see fit. In this case, pass it in to MIDIPacketListAdd as a raw byte buffer.

Excellent! With SimpleSynth open, let's give it a try, Mac folks.

```
midi = LiveMIDI.new
midi.note_on(0, 60, 100)
sleep(1)
midi.note_off(0, 60)
sleep(1)
midi.program_change(1, 40)
midi.note_on(1, 60, 100)
sleep(1)
midi.note_off(1, 60)
```

All that leaves is Linux!

Interfacing with ALSA

ALSA provides several ways to sequence MIDI events. It provides a higher-level API (the *sequencer* API) that is similar to CoreMIDI. It also provides a lower-level API (the *raw* API) that is similar to the Windows Multimedia system API.

Unfortunately, because of its use of complex C structs and macro functions (which don't exist as runtime functions for Ruby DL to interact with), the higher-level API is a bad fit for Ruby DL. However, you can use a special feature of the raw API to be full citizens in the world of MIDI routing graphs.

Just like the other implementations, you'll start with a module named C.

```ruby
class LiveMIDI
  module C
    extend DL::Importable          Fiddle :: Importer
    dlload 'libasound.so'

    extern "int snd_rawmidi_open(void*, void*, char*, int)"
    extern "int snd_rawmidi_close(void*)"
    extern "int snd_rawmidi_write(void*, void*, int)"
    extern "int snd_rawmidi_drain(void*)"
  end
end
```

The one tricky thing here is that your Linux distribution may not include a symlink from the libasound.so name to the actual version you're running (both typically live in the /usr/lib directory). In this case, you should change the dlload line to specify an exact version or even a full path to the dynamic library.

Writing your initialize and close methods should be old hat by now:

```ruby
class LiveMIDI
  def open
    @output = DL::PtrData.new(nil)
    C.snd_rawmidi_open(nil, @output.ref, "virtual", 0)
  end

  def close
    C.snd_rawmidi_close(@output)
  end
end
```

Notice that you've passed the string "virtual" into the constructor. This tells ALSA to create a sequencer endpoint, even though you're using the raw API.

With the addition of your message method, you're done!

```ruby
class LiveMIDI
  def message(*args)
    format = "C" * args.size
    bytes = args.pack(format).to_ptr
    C.snd_rawmidi_write(@output, bytes, args.size)
    C.snd_rawmidi_drain(@output)
  end
end
```

Again, you can use the pack trick to get the bytes you'd like to write out. But make sure to call snd_rawmidi_drain to flush out your messages.

Now, in order to try this out, you're going to need some assistance. First of all, just as you used SimpleSynth under OS X, you're going to use a program called TiMidity under Linux. Start by installing TiMidity from your distribution's package manager. Then run it with the following options:

```
timidity -iA -B2,8 -Os
```

The -i knob tells TiMidity to read its input from an ALSA sequencer. The -B knob adjusts the buffer to prevent stutters, and the -Os knob tells it to output the generated audio via ALSA.

Next, because you haven't written any connection code, you're going to need to manually connect your Ruby LiveMIDI object's output port to TiMidity's input port. There are a number of utilities to do this, but I recommend qjackctl. Launch it, click the Connect button to open the connections window, and select the MIDI tab. Select TiMidity in the right-hand list. As soon as you launch your script (you'll put a call to the sleep method at the beginning), an entry starting with the word "Client" should appear on the left. Select it and click the Connect button. A line should be drawn between the two of them, and they should now be linked (see Figure 2-2).

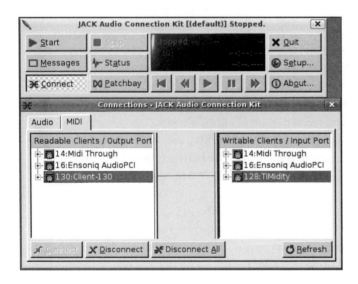

Figure 2-2. *Connecting your ALSA client to TiMidity*

Of course, if you prefer, you may also use the `aconnect` command-line utility that ships with ALSA. Here's the test code:

```
midi = LiveMIDI.new
# Wait for user to connect
sleep(8)
midi.note_on(0, 60, 100)
sleep(1)
midi.note_off(0, 60)
sleep(1)
midi.program_change(1, 40)
midi.note_on(1, 60, 100)
sleep(1)
midi.note_off(1, 60)
puts "Done"
```

And with that, you've built a MIDI interface for all three major operating systems. You've played your first few notes over the speakers. Ready to start your first music project?

Building a Metronome

The first project will be building a metronome. A *metronome* makes a small noise at regular intervals. It's a great tool for developing an internal sense of tempo. Many MIDI systems support the ability to schedule events in time. To keep things simple, none of your wrappers expose this functionality. With that said, if you're going to implement a metronome, you're going to need some kind of timer! And if you want to play music, you're going to need to trigger and release notes at specific times.

First, some definitions. I'm going to use the terms *bang* and *interval* a lot. A bang is a regularly scheduled action, and an interval is the time between bangs. The term bang was popularized by Alex Mclean in his article "Hacking Perl in Nightclubs" (August 31, 2004, www.perl.com).

The interval represents the smallest musical duration in your computer music composition. You could specify intervals directly to your software. However, in the world of music, tempos are often expressed in beats per minute because it's easier to conceptualize. A bang is not necessarily the same as a beat because a bang must be the smallest note resolution, whereas beats are not required to be the smallest note used in a piece. Bangs are not beats, but beats per minute is a useful measure, so I'll use *bangs* per minute instead. If you want 120 quarter note beats per minute and want to use sixteenth notes, you'll need 480 bangs per minute. Dividing 60 seconds by the number of bangs per minute, gives your interval (the time between bangs).

Unfortunately, Ruby isn't good at precise timing. Even ignoring major timing problems like garbage collection, Ruby performance is sometimes erratic. But don't worry too much. You may hear a hiccup occasionally, but provided you have a fast system, this shouldn't be much of a problem. Running your Ruby process with high priority can help too.

Tip On Linux or Mac OS X, prefixing your commands on the terminal with `sudo nice -n -20 . . .` runs them at the highest priority.

Keeping Time

Here's the strategy for doing reasonable sleep/wake timing in Ruby. The Timer class will be initialized with a resolution. This resolution should be significantly smaller than the smallest unit of time you want to measure. So, given the tick duration of 60/480 seconds I just mentioned, you'd divide that by 10 and use that as our resolution. This means that you'll never be off by much more than a 1/10 of a tick. You can increase this number for better resolution at a performance cost.

The Timer class simply provides an at method that schedules a callback for the provided block. Here's an example:

```
timer = Timer.new(0.01)
timer.at(Time.now + 1) { puts "hello" }
```

You give your Timer a 1/100 of a second resolution, and then tell it to puts "hello" one second from now. Here's how it works. In order to prevent a Timer from blocking all execution, you want to put its run loop inside a second Ruby Thread that loops forever, calling sleep when required and regularly calling its private dispatch method.

```
class Timer
  def initialize(resolution)
    @resolution = resolution
    @queue = []

    Thread.new do
      while true
        dispatch
        sleep(@resolution)
      end
    end
  end
end
```

The Timer class's Thread instance starts immediately and runs the private dispatch method that triggers the callbacks. This Thread sleeps for the resolution before running dispatch again. This is repeated forever.

Meanwhile, the dispatch method just checks to see if any scheduled events need to be executed. This busy loop does unnecessary work, but the overall CPU cost is tolerable, and it gets you moderately accurate resolution. The sleep intervals keep the total cost much lower than it would be otherwise.

```ruby
class Timer
  private
  def dispatch
    now = Time.now.to_f
    ready, @queue = @queue.partition{|time, proc|  time <= now }
    ready.each {|time, proc| proc.call(time) }
  end
end
```

The method records the time when it begins. This makes sure that it won't ever accidentally release a later event and not release a previous event because of the delay involved in sequentially checking each scheduled event. It also passes in the time the callback is expected to be called at. I'll talk about why that is in the section titled "Fixing Your Timer Drift."

But what about a method to add an event?

```ruby
class Timer
  public
  def at(time, &block)
    time = time.to_f if time.kind_of?(Time)
    @queue.push [time, block]
  end
end
```

Let's try out that example you wrote before.

```ruby
timer = Timer.new(0.01)
timer.at(Time.now + 1) { puts "hello" }
```

It works! So how do you implement your metronome? Well, the good news is that a metronome is basically a timer with a little bit extra.

A Working Metronome

Here's the actual implementation:

```ruby
class Metronome
  def initialize(bpm)
    @midi = LiveMIDI.new
    @midi.program_change(0, 115)
    @interval = 60.0 / bpm
    @timer = Timer.new(@interval/10)
    now = Time.now.to_f
    register_next_bang(now)
  end

  def register_next_bang(time)
    @timer.at(time) do
      now = Time.now.to_f
      register_next_bang(now + @interval)
      bang
    end
  end

  def bang
    @midi.note_on(0, 84, 100)
    sleep(0.1)
    @midi.note_off(0, 84, 100)
  end
end
```

The class uses the bangs per minute convention. Also note how each time register_next_bang is called, it registers the next callback immediately, and then calls bang. It plays a C two octaves up from middle C, played on channel 0 using the General MIDI woodblock instrument. Want to hear what it sounds like?

```ruby
m = Metronome.new(60)
# Sleep here to keep the program running
sleep(10)
```

If you pass in 120, you'll get 120 bangs per minute, so your metronome will tick every half second. Mostly. It turns out you have a small problem with drift.

Fixing Your Timer Drift

If a particular callback is even a little bit late (and with the way the timing is implemented, this will happen), the next callback time will be calculated from the time the block is triggered instead of when it was supposed to be triggered. This causes the metronome to lag farther and farther behind as time goes on. Each interval still sounds basically the right length, but a program making music using an accurate clock would soon get out of phase with this code. The fix is to stop ignoring the time passed into the callback. If you use that as a base instead of the current time, you can circumvent the drift problem:

```ruby
class Metronome
  def register_next_bang(time)
    @timer.at(time) do |this_time|
      register_next_bang(this_time + @interval)
      bang
    end
  end
end
```

It's going to be a pain, though, if you need to manually sleep after each note_on just so that you can call note_off again. Instead, let's add a play method to the LiveMIDI class that understands durations.

Writing the Play Method

If you're going to manage the timing of note_off messages yourself, you're definitely going to need a Timer. Which means you'll need to pass in beats per minute so you can choose a small enough Timer resolution. You'll need to create this Timer during initialization:

```ruby
class LiveMIDI
  attr_reader :interval
  def initialize(bpm=120)
    @interval = 60.0 / bpm
    @timer = Timer.new(@interval/10)
    open
  end
end
```

The play method needs to take an additional duration parameter. I've decided to insert the duration parameter before velocity, since velocity is the one parameter that it's possible to come up with a good default for. You'll set the default velocity to 100, which is louder than the previous default of 60, but it leaves a little room before you hit the maximum of 127.

```ruby
class LiveMIDI
  def play(channel, note, duration, velocity=100, time=nil)
    on_time = time || Time.now.to_f
    @timer.at(on_time) { note_on(channel, note, velocity) }

    off_time = on_time + duration
    @timer.at(off_time) { note_off(channel, note, velocity) }
  end
end
```

It's obvious why you're using the Timer class for the note_off messages (since you need to defer the note shutoff). But it's not instantly clear why you're scheduling the note_on messages as well. Because timing can be so erratic, it's sometimes advantageous to use *runahead*—by figuring out which notes you'll play and scheduling them ahead of time, you can avoid accidentally taking too long to select the next note when it is supposed to be played. If the time parameter is supplied, the note_on message won't be triggered until then. The note_off time will always be relative to the note_on time.

With the play method finished, you can rewrite your Metronome class's initialize and tick methods to look like this:

```ruby
class Metronome
  def initialize(bpm)
    @midi = LiveMIDI.new(bpm)
    @midi.program_change(0, 115)
    @interval = 60.0 / bpm
    @timer = Timer.new(@interval/10)
    now = Time.now.to_f
    register_next_bang(now)
  end

  def bang
    @midi.play(0, 84, 0.1, Time.now.to_f + 0.2)
  end
end
```

Avoiding Too Many Timers

Hmm, but now you've got an interesting situation. You have two Timer instances running simultaneously (the metronome's and the synthesizer's). This isn't technically wrong, but it increases system load (and therefore the rate of hiccups and timing problems).

You could solve this with an accessor for the LiveMIDI @timer instance variable. Then, inside Metronome, you could schedule events using that timer. But that's an awfully big abstraction violation. More to point, what if you have more than one instance of the LiveMIDI interface running?

Instead, let's modify the Timer class itself. Let's provide a way for everyone to easily share Timer instances. You're going to add a get class method that returns a shared Timer instance when it can (the Singleton design pattern, the most reviled of all patterns).

But wait! What if your Timer instances want to use different intervals? If this code were really fancy, you'd find the least common denominator and then dynamically change the already running Timer's interval. Instead, why not just share Timer instances that use the same interval?

```ruby
class Timer
  def self.get(interval)
    @timers ||= {}
    return @timers[interval] if @timers[interval]
    return @timers[interval] = self.new(interval)
  end
end
```

Timer instances with different intervals won't synchronize their start times using this approach, so that's a great reason to make sure all the Timer instances you use have the same interval (so you only end up creating one).

Your LiveMIDI and Metronome classes can be changed as follows to take advantage of this class method:

```ruby
class LiveMIDI
  def initialize(bpm=120)
    @interval = 60.0 / bpm
    @timer = Timer.get(@interval/10)
    open
  end
end
```

```
class Metronome
  def initialize(bpm)
    @midi = LiveMIDI.new
    @midi.program_change(0, 115)
    @interval = 60.0 / bpm
    @timer = Timer.get(@interval/10)
    now = Time.now.to_f
    register_next_bang(now)
  end
end
```

Now your Ruby has less work to do.

Composing

The bad news is that even though computers are a powerful tool for composition, they can't teach music theory (and neither can I). If you're interested, most community colleges do offer music classes. But even if you aren't an expert, you can still have fun playing with computer music, especially when Ruby's involved!

Notation

Every profession has its own lingo and shorthand representations. Music has a very comprehensive and standard representation. Unfortunately, sheet music is mainly visual. Luckily, a number of people have come up with ways to represent musical notes in plain old ASCII text (of the sort you write code in). The details vary a little, but the idea is the same. You'll build your own system here to make life easier. I'll talk more about what a comprehensive solution might look like in the section titled "Taking Patterns Further," but let's start with a simple pattern system.

Patterns

Patterns use sequential characters to represent events. Patterns are really great for drums, but can be used all over. Consider the following:

```
Kick:  *---**--
Snare: --*---*-
```

You'll hear this pattern in a second, and it should be instantly recognizable from many popular songs. But visually, you also get an immediate understanding of the timing and relationships of the drumbeats. In order to turn them into patterns, you'll need to the take the strings apart. Let's start by breaking them into individual characters:

```ruby
class Pattern
  def parse(string)
    characters = string.split(//)
    no_spaces = characters.grep(/\S/)
    return no_spaces.map do |char|
      case char
        when /-/ then nil
        when /\D/ then 0
        else char.to_i
      end
    end
  end
end
```

A quick demo is in order.

```ruby
p = Pattern.new
p.parse('*--- **--') ➤ [0, nil, nil, nil, 0, 0, nil, nil]
```

What's that final clause doing with char.to_i, though? Consider this example:

```ruby
p.parse('0--- 12–') ➤ [0, nil, nil. nil, 1, 2, nil, nil]
```

What's interesting about this is that the patterns can represent more than just on (*) or off (-). By allowing numbers, you're able to represent notes as well. I'll come back to this in just a few paragraphs, but let's get the Pattern class usable first.

You'll make the parse method private, since it's just a helper for the constructor. The constructor will do little more than save the produced list.

```ruby
class Pattern
  def initialize(base, string)
    @base = base
    @seq = parse(string)
  end
end
```

I'd explain the @base variable, but the next method will do a better job than I can.

```ruby
class Pattern
  def [](index)
    value = @seq[index % @seq.size]
```

```
      return nil if value.nil?
      return @base + value
    end
  end
end
```

Tip Having a method named [ ] lets you index into instances using the same syntax that arrays and hashes use.

Once you've created a sequence, you can index into it and get back one of the numbers in the sequence plus the base you used to create the sequence (nil is kept as nil). This way you can use your simple on/offs to represent the pattern for a single drum in either of these ways:

```
beat_using_symbols = Pattern.new(36, '*--- **--')
beat_using_zeroes = Pattern.new(36, 'O--- OO--')
```

Both represent the same pattern, and as long as they are ultimately played through a channel that is mapped to drums where the 36 is a valid note (for example, the kick drum), you'll get the sound you're looking for. Because you modulo the index by the sequence size, the pattern will repeat as the index increases. Of course, you'd also like to be able to get the length of the pattern.

```
class Pattern
  def size
    return @seq.size
  end
end
```

Patterns are good for more than just drums. The way it's written, patterns can contain more than a single note.

```
Pattern.new(60, '4202 444- 222- 477-') ➤ [4, 2, 0, 2, 4, 4, 4, nil, 2, 2, 2, nil, 4,
7, 7, nil]
```

Recognize that as "Mary Had a Little Lamb"? It looks a little different this way. Of course, you'd really rather not have gaps at the end of the last three measures. You'd rather have those notes on the third beat be half notes and last for two beats instead. If you're willing to sacrifice some simplicity, you can add the concept of durations to the Pattern class.

From now on, your sequences will have a pair at each slot. The first item will be the note number and the second will be the note duration. The durations are expressed in pattern slots, not raw times, since there is no notion of real time inside the `Pattern` class.

```ruby
class Pattern
  def parse(string)
    characters = string.split(//)
    no_spaces = characters.grep(/\S/)
    return build(no_spaces)
  end

  def build(list)
    return [] if list.empty?
    duration = 1 + run_length(list.rest)
    value = case list.first
      when /-|=/ then nil
      when /\D/ then 0
      else list.first.to_i
    end
    return [[value, duration]] + build(list.rest)
  end

  def run_length(list)
    return 0 if list.empty?
    return 0 if list.first != "="
    return 1 + run_length(list.rest)
  end
end
```

Before I talk about the new `parse` method, consider the `rest` method you've used on an `Array` instance. This method isn't part of standard Ruby (even though it nicely complements the `first` method by returning all elements except the first). You'll be using it throughout the book, so keep the following definition somewhere handy:

```ruby
module Enumerable
  def rest
    return [] if empty?
    self[1..-1]
  end
end
```

Defining it inside the `Enumerable` module (where all the common collection methods live) means that any collection type that mixes in `Enumerable` will get the `rest` method for free.

Okay, returning to the new `parse` method. Now notes can be extended by following them with an equal sign (=). This is exclusive (you can't extend a note on top of another note) for clarity. Anyone interpreting the values returned from a pattern will now need to remember to make use of the duration. Here's how'd you write "Mary Had a Little Lamb" now:

```
Pattern.new(60, '4202 444= 222= 000=')
```

Why'd I choose =? No good reason. A period (.) or plus sign (+) might have been good choices, but both already have meanings in conventional music theory, so it seemed better to choose a neutral glyph. You should feel free to use whatever makes the most sense to you.

You'll also need to change the way the [ ] method adds in the base note value:

```ruby
class Pattern
  def [](index)
    value, duration = @seq[index % @seq.size]
    return value, duration if value.nil?
    return @base + value, duration
  end
end
```

Playing Songs

Okay, what do you need to play a pattern out loud?

```ruby
class SongPlayer
  def initialize(player, bpm, pattern)
    @player = player
    @interval = 60.0 / bpm
    @pattern = Pattern.new(60, pattern)
    @timer = Timer.new(@interval / 10)
    @count = 0
    play(Time.now.to_f)
  end

  def play(time)
    note, duration = @pattern[@count]
    @count += 1
    return if @count >= @pattern.size
```

```
      length = @interval * duration - (@interval * 0.10)
      @player.play(0, note, length) unless note.nil?
      @timer.at(time + @interval) {|at| play(at) }
    end
  end
end
```

The class stops playing when it exceeds the length of the pattern; and when it plays notes, it stops them a little before the next note (to help avoid the possibility that a delayed note off message might turn off a note that just started). And the pattern?

```
bpm = 120
midi = LiveMIDI.new(bpm)
SongPlayer.new(midi, bpm, "4202 444= 222= 477=")
sleep(10)
```

Mary's little lamb!

■**Tip** If you're still hearing the woodblock sound from the metronome example, you probably want to reset your MIDI synthesizer (SimpleSynth or TiMidity) or at least change channel 0 back to the piano.

Tempo Tap

An interesting modification to these sorts of patterns (especially if you play a musical instrument and are looking to use the computer for accompaniment) is to play notes every time you "tap" instead of linking the notes to some inexorable timer.

With the right glue, you could use a MIDI keyboard (a piano-like keyboard that sends MIDI messages) or pedals to provide the tap; but you should keep it simple for now and just use the Return key. Every time you tap it, the code will play the next note in the sequence. You don't need to bother with any sort of beats per minute measure, since the user will be providing the tempo himself. Instead, the constructor is parameterized on the length of time to play an activated note (similar, but not quite the same thing).

```
class Tapper
  def initialize(player, length, base, pattern)
    @player = player
    @length = length
    @pattern = Pattern.new(base, pattern)
    @count = 0
  end
```

```
  def run
    while true
      STDIN.gets
      note, duration = @pattern[@count]
      @player.play(0, note, @length * duration) if note
      @count += 1
    end
  end
end
```

Cool, now you can tap along as you play (well, as long as you don't mind putting your keyboard on the floor and stomping on it while you jam on your guitar).

```
midi = LiveMIDI.new(120)
midi.program_change(0, 16)
t = Tapper.new(midi, 0.5, 60, "4202 444= 222= 477=")
t.run
```

Taking Patterns Further

Admittedly, the system you've put together is limited in some ways. It can't represent more than ten half steps, which isn't even a full octave. If you want more flexibility, you'll probably want a space delimited pattern format. Changing your call to split to /\s+/ could switch you over. Since you'd be giving up the use of space as a separator, you could make the single pipe symbol (|) a throwaway character to replace it (this code doesn't work, of course).

```
ep = ExtendedPattern.new(0, "64 62 60 62 | 64 64 64 = | 62 62 62 = | 60 60 60 =")
```

Another feature might be to add the ability to specify notes using the form e4 to represent the fourth octave E. A simple lookup table could do the translation. The defining characteristic of the pattern syntax, though, is that each position represents a unit of the smallest time interval (even though the pattern has no knowledge of the time signature itself). But if you play the "Mary Had a Little Lamb" pattern at 120 bpm, and the smallest notes you use are quarter notes, you can calculate the exact time interval for each pattern position.

Of course, now imagine a piece that uses sixteenth notes. A whole note is going to be a real pain to write each time you need one ("60 = = = = = = = = = = = = = = ="). With some changes to the parser, though, you could add the ability to use duration prefixes. Consider the following mapping:

```
times = {
  's'  => 1,
  'e'  => 2,
  'de' => 3,
  'q'  => 4,
  'dq' => 6,
  'h'  => 8,
  'dh' => 12,
  'w'  => 16,
  'dw' => 24,
}
```

A middle C sixteenth note would be written 's60' or 'sc5' while a whole note would be written 'w60'. A dotted quarter note would be 'dq60'. But what about chords? Obviously, you can just run multiple patterns simultaneously.

```
p1 = ExtendedPattern.new('c5')
p2 = ExtendedPattern.new('e5')
p3 = ExtendedPattern.new('g5')
```

Another way would be to use the + symbol to join notes that should be played simultaneously.

You won't be implementing the ExtendedPattern class in this chapter, but these are all features you might want to consider if the original Pattern class is too constraining and you feel like striking out on your own. This level of control gets you much closer to the level of expression required for complex composition.

Saving Your Music

Accompanying the MIDI music interface is a corresponding file format. The file format looks very similar to the MIDI wire protocol with some extras. But instead of worrying about the details of the format, you'll use the excellent Ruby midilib library. The midilib library can easily be installed from RubyGems with the following command:

```
gem install midilib
```

You're going to implement an alternate class named FileMIDI that you can use instead of the LiveMIDI interface when you want to save your products. FileMIDI will use the classes inside the midilib MIDI module. Your initialize method looks like this:

```ruby
class FileMIDI
  attr_reader :interval

  def initialize(bpm)
    @bpm = bpm
    @interval = 60.0 / bpm

    @base = Time.now.to_f
    @seq = MIDI::Sequence.new

    header_track = MIDI::Track.new(@seq)
    @seq.tracks << header_track
    header_track.events << MIDI::Tempo.new(MIDI::Tempo.bpm_to_mpq(@bpm))

    @tracks = []
    @last = []
  end
end
```

Start by setting up a simple MIDI Sequence that contains one Track. You have to set up the Tempo for that Track and call the super class's initialize method, but unlike the LiveMIDI class, you don't need to instantiate a Timer.

note_off messages don't need to be delivered at their actual time. It's enough to simply write it to midilib's sequence, and it will do the appropriate interleaving. Of course you still won't be able to produce MIDI files faster than real time because of the way timing is handled.

The program_change method is kind of interesting. You create a new Track each time it's called, write out the program_change method to it, add the Track to the Sequence, and then store it in an array indexed by channel. When it comes time to play a note, you can retrieve the right track for the specified channel by looking into the array. All the tracks get written out eventually.

```ruby
class FileMIDI
  def new_track(channel)
    track = MIDILIB::Track.new(@seq)
    @tracks[channel] = track
    @seq.tracks << track
    return track
  end

  def program_change(channel, preset)
    track = new_track(channel)
```

```
      # Bind the preset to channel 0, since each channel has its own track
      track.events << MIDILIB::ProgramChange.new(0, preset, 0)
    end
  end
```

Here's the play method. You'll see the seconds_to_delta method in a second.

```
class FileMIDI
  def channel_track(channel)
    @tracks[channel] || new_track(channel)
  end

  def play(channel, note, duration=1, velocity=100, time=nil)
    time ||= Time.now.to_f
    on_delta = time - (@last[channel] || time)
    off_delta = duration * @interval
    @last[channel] = time
    track = channel_track(channel)
    track.events << MIDILIB::NoteOnEvent.new(0, note, velocity,➡
seconds_to_delta(on_delta))
    track.events << MIDILIB::NoteOffEvent.new(0, note, velocity,➡
seconds_to_delta(off_delta))
  end
end
```

Events are dropped into the tracks with a time delta that describes how long they come after the last event. Wait, but if you're already passing in deltas, what's the seconds_to_delta method doing? Unsurprisingly (given what you've seen so far), MIDI times are represented in a special format. Luckily, using seconds_to_delta converts the floating point seconds delta into a real MIDI time delta.

```
class FileMIDI
  def seconds_to_delta(secs)
    bps = 60.0 / @bpm
    beats = secs / bps
    return @seq.length_to_delta(beats)
  end
end
```

To cap it off, you'll want a save method that writes out a MIDI file:

```
class FileMIDI
  def save(output_filename)
    File.open(output_filename, 'wb') do |file|
      @seq.write(file)
    end
  end
end
```

Let's use the SongPlayer class with the FileMIDI to save a copy of "Mary Had a Little Lamb."

```
bpm = 120
midi = FileMIDI.new(bpm)
SongPlayer.new(midi, bpm, "4202 444= 222= 477=")
sleep(10)
midi.save("mary.mid")
```

Okay, so sleeping until it's time to call save is a little silly, but it works. Try playing mary.mid with your computer's MIDI player.

Ahead-of-time composition is not the only way to make computer music. The rest of this chapter is dedicated to a (regrettably brief) tour of some of the more avant-garde applications of computer music, including live coding.

Live Coding

Live coding is computer programming as a performance art. Typical performances involve the live synthesis of music or visuals for an audience. If that sounds strange to you, just wait until you see it!

Of course, historically, there is nothing odd about live coding. Humans have been doing improvisational art since the beginning. It's only natural that as you build more powerful creative tools, the tools become part of the improvisational process. As the most flexible tool yet created, computers are becoming a common artistic tool. Most live coding is still done by laptop musicians, but coders are also exploring the full range of visual effects made possible by screen projection, as well as audience driven performance art.

The web site TOPLAP has become a hub for many of these artists. According to the front page, TOPLAP stands for "(Temporary|Transnational|Terrestrial|Transdimensional) Organisation for the (Promotion|Proliferation|Permanence|Purity) of Live (Algorithm| Audio|Art|Artistic) Programming." For more information about live coding, you should visit their web site at http://toplap.org and sign up for their mailing list if you are interested.

Interfaces for Live Coding

The first question about live coding is always, What are you going to use for an interface? Some languages, like Impromptu (a Scheme-based audio environment) provide their own live editor that interfaces with the language's run time. Other languages, like ChucK, provide both command-line interfaces as well as advanced Integrated Development Environments (IDEs) with 3D effects and visualization tools for performances.

All you really need, though, is a text editor and the ability to *hot swap* code (replace parts of a running program). You'll be taking this simple approach and building a monitor that watches your source file. Whenever you modify and save the file, the monitor will notice and reload the source. If the load is successful (no syntax errors, etc.), then the new code will be swapped in for the old code.

This approach was described in depth by Alex Mclean in his Perl.com article "Hacking Perl in Nightclubs." His system is more powerful than what you'll be putting together, since he built his own editor that gives his programs the ability to rewrite their own source code. But this system should give you all the power you need for the moment!

Here's an example of what your live code source might look like. Save this to a file named live.rb.

```
bpm(120)
midi = LiveMIDI.new(bpm)
midi.program_change(0, 40)
bang do |b|
  midi.play(0, 60, 1) if b % 2 == 0
end
```

This code will be evaluated using instance_eval, so calls like bpm() are actually method calls on the target object. The bpm method requests that the system trigger 120 times per minute. It's then used on the next line to request the current bangs per minute number.

The most important feature of this code is the bang callback. Every time a new time slice passes, the bang callback is triggered, giving the code a chance to do something. In this example, you play middle C on the violin every other bang. In order to make this work, you're going to need a class to read and execute your source code, as well as a class to manage the callbacks.

The Player class will do the hard work of managing the callbacks. It will support two kinds of callbacks: the standard bang callbacks, as well as close callbacks that are triggered when the player is being unloaded or shutting down. You might as well call the close callbacks *closebacks* to distinguish them. The initialize method will give you a default bpm of 120 and call reset to clear both the callbacks and closebacks.

```ruby
class Player
  attr_reader :tick
  def initialize()
    bpm(120)
    reset
  end

  def reset
    @callbacks = []
    @closebacks = []
  end

  def bpm(beats_per_minute=nil)
    unless beats_per_minute.nil?
      @bpm = beats_per_minute
      @tick = 60.0 / beats_per_minute
    end
    return @bpm
  end
end
```

The bang and close methods let you add callbacks. They'll support adding blocks in the block slot or any object that supports a call passed in as an argument.

```ruby
bang do
  # Play something here
end


bang(object_that_bangs)
```

The methods to implement this along with the methods that trigger these callbacks (and closebacks) look like this:

```ruby
class Player
  def bang(callback1=nil, &callback2)
    @callbacks.push(callback1) if callback1
    @callbacks.push(callback2) if callback2
  end

  def close(closeback1=nil, &closeback2)
    @closebacks.push(closeback1) if closeback1
    @closebacks.push(closeback2) if closeback2
  end
```

```
  def on_bang(b)
    @callbacks.each{|callback| callback.call(b) }
  end

  def on_close
    @closebacks.each{|closeback| closeback.call }
  end
end
```

That's it. But wait, who calls the on_bang method? That responsibility lies with the Monitor class. The monitor is the heart of your live coding system. It is responsible for watching the source code file for changes, loading it into a Player object, and then calling on_bang every tick.

```
class Monitor
  def initialize(filename)
    raise "File doesn't exist" if ! File.exists?(filename)
    raise "Can't read file" if ! File.readable?(filename)

    # Reload timer is independent of other times - every half second should be fine
    @timer = Timer.get(0.5)
    @filename = filename
    @bangs = 0
    @players = [ Player.new() ]

    load
  end
end
```

First you need to make sure the file exists and is readable. Raising String instances is probably fine here (instead of using real exceptions), since this is a top-level module and no one is intended to catch them.

Also note the Monitor keeps the master bang counter in @bangs. This bang counter won't reset when the file changes and a new player is loaded. This is important. If the counter was reset, you would lose your place in the song. The bang counter provides a reference, since all time is measured in bangs, so newly loaded code will evaluate where the old code left off.

You keep a stack of loaded Player objects in @players. This way, if you load code with a syntax error, you can revert to an old Player object. You put a Player instance with no loaded code at the bottom so there is always at least one valid Player.

The load method you call at the end of the initialize method needs to read the code in and call instance_eval on it into a new object on the stack:

```ruby
class Monitor
  def load()
    code = File.open(@filename) {|file| file.read }

    dup = @players.last.dup
    begin
      dup.reset
      dup.instance_eval(code)
      @players.push(dup)
    rescue
      puts "LOAD ERROR: #{$!}"
    end

    @load_time = Time.now.to_i
  end
end
```

In the case of a syntax error, the new Player instance doesn't get pushed onto the stack, so things continue with the old Player object.

How do you know when you need to reload the code? Notice that the monitor kept track of the load time in the preceding code using the @load_time variable. The modified? method compares it to the modified time on the file.

```ruby
class Monitor
  def modified?
    return File.mtime(@filename).to_i > @load_time
  end
end
```

All that's left is to put together the run loop that will manage everything:

```ruby
class Monitor
  def run(now=nil)
    now ||= Time.now.to_f
    load() if modified?

    begin
      @players.last.on_bang(@bangs)
    rescue
      puts "RUN ERROR: #{$!}"
      @players.pop
      retry unless @players.empty?
    end
```

```
      @bangs += 1

      @timer.at(now + @players.last.tick) {|time| run(time) }
    end
  end
```

The now parameter indicates when run is supposed to have been started. Since you probably won't provide this when starting the monitor running, make it optional and set it to the current time if it's nil. Reload the file if it is modified; otherwise, it's time to call on_bang on the player at the top of your @players stack.

As with the load method, you need to be vigilant to make sure an error doesn't kill the entire system. If you get a runtime error, remove this player and try to use the previously loaded Player object. If an error also occurs in that Player object, you'll keep retrying until the stack is empty.

All that's left is to increment @bangs and schedule the next run method with your Timer. Of course, it'd be nice to be able to call a version of the run method that runs forever and prevents Ruby from exiting so that you can live code.

```
class Monitor
  def run_forever
    run
    sleep(10) while true
  end
end
```

Okay, let's look at some live coding examples. Say you start with the following code:

```
require 'music'

bpm(120)
midi = LiveMIDI.new(bpm)
midi.program_change(0, 40)
bang do |b|
  midi.play(0, 60, 1) if b % 2 == 0
end
```

Save it to a file named live.rb. Then run the following command (assuming you've named the file with the rest of your code music.rb):

```
ruby -e "require 'music'; Monitor.new('live.rb').run_forever"
```

Your monitor should load the file, and on every other bang, you'll play middle C over channel 0 to preset 1. Of course, it's a pain to manually manage channel numbers, but there are some small improvements that you can make to express this more naturally.

Improvements for Live Coding

First of all, creating a new LiveMIDI instance each time the file is reloaded is silly. In particular, it can cause problems for your connection-based MIDI systems. So you'd like to reuse instances across reloads. Adding a class method to the LiveMIDI class for reuse and a means for it to change the bpm will let you reuse instances in most cases.

```ruby
class LiveMIDI
  attr_accessor :bpm

  @@singleton = nil
  def self.use(bpm)
    return @@singleton = self.new(bpm) if @@singleton.nil?
    @@singleton.bpm = bpm
    return @@singleton
  end
end
```

What about all the raw channel numbers you've been using? The introduction of a simple proxy class can really improve the readability.

```ruby
class Instrument
  def initialize(midi, channel)
    @midi = midi
    @channel = channel
  end

  def play(*args)
    @midi.play(@channel, *args)
  end
end
```

This would let you rewrite the code like this:

```ruby
bpm(120)
midi = LiveMIDI.use(bpm)
midi.program_change(0, 40)
melody = Instrument.new(midi, 0)
bang do |b|
  melody.play(60, 1) if b % 2 == 0
end
```

But this still isn't as clear as it could be. Let's add a new `instrument` method to `LiveMIDI` and make a few changes to the rest of the infrastructure to support it. Feel free to make similar changes to the `FileMIDI` class to keep them compatible, but it's not required.

```ruby
class LiveMIDI
  def self.use(bpm=120)
    return @@singleton = self.new(bpm) if @@singleton.nil?
    @@singleton.bpm = bpm
    @@singleton.reset
    return @@singleton
  end

  def initialize(bpm=120)
    self.bpm = bpm
    @timer = Timer.get(@interval/10)
    @channel_manager = ChannelManager.new(16)
    open
  end

  def instrument(preset, channel=nil)
    channel = @channel_manager.allocate(channel)
    program_change(channel, preset)
    return Instrument.new(self, channel)
  end

  def reset
    @channel_manager.reset
  end
end
```

This is a big improvement because channels are now automatically allocated, and the `Instrument` object is created inside the method. The `ChannelManager` class is basically just a queue containing the numbers 0 through 15. Each `allocate` call dequeues a channel number. If the channels are released, the channel number goes back on the queue. You don't need to worry about releasing them yourself, though. Just make sure that when the code is reloaded, the `ChannelManager` is reset.

```ruby
class ChannelManager
  def initialize(total)
    @total = total
    reset
  end
```

```
  def reset
    @channels = (0...@total).to_a
  end

  def allocate(channel=nil)
    raise "No channels left to allocate" if @channels.empty?
    return @channels.shift if channel.nil?
    raise "Channel unavailable" unless @channels.include?(channel)
    @channels.delete(channel)
    return channel
  end

  def release(channel)
    @channels.push(channel)
    @channels.sort!
  end
end
```

This extra code lets you rewrite the live coding example as follows:

```
bpm(120)
midi = LiveMIDI.use(bpm)
melody = midi.instrument(40)
bang do |b|
  melody.play(60, 1) if b % 2 == 0
end
```

Okay, you're playing a C on the violin every other bang. Let's add drums using the Pattern class you wrote before. By default, the ChannelManager allocates an arbitrary channel. But it also allows the user to request a channel. This is because General MIDI has a special convention for drums. Channel 10 (what you call channel 9, since you start numbering at 0 like a good computer scientist) is dedicated to drums. Each note represents a different drum sound.

So when you want to use a full drum kit, make sure to specify channel 9. It doesn't even matter which preset instrument you request. Just ask for the right channel.

```
bpm(120)
midi = LiveMIDI.use(bpm)
drums = midi.instrument(0, 9)
pattern = Pattern.new(36, "x--- x-x-")
bang do |b|
  note, duration = pattern[b]
  drums.play(note, duration) if note
end
```

Once again, a little extra work can shorten this up and make your live coding more agile. You add a `pattern` method to the `Instrument` class that creates a `Pattern` instance, and then, rather than returning it, returns a `proc` that can be passed into the `bang` method and called directly!

```ruby
class Instrument
  def pattern(base, string)
    pattern = Pattern.new(base, string)
    interval = midi.interval
    return proc do |b|
      note, duration = pattern[b]
      length = interval * duration - (interval * 0.10)
      play(note, length) if note
    end
  end
end
```

Here's the new version:

```ruby
bpm(120)
midi = LiveMIDI.use(bpm)
drums = midi.instrument(0, 9)
bang drums.pattern(36, "x--- x-x-")
```

If you save your file now, the kick drum pattern plays alongside the violin Cs. Next, let's add the hi-hat and a slightly more complicated melody.

```ruby
bpm(120)
midi = LiveMIDI.use(@bpm)
melody = midi.instrument(40)
drums = midi.instrument(0, 9)
bang melody.pattern(60, "4-00 4==2")
bang drums.pattern(36, "x--- xx--")
bang drums.pattern(40, "--x-")
```

Very cool, huh? I do have one caution, however. Patterns are a great tool and are one of the easiest ways to compose or accompany yourself. But it's only the most basic version of live coding. Many serious live coders strive for their code itself to be art (instead of simply a tool for making art). For this reason, most live coders focus on live coding generative music (music composed by algorithm).

Generative music has fascinated since even before the computer revolution. John Cage is particularly famous for his experimentation with aleatoric music starting in the early 1950s. Aleatoric music is a subtype of generative music. Like generative music, aleatoric music is composed or played through a predefined algorithm; however, in the case of aleatoric music, that algorithm must use a source of randomness to make decisions.

There is a rich tradition to generative music, but it is beyond the scope of this chapter. If you find the idea interesting, please do pursue it further!

Summary

In this chapter, you built a MIDI interface for playing music on all three major computing platforms. You then used this interface to build a metronome, play music, accompany us, and even turn your computer itself into an instrument for live coding. In the process, you mastered the world of dynamic linking interfaces, learned about the MIDI protocol, and worried about some of the implications of time-keeping for music.

Obviously, the world of computer music software is quite large. There are any number of ways to continue your work inside Ruby. There are more ways to interact with your MIDI subsystem, build better pattern systems, and experiment with algorithmic composition. But to really unlock the possibilities, you'll want to interact with external systems.

Perhaps the most interesting standard is called Open Sound Control (OSC). OSC is a simple network protocol for music applications. A whole host of applications support it, including Pure Data (Pd) and SuperCollider. Best of all, there are several modules available to send and receive OSC messages from Ruby including the osc and rubyosc modules. Your operating system's MIDI subsystem also provides access to a whole new class of systems.

And, of course, feel free to combine this project with other projects in the book. Music definitely goes with animation, but it also goes with games, Lisp, and even parsing (as you've seen in the Pattern class). Like all good hobbies, computer music and live coding can be addictive. Consider yourself warned!

CHAPTER 3

■■■

Animating Ruby

Think back to writing your first computer program. If you're from the right era (when BASIC was popular), it probably looked like this.

```
10 PRINT "Hello World!"
```

Or if you were going to be one of those problem programmers, it might have looked something like this.

```
10 PRINT "Hello World!"
20 GOTO 10
```

But do you remember your second program? A lot of folks dove straight into graphics, animation, and art. I still remember mine. It was the classic, randomly colored bubbles demo. It was simple, it was mesmerizing, and it was written in GWBasic.

It's often lamented that modern programming environments make it too hard to get started on programming projects like these. While this is true, some innovations have also made things easier. Thanks to copy and paste, there's no need to painstakingly transcribe BASIC code out of books, and these days tutorials and FAQs are freely available on the Web. But finding an accessible drawing API for your programming language and operating system combination can be difficult. And languages seldom ship with a blessed implementation.

Thankfully, with the right tools under your belt and a little work on your part, Ruby makes animation easy. In this chapter, you'll have a look at creating animations using Ruby, scalable vector graphics (SVG), templating, and coroutines.

Scalable Vector Graphics

Modern operating systems don't let you just poke video memory any more, drawing lines directly to the display. There are some great modern APIs for drawing, but many of them are operating-system specific, and most require building a native code module for Ruby.

Luckily, you don't need one of those drawing frameworks to do your animation. There's an excellent W3C (World Wide Web Consortium) standard called *scalable vector graphics.* SVG is XML based, freely documented, and there are implementations and viewers for all major operating systems (including the popular Firefox web browser). Because lines and shapes are described by XML, SVG can be easily generated from any language with an XML library or even simple text output.

SVG Basics

The basics of SVG are simple. Like XHTML or any other XML document type, SVG images consist of a series of nested tags. Most SVG documents will look something like this:

```
<?xml version="1.0"?>
<!DOCTYPE svg PUBLIC "-//W3C//DTD SVG 1.1//EN"
  "http://www.w3.org/Graphics/SVG/1.1/DTD/svg11.dtd">

<svg width="800" height="800" xmlns="http://www.w3.org/2000/svg" ➥
xmlns:xlink="http://www.w3.org/1999/xlink">

<!--CONTENT WOULD GO HERE -->

</svg>
```

The document begins with a header indicating that it uses XML version 1.0, and then sets the document type to SVG and includes the official SVG document type description (DTD) that can be used to catch simple formatting errors in the image. The actual meat goes between the `<svg>` opening and closing tags. Note that the `<svg>` opening tag puts you inside the SVG namespace and sets the height and width. It also opens up the *XLink* namespace (a separate XML standard that is optionally used by certain SVG features).

Setting the height and width probably isn't exactly like what you're used to in other image formats. Because SVG descriptions are mathematical, SVG images can be grown or shrunk with no loss of clarity or pixilation. So when you set the height and width, you're just defining the units that you'll use inside the SVG canvas (although SVG viewers will respect the outermost height and width attributes at display time).

Since I've chosen 800 by 800, if I define a shape with width 400, it will take up half of the horizontal space. So let's get to the interesting bit and see what you can put inside the `<svg>` tag.

SVG Shapes

Here's the code for a rectangle.

```
<rect x="200" y="200" width="400" height="400" fill="#FF0000" ➥
stroke-width="1" stroke="#000000" />
```

Immediately you'll notice that rectangles have a height and width just like the `<svg>` container node. SVG reuses attribute names whenever possible. The notion of x and y positional attributes should be familiar. The rectangle shown in Figure 3-1 sits right in the middle of the image.

Figure 3-1. *A rectangle defined with SVG*

You can use hex notation to color your images. The `fill` attribute sets the body color, and the `stroke` attribute sets the border color for the rectangle. And finally, the `stroke-width` attribute sets the width of the border to 1.

■**Tip** With hex color notation, the first two digits of the hex number represent the red value (#FF0000), the second two represent the blue value (#00FF00), and the third represents the green (#0000FF). Black contains no red, no green, and no blue (#000000), and white has the full values of all (#FFFFFF). Other colors can be created by varying the values of each color. For example, #FF33CC produces a strange magenta color.

SVG has an enormous number of node types you can use to draw images. A full list can be found in the SVG specifications. The most recent nondraft specification is version 1.1, which is available at `www.w3.org/TR/SVG11/`.

Let's start by looking at a few more interesting node types. For example, polygons are one of the most versatile SVG objects. Polygons can have many of the attributes you're used to, like x, y, height, width, fill, and so forth. But they also introduce a points attribute. The points attribute is a list of x, y pairs that describe the perimeter of the polygon. Here's an example:

```
<polygon fill="#00FF00" stroke="#000000" stroke-width="2" ➥
points="0,0 200,0 300,200 100,200" />
```

Remember, the polygons connect the last point in the list to the first automatically. Figure 3-2 shows what the polygon would look like.

Figure 3-2. *A polygon defined with SVG*

Note Some consider it a questionable design decision that SVG uses a special string formatting convention to encode the points of the polygon. A more native way to do this in XML might have been to use subnodes of type `<point>` that describe the path of the polygon. However, the SVG way is probably easier to write and takes up less space.

If you wanted to embed bitmapped images (or even other SVG images) in your SVG, you could use the `<image>` tag. Nonscalable graphics will be scaled to the best of the viewer's ability if they are presented at a non-native zoom. As with other tags, `<image>` has positional and size attributes. Files are referenced using the XLink standard's `href` attribute (short for *hypertext reference*), which should look familiar to anyone with HTML experience. Of course, because `href` comes from a different XML namespace, you'll need to prefix it with `xlink:` when you use it. This is the reason I opened the XLink namespace in the initial `<svg>` tag. I won't be using this in the simple animations, but if you try your hand at more sophisticated animations after reading this chapter, the `<image>` tag is a boon.

```
<image x="200" y="200" width="100" height="100" xlink:href="other.bmp" />
```

Obviously, these are just some of the basic tags. More sophisticated tags that describe curves (like cubic splines) can be used to create truly breathtaking images like the famous SVG tiger, but they can also be quite complicated.

Well, that's enough of an introduction to SVG to get you started. Let's dive in now with a simple animation.

The Animator

Most of the programs you could use to convert your pictures into animations expect a traditional rasterized image (JPEG seems to be the most popular format). In order to rasterize your pictures, though, you'll need to put together a complete SVG file.

Note A rasterized image consists of a two-dimensional matrix of pixel values. While vector images are represented using abstract concepts like lines or shapes, a rasterized image has been converted solely to pixels.

This file will be the responsibility of the `Animation` class. Animations keep track of the SVG objects that belong to them. When it is time to render a new frame, the animation is responsible for calling the render method on each component and combining the returned SVG into a single image.

In addition, Animation objects will manage and track time increments during the animation. The class will provide a callback system so that programmers can script actions (for example, updating the appearance or location of animated objects).

You'll be able view and debug your SVG images using the excellent Firefox web browser, the Adobe SVG Viewer, or any number of other SVG-compatible applications. Later, when you knit the images into movies, you'll use operating system–specific applications, but there are solutions for Mac, Linux, and Windows.

Let's take this opportunity to dive into the Animation class with the following code:

```
class Animation
  attr_reader :frame, :width, :height, :objects

  def initialize(width, height)
    @width    = width
    @height   = height
    @objects  = []
    @frame    = 0
    @step_callbacks = []
    @at_callbacks = Hash.new {|hash, key| hash[key] = [] }
  end
end
```

I'll initialize the class with a width and a height to specify how big the animation will be. The initializer also prepares other instance variables, including two to store callbacks, one for the frame number, and, most important, a list of objects to dump to SVG in each frame. The frame, height, width, and objects list are all made publicly accessible so that objects in the animation can ask the animator questions about the current frame, dimension, or even their fellow objects during callbacks.

Notice how the @at_callbacks hash table is initialized using a block. This block will be called every time the hash is indexed with a nonexistent key. It gives you a chance to insert a default value into the hash table.

■**Caution** Another popular method for providing hash table defaults is to pass in a default value to the new method like this: Hash.new([]). Think carefully before writing something like that! In the preceding example, the empty array will be returned for nonexistent keys, but the value won't actually be inserted into the hash. What's worse is that all nonexistent keys will return the exact same Array object (so mutations of that one return value affect all others)!

While you're at it, let's take the time to implement an add method that will insert objects into the animation.

```ruby
class Animation
  def add(obj)
    @objects.push(obj)
  end
end
```

But how do you turn these Ruby objects into an animation? You're going to need to create an SVG image for each frame and save them individually.

Rendering the Animation

When you're ready to render the animation, call the `run` method with an output directory and a number of frames to output, which is shown in the following code snippet:

```ruby
animation = Animation.new(800, 800)
animation.run("myfirstanimation", 5)
```

With no objects, this will be a pretty boring animation. You'll get five blank frames. The `run` method's implementation is simple (but only because I've put the hard work in a helper function):

```ruby
class Animation
  def run(dir, frames)
    Dir.mkdir(dir) rescue nil
    digits = frames.to_s.size

    frames.times do |n|
      @frame = n
      file = frame_id(n, digits)
      filename = File.join(dir, file)

      run_callbacks
      render(filename)
    end
  end
end
```

The method begins by creating a directory to save the images in. But if you've run this animation before, the directory will already exist and the `mkdir` method will throw an exception. Putting a `rescue` modifier after `mkdir` prevents the program from stopping if an exception is thrown. Writing it this way is concise because it avoids `begin` and `end` statements as well as several line breaks.

The other thing you need to do (and this may seem silly at first) is to figure out how many digits it will take to represent the number of frames you'll use. So if you're going to render 100 frames, you'll need three digits; therefore, your first frame's file name will be 000.jpg. This is important because a lot of the tools used to turn the individual frames into a movie require the file names to be sorted alphabetically.

By always padding with the needed digits, you ensure that "100" is not sorted before "11" and this will make your life a lot easier in the long run. The frame_id method turns the number and the digits into an appropriately padded string using the sprintf method:

```
class Animation
  def frame_id(frame, digits)
    sprintf("%.#{digits}d", frame)
  end
end
```

Inside the animation loop, setting the @frame instance variable also means that calls to the frame accessor will always return the right value. I want to talk about the run_callbacks and render methods in the next few sections, but here's a quick digression.

Instead of writing your times iterator with a parameter named n, and then storing n in @frame, you could have written it like this:

```
frames.times do |@frames|
. . .
end
```

Code like preceding example is appearing more frequently in the Ruby community. It relies on the fact that closure parameters exist in their parent scope as previously discussed in Chapter 2. I'm occasionally tempted to use this style myself and shorten my code.

Unfortunately, it's often confusing, especially when used on temporary variables (as opposed to the preceding instance variables). More important, the creator of Ruby, Yukihiro Matsumoto (affectionately known to the Ruby world as Matz), has said he'd like to fix this "feature" and have block parameters exist inside their own scope. The change is probably for the best, too, because the current behavior can be quite surprising and sometimes leads to bugs that are difficult to diagnose.

Registering and Running Callbacks

You'll need the ability to run user-specified code at times (to control the animation). It would be simple enough to call a step method on each registered object when the animation advances. But instead, you should embrace the Ruby way and register blocks. The blocks can manipulate, add, or remove objects from the animation.

I'll provide two means of registering blocks as callbacks. The first allows you to trigger an event at a specific time.

```
animation.at(4) { puts animation.frame }
```

This callback will only be called while constructing frame 4, and you can see how it uses the frame method to get the current frame and print it.

The other kind of callback is invoked on every frame change. This doesn't mean these callbacks need to do something every time they wake, but they have the opportunity. The following example prints the number of every frame.

```
animation.step { puts animation.frame}
```

The code for the registration methods is small. Thanks to the auto-initializer block you provided the hash with, it is always safe to assume a location in the hash contains a list.

```
class Animation
  def at(frame, &callback)
    @at_callbacks[frame].push(callback)
  end
end
```

The step callback is almost identical:

```
class Animation
  def step(&callback)
    @step_callbacks.push(callback)
  end
end
```

step just stores the callback in its list. The at method keeps a list of callbacks for each frame in a hash table in order to support multiple callbacks attached to the same frame. Triggering the callbacks is equally simple.

```
class Animation
  def run_callbacks
    @step_callbacks.each{|cb| cb.call }
    @at_callbacks[frame].each {|cb| cb.call }
  end
end
```

Notice how every step callback ever registered is called, but only the current frame's at callbacks are invoked.

So far, the process of rendering the frames themselves has been ignored. Here's where your knowledge of SVG comes in handy. You're going to need to output all the standard SVG headers and footers each time. You could embed these as text fragments and print them before and after everything else. But let's use a single string along with embedded Ruby templating (ERB) instead.

Embedded Ruby Templating

ERB is an elegant Ruby templating language that ships with the standard distribution. Some purists say it gives too much freedom for a templating system (since you can include arbitrary Ruby code), but it's a fantastic tool for combining and arranging text fragments. It's mostly used for HTML templating, so the template tags look a bit like XML, but it's perfectly usable for all types of textual content.

■**Tip** If you've used Ruby on Rails, ERB should look familiar. All those RHTML files you've been writing are actually ERB!

```
require 'erb'
class Animation
  Template = ERB.new(<<-END)
<?xml version="1.0"?>
<!DOCTYPE svg PUBLIC "-//W3C//DTD SVG 20010904//EN" ➥
"http://www.w3.org/TR/2001/REC-SVG-20010904/DTD/svg10.dtd">
<svg width="<%= width %>" height="<%= height %>" xmlns="http://www.w3.org/2000/svg">
<% objects.each do |obj| %>
  <%= obj.render(frame) %>
<% end %>
</svg>
  END
end
```

The Template variable is declared as a class constant (the capital letter it starts with tells you that it's a constant). Although you often see constants used in modules, they are perfectly legal inside classes (Class is a subclass of Module anyway).

Template is initialized with a new ERB template, which is initialized with a HereDoc string (which starts with the funny <<-END statement). HereDoc lets you embed arbitrary text blocks in your code that continue until the end word is encountered (I use END in the preceding example). As you can see, you're even allowed to close your parenthesis before starting the HereDoc on the next line.

Four of the previous lines contain templating directives. Your <svg> tag is templated on both its height and its width.

```
<svg width="<%= width %>" height="<%= height %>" xmlns="http://www.w3.org/2000/svg">
```

The syntax for a text replacement is <%= SOME RUBY EXPRESSION %>. Arbitrary Ruby code can be placed inside the template tag (although often a single variable or method call is sufficient). The result of its evaluation is substituted for the template expression in the final document.

The next three templating lines are a little more sophisticated:

```
<% objects.each do |obj| %>
  <%= obj.render(frame) %>
<% end %>
```

Unlike <%= %> template tags, <% %> tags don't get replaced with their evaluation. Instead, they disappear from the final document entirely. Don't think, however, that this means they have no effect. For example, in the preceding code, you can see how an iteration expression can be put inside these tags, and then a substitution tag can be used between them to repeat its substitution over and over again. <% %> template tags are also extremely useful for conditional expressions:

```
<% if foo %>
  Foo is true.
<% end %>
```

I won't use conditional expressions here, but you can see how they'd be useful. I'll talk more about the process by which these expressions are evaluated and how the final template text result is produced in the following "Binding Objects" section. But first, look at the process by which the SVG is rendered.

Rendering the Frames

The render method is responsible for outputting each frame. You open an SVG file for writing, and then fill it with the results of your template. Finally, you convert the SVG file into a JPEG so you can easily knit the frames into a video, as shown in the following snippet of code:

```
class Animation
  def render(filename)
    File.open("#{filename}.svg", "w") do |file|
      file.write(Template.result(objbinding))
    end
    system("convert #{filename}.svg #{filename}.jpg")
    # Un-comment the next line to delete the intermediate SVG
    # File.unlink("#{filename}.svg")
  end
end
```

ImageMagick's convert utility does the conversion. Convert is able to translate almost any image format into almost any other. There are plenty of other converters that may support different subsets of SVG features. ImageMagick, Apache Batik, rsvg, and the Cairo rendering library all provide programs to perform this conversion. Use whatever is easiest and available for your operating system.

Unless you have problems with ImageMagick on your operating system (or need better SVG support), I recommend it for now. It is available for most platforms at www.imagemagick.org, or it can be installed from a packaging system on Linux (use your distribution's packaging system) or Mac (try MacPorts).

If you'd like to remove the intermediate SVG files, calling File.unlink is simple enough. But what is this objbinding passed into the Template?

Binding Objects

The RDoc (standard Ruby documentation format) page for ERB states that the result method of an ERB instance takes a Binding object. What is a Binding object? If you poke around, you'll notice that the Binding class is documented in the Ruby Core API Documentation. But the documentation is sparse. Binding doesn't support any methods beyond those provided by Object. So what's a Binding object used for?

Binding objects represent the visible scope from some location. They have no methods because they are intended to be opaque. You can capture the current bindings at any time with the binding kernel method.

```
mybinding = binding()
```

This Binding can then be passed to a very few other methods, one of which is eval. Consider this example.

```
def binding_with_foo
  foo = 7
  return binding
end
```

```
bf = binding_with_foo
eval("foo") ➤ NameError: undefined local variable or method 'foo' for main:Object.
eval("foo", bf) ➤ 7
```

So a `Binding` object remembers all the variables you could see at the time it was created. By accepting a `Binding` object, ERB lets you determine in exactly what context your embedded Ruby expressions are evaluated.

■**Tip** The Ruby Extension project, which provides additional useful methods for a variety of core Ruby classes, has several new pure Ruby methods for the `Binding` class that make it less opaque. These include `[]` and `[]=` methods to access inner variables, as well as `defined?`, `eval`, `local_variables`, and the very powerful `of_caller`, which lets you get the bindings of the method that called you. Many of these methods are implemented using `eval` and strings containing Ruby expressions.

You need to be careful where you get your `Binding` objects from. If you simply call the kernel `binding` method when you invoke `results` on the template, both the `filename` and `file` variables would already be defined in the method. In this case, since you use neither name inside your template, no damage would be done. However, in web application templating, this could lead to bugs. You can get a mostly clean environment with the following trick:

```
class Animation
  def objbinding
    return binding
  end
end
```

This method has no arguments and no variables, so it gives you as clean of an environment as possible. You then capture that environment as a binding and pass into ERB. All you need to worry about now is calling one of the object's instance methods by accident. This is easy, unfortunately, because Ruby goes out of its way to make internal method calls look identical to temporary variable accesses. Keeping this in mind can help avoid these mistakes.

Since you have methods to access the animation's height, width, current frame, and contents, you have everything you need to fill in the template.

Wrapping SVG with Objects

You can easily create a thin wrapper to represent the SVGObjects class.

```
class SVGObject
  def initialize(name, attrs={})
    @name = name
    @attrs = attrs
    @contents = []
  end
end
```

The name argument will be the XML node name, and the attrs will be its attributes. Thus SVGObject.new(:rect, :x => 0, :y => 0, :width => 100, :height => 100) becomes <rect x="0" y="0" width="100" height="100">.

Attributes can be read or set using the [ ] and [ ]= methods, and nested objects can be added with the add method.

```
class SVGObject
  def [](key)
    @attrs[key]
  end

  def []=(key, value)
    @attrs[key] = value
  end

  def add(obj)
    @contents.push(obj)
    return self
  end
end
```

And at render time, the render method converts the objects straight into SVG.

```
class SVGObject
  def render(frame)
    attrs = @attrs.map{|k, v| %Q{#{k}="#{v}"} }.join(' ')
    body  = @contents.map{|obj| obj.render(frame) }.join("\n")

    return %Q{<#{@name} #{attrs}>#{body}</#{@name}>}
  end
end
```

Though not strictly necessary, the move_to and move_by methods are convenient ways to manipulate x and y coordinates.

```ruby
class SVGObject
  def move_by(xd, yd)
    raise "Has no coordinates" unless @attrs[:x] && @attrs[:y]

    @attrs[:x] = @attrs[:x] + xd
    @attrs[:y] = @attrs[:y] + yd
    return self
  end

  def move_to(x, y)
    @attrs[:x] = x
    @attrs[:y] = y
    return self
  end
end
```

You can use instances of these SVGObject subclasses anywhere you need simple access to SVG shapes. For example, consider this subclass that draws a rectangle:

```ruby
class Rect < SVGObject
  def initialize(x=0, y=0, width=100, height=100, attrs={})
    attrs[:x] = x
    attrs[:y] = y
    attrs[:width] = width
    attrs[:height] = height
    super(:rect, attrs)
  end
end
```

Of course, SVGObject subclasses can be significantly more complex as well.

Drawing One Cube

Let's use your SVG wrapper to draw a cube, using the special SVG <g> tag to bundle polygons together. You'll be using an isometric view of your cubes. Isometric perspectives are interesting because they let you create recognizably 3D environments without using foreshortening (at a slight cost to accuracy—there is some subtle distortion). This effect works because each edge of the cube is drawn as the same length. It's especially popular in older video games because it simplifies a rendering engine dramatically. In fact, you won't be using exact isometric dimensions, but the numbers should be close enough to preserve the effect (the cube edges will be 25 × 25 × 22.4). You can check this using the following polygon descriptions.

In turn, because of this perspective, some extra math is required to convert your simple grid index x and y values into real SVG coordinate x and y values.

```ruby
class Cube < SVGObject
  def initialize(x, y, z)
    super(:g)
    # 3D coordinates, _not_ SVG coordinates
    @x, @y, @z = x, y, z

    svgx = (x * 20) + (y * -20)
    svgy = (x * 10) + (y * 10) - (z * 20)
    self[:transform] = "translate(#{svgx}, #{svgy})"
    self[:fill]   = "#FEFEFE"
    self[:stroke] = "#000000"
    self[:'stroke-width'] = 1

    add(SVGObject.new(:polygon, :points => "0,10 20,20 40,10 20,0"))
    add(SVGObject.new(:polygon, :points => "0,10 0,35 20,45 20,20"))
    add(SVGObject.new(:polygon, :points => "20,20 20,45 40,35 40,10"))
  end
end
```

Inside the cube you describe three polygons, one for each of the visible faces (see Figure 3-3). By setting attributes like the fill, stroke, and stroke-width in the <g> tag, you change them for the cube faces as well. Most important, you'll use the translate transformation to position the cube at the appropriate geometric position, shifting the cube left, right, up, or down accordingly.

Figure 3-3. *A simple (almost) isomorphic cube*

Drawing Many Cubes

In the following sections, you're going to focus mostly on animating simple geometric shapes. Let's make a pro-Ruby animation you can share with your friends. Heck, you can even put it to music. If you've composed something from the previous chapter, this could be the music video to accompany it.

Timing the video to the music won't be a problem. For example, if the music has 120 BPM, this comes out to two beats per second. If the song had four beats per measure, you have a new downbeat every two seconds, and each new beat is triggered every half second. You just need to make sure the final video frame rate is a ratio of that interval so that you get a frame change on each beat, and if required, you can scale the number of frames up or down as demanded.

Domain-Specific Languages

If you've spent enough time in the Ruby community, you've probably heard more than you intended about domain-specific languages (DSLs). DSLs are a great tool, and since their stunning rise to popularity, they've been getting a lot of press.

Martin Fowler divides DSLs into two categories, internal DSLs and external DSLs. *Internal DSLs* are nothing more than your programming language along with whatever definitions and extensions you've added to make describing your problem domain easiest. Most Ruby DSLs are of this type (although they take a wild joy in stretching poor Ruby's syntax). Lisp DSLs are probably best described as internal DSLs as well, although as you saw in Chapter 2, macros and s-expressions give you extraordinary power to change how the language is evaluated, raising some question here.

External DSLs are also designed for a specific problem domain, but instead of being written in the syntax of the host programming language, they are actually mini-languages that the host language knows how to evaluate.

Frustratingly, you sometimes see DSLs in Ruby code where they don't belong. Often they are used to avoid writing a parser, hijacking Ruby's own syntax. Unfortunately, this technique tends to collapse when stressed. Here is an example DSL you might be tempted to use in Chapter 5 to configure the monsters in your turn-based strategy game:

```
monster "Dragon" do
  hp 10
  attack 7
  defense 0.5
end
```

I love how readable the preceding code is. It could be understood by a novice. It almost looks like it could be written by a novice. But could it actually be? That's a good question. Copying and pasting might be possible, but as soon as you ask the novice to start remembering the format, they'll begin to have questions. For example, what does the word do mean after the monster's name? And why is the name in quotes, when nothing else is? Why do decimal numbers have to start with a leading zero? The answer to all these questions is, of course, because you are using Ruby syntax (even if you're pretending not to).

Or in a worse scenario, let's say a naïve user decides to give the dragon a new attribute:

```
monster "Dragon" do
  hp 10
  attack 7
  defense 0.5
  breathes "FIRE!"
end
```

Assuming the user manages to put FIRE! in quotes, he'll get an undefined method error for breathes. On the other hand, if he accidentally calls a preexisting method, the results can be even more interesting:

```
monster "Dragon" do
  hp 10
  attack 7
  defense 0.5
  chomp knights
end
```

Although that's not the weirdest error he could generate, consider this:

```
monster "Demon" do
  require binding
end
```

With those warnings out of the way, are you ready to commit the same sin? I rationalize it by telling myself that this code is intended for experts only (but do try to feel a little guilty).

An example of the internal DSL you'd like to be able use is written in the GridDrawer.new block:

```
anim = Animation.new(800, 800)
cubes = SVGSorted.new
anim.add(cubes)
```

```
griddrawer = GridDrawer.new(cubes) do
  north(2)
  east(2)
  south(2)
  west(2)
  up(2)
end
anim.step{ griddrawer.step }
anim.run(20)
```

Implementing GridDrawer

GridDrawer performs the same function as an Etch A Sketch, and its core implementation is simple. It is passed a container to which it adds cubes based on the user's commands. You can create a GridDrawer with this container, a set of initial coordinates, and a list of commands like this:

```
griddrawer = GridDrawer.new(cubes, 4, 4, 0) do
  north
  north
  east
  east
  up
end
```

The GridDrawer will populate your cubes container with each executed command. The code block provided to the constructor is the list of commands. The block is instance_evaled on the GridDrawer object, so method calls like north in the block are invoked on the object itself, which is accomplished like this:

```
self.instance_eval(&@block)
```

A first take at implementing the navigation method north follows. This code assumes a draw method that places a cube at the coordinates described by the cube drawer's x, y, and z coordinates.

```
def north
  @y -= 1
  draw
end
```

■**Note** SVG defines 0, 0 to be the top-left corner of the view. These cubes use the same orientation (although a different scale). In the preceding code, north is defined to be the top-right corner of the monitor.

You need to repeat this method stub for each direction: north, south, east, west, up, and down. This scales poorly as you expand the code each of these method shares. For example, if you'd like to able to specify long runs of drawing in a particular direction, it would be nice to be able to write the following:

```
griddrawer = GridDrawer.new(cubes, 4, 4, 0) do
  north(2)
  east(2)
  up
end
```

The change is simple enough:

```
def north(n=1)
  n.times do
    @y -= 1
    draw
  end
end
```

But propagating this code to all the other directional methods is beginning to look a bit tedious. You should immediately look at refactoring the directional methods. If you're willing to move the looping and coordinate arithmetic into draw, you can shorten things down to just this:

```
def north(n=1)
  draw(n, 0, -1, 0)
end
```

You're also going to use directives like northwest to draw a cube one unit north and one unit west. The definition of northwest would look like the following:

```
def northwest(n=1)
  draw(n, -1, -1, 0)
end
```

It might also, of course, be nice to support n for north, nw for northwest, u for up, and so on. You could add each of these definitions, but this will lead to repetition and become frustrating as you add more methods. Luckily, Ruby allows you to move one level up the abstraction hierarchy (beyond what some other languages can do) and write methods to implement other methods.

Metaprogramming

In the pursuit of DRY (don't repeat yourself), you're going to write a class method that will help you define each of these directional methods. Ideally, you'll be able to write something like the following when you're done.

```ruby
class GridDrawer
  def_draw :north, :n, :y => -1
  def_draw :south, :s, :y => +1
  def_draw :west,  :w, :x => -1
  def_draw :east,  :e, :x => +1
  def_draw :down,  :d, :z => -1
  def_draw :up,    :u, :z => +1

  def_draw :northwest, :nw, :y => -1, :x => -1
  def_draw :northeast, :ne, :y => -1, :x => +1
  def_draw :southwest, :sw, :y => +1, :x => -1
  def_draw :southeast, :se, :y => +1, :x => +1
end
```

First though, you'll need to define the def_draw class method on GridDrawer. You need it to be in the source above the location where it's called, and since it is a class method, let's go ahead and just put it at the top of the class definition.

```ruby
class GridDrawer
  protected

  def self.def_draw(*names)
    delta = {}
    delta = names.pop if names.last.kind_of?(Hash)
    delta.default = 0
    x, y, z = delta.values_at(:x, :y, :z)

    names.each do |name|
      self.class_eval("def #{name}(n=1); draw(n, #{x}, #{y}, #{z}); end")
    end
  end

  public
end
```

What's going on here? First of all, notice that def isn't defining an instance method. By prefixing the method name with self, you make the method a class method. In other words, the method exists on the class object GridDrawer itself instead of on the objects created by calling GridDrawer.new. If you wanted to call the class method outside of the GridDrawer, you'd need to write the following.

```
GridDrawer.def_draw(:north, :n, :y => -1)
```

But since this method is for internal use and not really part of the exported API, you make the method protected so that no one will add new drawing methods without at least understanding that you didn't plan for such behavior.

The def_draw method takes a variable list of parameters, which are called names. In fact, though, the last item in the list may not be a name. If it is a hash, then you'll assume it was meant as a group of keyword arguments defining the deltas to move in each direction (x, y, and z). This is a peculiarity of Ruby.

Ruby doesn't have variable keyword arguments, but Matz allowed unenclosed (by braces) hash literals to form a hash when used as part of an argument list. This doesn't work outside of argument lists.

```
:x => -1 ➤ SyntaxError: compile error
```

It does, however, let you emulate variable keyword arguments in a method call. By writing your method this way, you accept a variable number of names, plus an optional and variable set of coordinate deltas specified like keyword arguments. If no deltas are specified, the delta variable will contain an empty hash. Either way, you instruct the hash to provide a default value of 0 if the key is not found, and then unpack the deltas from the hash table for easy use later.

Ultimately, though, the class method needs to dynamically add the methods to its own class. You could use the define_method method, but in this case it will probably be quicker to eval a string that contains the method definition. You can use class_eval here to make sure the definitions you add get added to the class itself. The code generates methods that would look like the following if they weren't defined on one line using semicolons:

```
def north(n=1)
  draw(n, 0, -1, 0)
end
```

By creating a method that generates these other methods, you've reduced the overall length of your app and made further changes quicker (because you don't need to change each method). You now have the ability to write code using your DSL, but you'll need to implement the draw method before it will work.

The Draw Method

You know the draw method needs to take a number of repetitions as well as the x, y, and z deltas to move the pen. You're going to need to move the current coordinates and place a cube once for each repetition. These coordinates will need to be stored in instance variables, so let's start with an initializer for GridDrawer.

```
class GridDrawer
  def initialize(object_class, container, x=0, y=0, z=0, &block)
    @object_class = object_class
    @container = container
    @pen = true
    @x   = x
    @y   = y
    @z   = z

    @block = block
  end
end
```

A new GridDrawer is initialized with two crucial objects. The first is the class of the objects you'll be drawing with (the Cube class, in this case). The second is an instance of a container object that will hold all the instances of the object class. You could have just integrated this code into the GridDrawer, but separating it like this leaves you some flexibility. You can also take optional starting coordinates for your "pen." The last parameter is a block that will eventually be called to make your DSL work. That's more than you need to get draw up and working, so let's have a look at that.

```
class GridDrawer
  def draw(rep=1, xd=0, yd=0, zd=0)
    rep.times do
      @x += xd
      @y += yd
      @z += zd
      @container.add(@object_class.new(@x, @y, @z)) if @pen
      wait
    end
  end
end
```

By giving draw's arguments default values, you let someone add a cube at the current square by calling draw with no parameters.

■**Caution** I've written this so that each cube is placed after the cursor is moved. I also tried writing it so that the cube is placed before the cursor is moved. Both ways ended up confusing me, but moving first seemed more intuitive.

Deferring Execution

In order animate this drawing, a new cube needs to appear in each frame. Without some way to defer execution, the first time you started running code from your DSL, all the cubes in the entire animation would be added, and your first frame would contain all the cubes you were ever going to add. Luckily, deferred execution is within reach. Notice the call to the undefined `wait` method inside `draw`?

You'll be using paused threads in order to pause execution, but continuations (a powerful, if sometimes baffling, language feature that Ruby provides) could also be used. Most programmers will find the thread-based approach easier to understand. Let's start by implementing a class along the lines of Ruby's `Generator` class. If you haven't used the `Generator` class, here's an example:

```
require 'generator'

generator = Generator.new do |g|
  9.times{|n| g.yield(n) }
end
generator.next ➤ 0
generator.next ➤ 1
. . .
generator.next ➤ 8
generator.next ➤ EOFError: no more elements available
```

■**Caution** Don't confuse `g.yield` with the Ruby keyword `yield`. Ruby's `yield` invokes an unnamed block parameter to a method. The generator `yield` defers its execution and returns any parameters it is passed.

The `Generator` class is implemented using continuations, and the source is a great read if you're interested in delving deeper. The deferred execution example will look somewhat similar, except you won't bother returning values when execution is suspended. You'll also `instance_eval` the initialization code block so that method calls are invoked on the object itself. Here's a usage example:

```
sleeper = Sleeper.new do
  puts 1
  sleep
  puts 2
  sleep
  puts 3
end

sleeper.next ➤ 1
sleeper.next ➤ 2
sleeper.next ➤ 3
sleeper.next ➤ nil
sleeper.next ➤ nil
```

See how the `sleep` method refers to the `sleeper` object? How will you implement this? It's actually pretty simple. First of all, your initializer needs to take a block argument and save it in an instance variable like the following:

```
class Sleeper
  def initialize(&block)
    @block = block
  end
end
```

Now, in order to pause execution, you're going to run this block in a new thread. By default, the `sleeper` object starts out asleep, so you won't call it until the first time `next` is called. If it's a successive call and the thread hasn't run out of work to do yet, you can reawaken the thread. For calls after the thread has run out of work, you do nothing. Throwing an exception would also be a reasonable thing to do here, but you'll be using a variant of this code in your animation where the correct response is to remain silent.

```
class Sleeper
  def next
    if ! @thread
      @thread = Thread.new { self.instance_eval(&@block) }
      Thread.pass until @thread.stop?
```

```
    elsif @thread.alive?
      @thread.run
      Thread.pass until @thread.stop?
    end

    return nil
  end
end
```

A new thread is created, and the block is instance_evaled in that thread. The next method then spins loops until the thread has stopped executing. It spins, repeatedly calling Thread.pass. Thread.pass is a class method that tells the current thread of execution to let other threads run instead for a while. A loop like this makes sure you don't waste time running as long as the subthread still has work to do.

The difference on successive calls is simply that the thread already exists, so you simply need to verify that it hasn't ended yet. Provided that it is still alive, you can simply run it and then wait for it to stop. Which brings us to the last bit of code, the sleep method:

```
class Sleeper
  def sleep
    Thread.stop
    return nil
  end
end
```

Thread.stop suspends the current thread, which will cause the next cycle through the spin loop in the next method to find that the subthread has stopped. By using instance_eval, you can call the sleep method from inside the block without needing to pass the sleeper object itself into the closure. Of course, this changes the scope of all method calls inside the block, so it's important to be aware of the change.

The other feature of note is the return statements at the end of both the next and sleep methods. These make sure the last evaluation of the methods is not returned as the result of the method, and that the return value remains nil.

Adding Deferred Execution to GridDrawer

Let's add the functionality of the Sleeper class into the GridDrawer class. You'll call the method that sleeps wait and method that resumes step, but other than that, the code should be mostly the same.

```
class GridDrawer
  def step
    if ! @thread
      @thread = Thread.new { self.instance_eval(&@block) }
      Thread.pass until @thread.stop?
    elsif @thread.alive?
      @thread.run
      Thread.pass until @thread.stop?
    end

    return nil
  end

  def wait
    Thread.stop
    return nil
  end
end
```

This not only provides the missing wait method, but it also evaluates the block using instance_eval so that the block can invoke methods like north, draw, and wait without needing to explicitly reference an object instance.

A Few More Helper Methods

Before finishing up the GridDrawer, let's add just a few more methods. In particular, it'd be nice to be able to move the drawing cursor without leaving a trail. Depending on the circumstances, here are some different methods to help:

```
class GridDrawer
  def pendown
    @pen = true
  end

  def penup
    @pen = false
  end

  def j(x, y, z); jump(x, y, z); end
  def jump(x, y, z)
    @x, @y, @z = x, y, z
  end
```

```
def m(xd, yd, zd); move(xd, yd, zd); end
def move(xd, yd, zd)
  @x += xd
  @y += yd
  @z += zd
end
end
```

You've provided a one-letter shorthand for jump and move as well. You could have done this using Ruby's powerful alias keyword (to actually clone the methods!), but keeping the synonyms powered by method calls means if someone wants to use a subclass or open classes to redefine the main definitions, the synonyms will be automatically changed as well.

Your First Animation

Let's take the GridDrawer out for a test drive and write a very special Ruby message. Here's your code skeleton:

```
anim  = Animation.new(800, 800)
bg    = Rect.new(0, 0, "100%", "100%", :fill => "#CCCCCC")
anim.add(bg)
cubes = SortedSVG.new
anim.add(cubes)

griddrawer = GridDrawer.new(cubes, Cube) do
  # Do something here!
end

anim.step{ griddrawer.step }
anim.step{ puts anim.frame }
anim.last("animation", 20)
```

You create your 800 by 800 animation, give it a neutral gray background using the rectangle class, and create a new SortedSVG container, which you'll use to keep your cubes ordered so that cubes farther "forward" are not drawn behind cubes that are farther back (not having this can lead to some really weird-looking shapes).

The SortedSVG object is a simple SVG <g> container that inherits from SVGObject with its add method overridden to keep the contents sorted in 3D space.

```ruby
class SortedSVG < SVGObject
  def initialize
    super(:g)
  end

  def add(obj)
    @contents.push(obj)
    @contents.sort!
    return self
  end
end
```

Since `SortedSVG` inherits from `SVGObject`, its render method will properly output the `@contents`. You'll also need to make sure the cube objects have a comparison method (sometimes jokingly called the "spaceship operator") that will sort them in 3D order. This ensures that the cubes "behind" other cubes are not accidentally drawn in front of them.

```ruby
class Cube
  attr_reader :x, :y, :z
  def <=>(other)
    return (x + y + z) <=> (other.x + other.y + other.z)
  end
end
```

Now for each frame, advance the `GridDrawer` one step and render the current frame. The animation is 20 frames long, but to save time, use the special `last` convenience method. The `last` method does all the animation steps just like `run`, but instead of rendering every frame, `last` only renders the final frame. For cumulative animations like these, this is a great tool and can save you a lot of rendering time.

```ruby
class Animation
  def last(dir, frames)
    Dir.mkdir(dir) rescue nil
    frames.times do |n|
      @frame = n
      run_callbacks
    end
    render("#{dir}/last")
  end
end
```

But what should the animation be? Let's write a little message.

```
griddrawer = GridDrawer.new(cubes, Cube) do
  move(5, 4, 0)
  draw
  north(6)
  east(2)
  se
  south(2)
  west(2)
  south
  se(2)
end

anim.step{ griddrawer.step }
anim.last("animation", 20)
```

Nice! It's like Etch A Sketch. One cube is added per frame to make the letter R. But this letter R (shown in Figure 3-4) seems like a pretty good candidate for abstraction. So let's subclass GridDrawer into LetterDrawer. That way if you want to use GridDrawer for another project, you won't need to strip the code for drawing letters out.

```
class LetterDrawer < GridDrawer
  def r
    move(0, 6, 0)
    draw
    north(6)
    east(2)
    se
    south(2)
    west(2)
    south
    se(2)
    move(3, -6, 0)
  end
```

Be careful here. You're using single-letter method names, and a few have already been defined (n, s, e, w) for directional navigation. Luckily, however, also provided are full-word method names like north and south, so if you overwrite the single-character versions, you'll still have access. Just make sure none of your code relies on n moving north if you go this route.

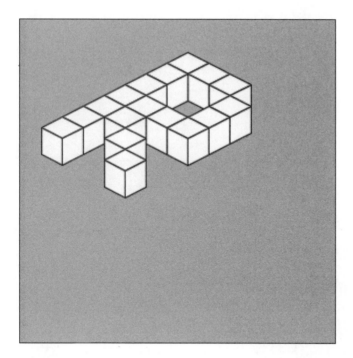

Figure 3-4. *The letter R*

The rest of the letters aren't very interesting, but they can be found in the full source. Let's look at how to initialize LetterDrawer. It's going to take a block just like a GridDrawer (because it is a subclass).

```
letterdrawer = LetterDrawer.new(Cube, cubes) do
  jump(5, -2, 0)
  r
  u
  b
  y

  jump(17, 8, 0)
  r
  u
  l
  e
  s
end
```

If you add in the logic to make this run, you'll be able to see your picture (see Figure 3-5).

```
anim.step{ letterdrawer.step }
anim.step{ puts anim.frame }
anim.last("animation", 132)
```

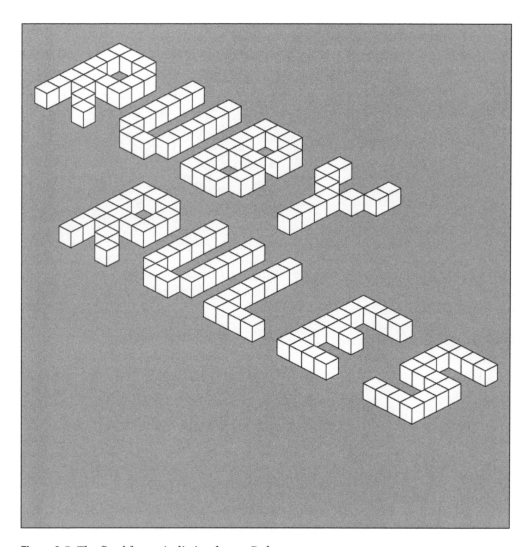

Figure 3-5. *The final frame is distinctly pro-Ruby.*

Pretty slick. Okay, let's make a movie, and then you'll see how you can make things more interesting.

Putting the Animations Together

Your operating system is going to determine how you stitch the images into a movie. There are a variety of tools to do the job, but some are better than others.

ImageMagick

Most of the utilities you'll be using only support JPG inputs. However, ImageMagick, which you've already used to do the SVG to JPG conversion, can obviously understand SVG perfectly. Here's an example of how to go straight from SVG to MPEG1, MPEG2, and AVI video files.

```
convert -delay 25 *.svg ruby.mpg
convert -delay 25 *.svg ruby.m2v
convert -delay 25 *.svg ruby.avi
```

The -delay option tells ImageMagick how long to show each frame. By showing each picture for 25 hundredths of a second, you get a frame rate of four frames per second.

When using these video formats, ImageMagick uses padding frames to get the appropriate frame rate. Using a more animation-oriented format like Multiple-image Network Graphics (MNG) allows ImageMagick to create a much smaller output file, with each frame only being represented once. Of course, MNG isn't supported by web browsers very well. But animated GIFs are!

```
convert -delay 25 *.svg ruby.mng
convert -delay 25 *.svg ruby.gif
```

Just make sure you always use the most up-to-date version of ImageMagick. ImageMagick SVG support is not complete, and the bugs can occasionally cause surprising visuals.

A final word of caution though: putting the video together with ImageMagick is very slow. If one of the following techniques works for you, you should probably go with that.

iMovie

Mac users have a great option for putting their videos together. Uncomment the line in your script that deletes the intermediate SVG files. This will let you easily lasso only the JPG files.

```
File.unlink("#{filename}.svg")
```

Run your program, then drag the JPG files from the Finder into the sources list of iPhoto and create a named photo album for them, as shown in Figure 3-6. When the import completes, retitle the album **Ruby Animation**.

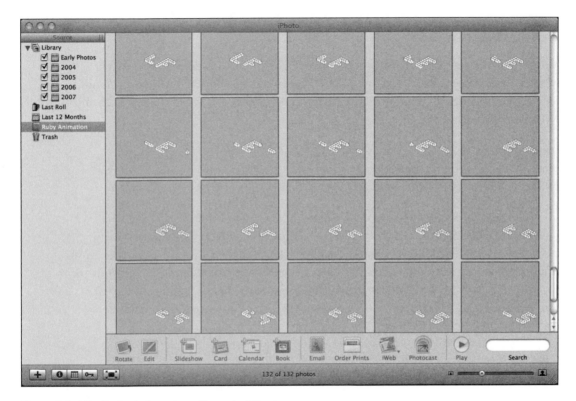

Figure 3-6. *The Ruby Animation album in iPhoto*

From inside iMovie, select the Media tab and the Photos option. Then select the album you just created from the drop-down box. Next, highlight all your images. Show the photo settings, and turn off the Ken Burns effect. Don't forget to set the speed slider (featuring a rabbit and turtle) to your frame length (set it 0:15 for a half second), as shown in Figure 3-7. Finally, click Apply and wait for the video to be rendered.

Now you can add audio tracks if you want by selecting Audio and then dragging songs down into one of the unused tracks.

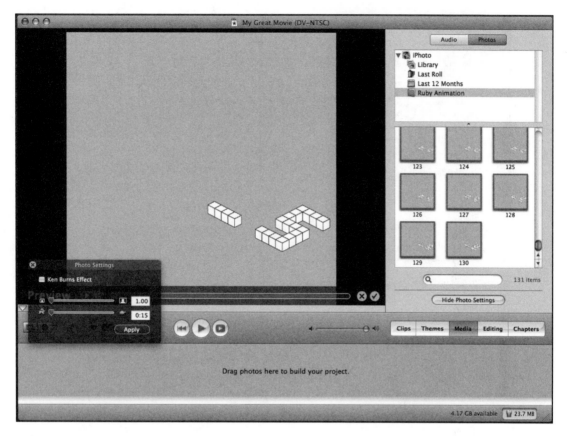

Figure 3-7. *Combining the frames in iMovie*

JPGVideo

On Windows, I found a tool called JPGVideo that can do the trick. Unfortunately, it is picky about input image formats. It demands 32-bit color depth and a nonindexed colorspace mode. You can download JPGVideo from the following web site: www.ndrw.co.uk/free/jpgvideo/

I found using the following ImageMagick convert command in the render method was enough to get JPGVideo working.

```
system("convert #{filename}.svg -colorspace HSL #{filename}.jpg")
```

Make sure the intermediate SVG files are deleted.

```
File.unlink("#{filename}.svg")
```

Click Configure to select your animation output directory, and then name your video. Click OK for the final rendering. There's a sample configuration in Figure 3-8.

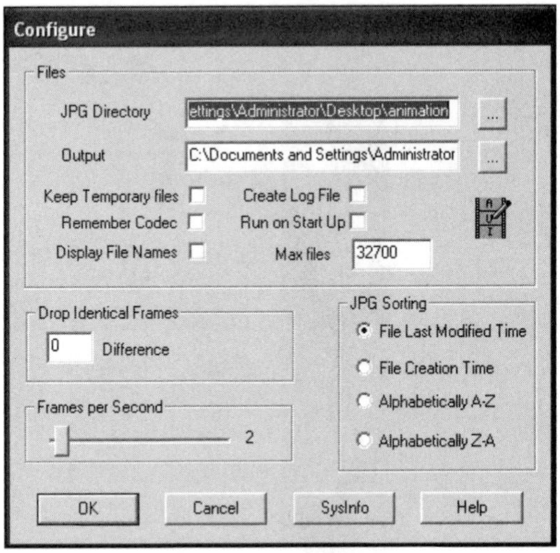

Figure 3-8. *JPGVideo configuration*

Don't Give Up

If none of these options works for you, don't give up. There are plenty of other software programs for putting these sorts of animations together. You should almost certainly be able to find one that works for you.

Spicing It Up

From here on out, the sky is the limit. It's up to your creative desires. For example, if you wanted to give your cube writing some depth, it's as simple as making the following change (pictured in Figure 3-9):

```
letterdrawer = LetterDrawer.new(cubes) do
  3.times do |z|
    jump(5, -2, z)
    r
    u
    b
    y
```

```
    jump(17, 8, z)
      r
      u
      l
      e
      s
    end
  end
end
```

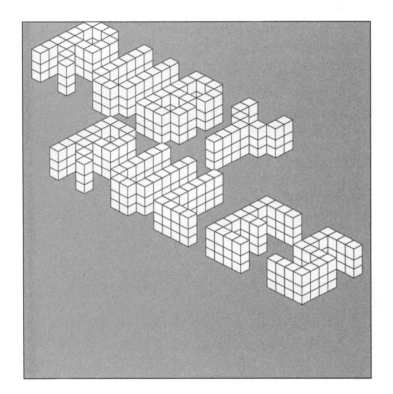

Figure 3-9. *Triple-high letters*

Or what if you want to make the drawing mechanism work the same as in the game Centipede, where only a certain number of cubes are ever drawn at any given time while moving through the animation? The SortedSVG structure seems like a good place to start. Let's make a new FixedSizeSortedSVG subclass. You still need to make sure to print your cubes in the proper 3D order, but you also need to keep around the order they were added to the structure so you can evict objects at the right time. Here's the code:

```ruby
class FixedSizeSortedSVG < SVGObject
  def initialize(size)
    super(:g)
    @size = size
    @fifo = []
  end

  def add(obj)
    @fifo.push(obj)
    @fifo.shift while @fifo.size > @size
    @contents = @fifo.sort
  end
end
```

Initialize the `FixedSizeSortedSVG` object with a size, and keep an FIFO (First In, First Out) queue around. Each time an object is added that would push over the size, you'll remove the oldest object from the list. But of course, if you want your `@contents` rendering to work, you'll need to make sure that `@contents` is always stored in 3D order; so use the sort method, which both orders the objects from the FIFO and makes a new copy of the list that you'll store in `@contents`.

```ruby
cubes = FixedSizeSortedSVG.new(20)
```

A snapshot of the results can be seen in Figures 3-10 through 3-12.

Figure 3-10. *Near the beginning of the animation*

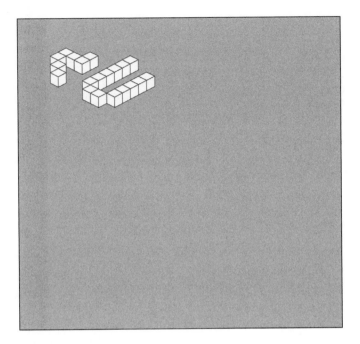

Figure 3-11. *Later on*

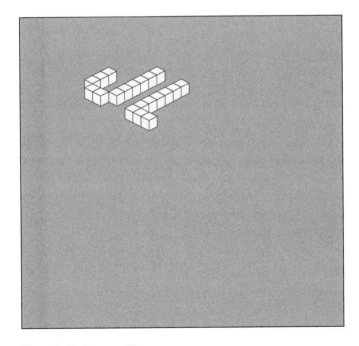

Figure 3-12. *Later still*

Okay, pretty cool, but let's put it in time with the music from Chapter 1. I like this Centipede version, but since there's a beat to match up with here, let's also have all the cubes visible every four beats. Once again, all it takes is a tweak to the cube storage class.

```ruby
class BeatSortedSVG < SVGObject
  def initialize(beats, size)
    super(:g)
    @size  = size
    @beats = beats
    @count = 0
    @all   = []
  end

  def add(obj)
    @all.push(obj)
    setup_contents
  end

  def step
    @count = (@count + 1) % @beats
    setup_contents
  end

  private
  def setup_contents
    if @count == 0 || @all.size < @size
      @contents = @all.sort
    else
      @contents = @all[-@size..-1].sort
    end
  end
end
```

And sure enough, now everything you've drawn is visible on the pulse beats, but the rest of the time it just looks like the Centipede version.

```ruby
cubes = BeatSortedSVG.new(4, 20)
anim.step{ cubes.step }
```

Summary

SVG images are really quite powerful. With nothing more than simple string manipulation, you built a Ruby animation framework. And with tricks like domain-specific languages and deferred execution, you've made something that is quite pleasant to use and script.

Of course, there are always more places to take the project. Once you've put your animation to music, you might want to try experimenting with colors! Remember, you can vary colors over time if you do it right. For example, see if you can make the cubes at the end of the Centipede-style cube chain gradually fade out instead of abruptly disappearing.

There's also a lot to be done using movement. What if the writing pulsed on the downbeat and jumped into the air? Or the writing exploded apart at the very end?

And, of course, if you find this sort of thing interesting, the next obvious step is to experiment with animated characters. Using the SVG `<image>` tag is a great way to add moving sprites and lush backgrounds. Or you could imagine coding a Ruby object that uses ERB templating to let you control how wide an SVG-drawn character's mouth is. From professional data visualization to cartoons in the style of Why The Lucky Stiff's *The Least Surprised*, the options are really limitless.

CHAPTER 4

■■■

Pocket Change: Simulating Coin Systems with Ruby

A lot of software today is written to help us *perform* tasks. But there exists an often unseen subcategory of software dedicated to the simple task of better *understanding* the world we live in.

Computer simulation is the art of building software models of real processes in order to learn more about them. It's a powerful tool for asking and answering questions, and it's used by scientists and engineers around the globe.

Scientific computing simulations are often written in fast execution languages like C or Fortran. Physicists simulating particles might require every ounce of computer power their machines have. But not all problems require this level of performance. In many cases, the trade-off between slower execution performance but faster development time can make higher-level languages like Ruby very compelling simulation tools.

Indeed, object-oriented programming languages (like Ruby) and simulation have a long history together. Simula-67, a language specifically designed for simulation, was the first to introduce the notion of objects to computer programming. So in this chapter, I'm going to ask one particular question and try to answer it with a simulation written in Ruby.

Here's the question: given prices in the United States, does our current set of coin denominations minimize the amount of change the average person carries around in his pocket? And if not, what are some better denominations of coins we could use?

In the process, you'll learn about simulations, but I'll also touch on algorithms for making change, how to speed up computation with dynamic programming, the perils of hash tables, optimal coin configurations, using searches to explore solution spaces, a work of fiction, and the coin replacement consensus.

Going Shopping

In order to run the change simulation, you're going to need to simulate a lot of purchases. During each of these purchases, a simulated consumer will pay the cashier using the change he is carrying (plus an unlimited supply of dollar bills). The cashier will then make change using the fewest coins possible. We'll track the average number of coins in the customer's pockets over time in order to gauge the success of various systems of coinage.

And if you want good results, you're going to need the prices from actual purchases. Luckily, I saved all my receipts for the past year or so. I've painstakingly entered 253 of these purchases into the computer.

You can find the full list in `prices.txt`. I've only included the portion of each price that is less than a dollar. I'm not going to worry about dollar bills at all, since I'll just assume there's an unlimited supply from the ATM.

I've also omitted purchases that cost some number of dollars but no cents, since they won't affect our change-making. And lastly, I've omitted my bagel purchases from the list. Spending $1.35 on a bagel and cream cheese every single morning has a serious potential to bias your results. Of course, if this were a real science experiment, you'd want to keep the bagels and increase the number of consumers sampled. But this price list should be sufficient for this investigation.

Randomizing the purchase data will help avoid fitting the solution too tightly to the specific order the receipts were entered in. (However, this also means we'll have to simulate more purchases in order to find a stable solution.) Let's start building the simulation by constructing an object that will let us randomly select a price from the list. All of the code in this chapter will reside in a single file. Title it `change.rb`.

```ruby
class Prices
  def initialize(*data)
    @data = data
  end

  def get
    @data[rand(@data.size)]
  end
end
```

This compact data structure takes a list of prices supplied on creation and gives you the ability to request one back at random. Here's a usage example:

```ruby
prices = Prices.new(1, 2, 3)
prices.get ➤ 2
prices.get ➤ 1
prices.get ➤ 2
```

It would also be useful to have `Prices` be able to feed a number of random prices into a block.

```
class Prices
  def each(count)
    count.times{ yield get }
  end
end
```

The each method can be used like this:

```
price_list = []
prices.each(4) {|price| price_list.push price }
price_list ➤ [1, 1, 3, 2]
```

Now let's read in the price file and put the prices into the random price object.

```
price_list = IO.readlines("prices.txt").map{|price| price.to_i }
prices = Prices.new(*price_list)
```

This price generator (based on real amounts, of course) gives the first part of what you need to simulate purchases. You're also going to simulate the customer who is paying for all these purchases, as well as someone capable of making change when the customer can't pay exactly.

How to Make Change

Making change at first seems like an easy problem. In the United States, we have four coins in common circulation, a 1-cent coin known as a *penny*, a 5-cent coin known as a *nickel*, a 10-cent coin known as a *dime*, and a 25-cent coin known as a *quarter*. For international readers, it's worth noting that there are 100 cents in a dollar (the fundamental monetary unit in the United States), and that the code we'll work with in this chapter will assume a coin system based on units of 1/100th of a dollar.

The Greedy Algorithm

In order to make change in the United States (and a great number of other countries for that matter), all you need to do is start with the largest coin denomination, take as many as you can without exceeding the amount of change you're making, and then proceed to the next smallest coin and repeat. Since we have a 1-cent coin, which is also the smallest unit used in U.S. prices, we're always able to make proper change. All our simulations will share this constraint that the coin systems must include a 1-cent coin.

Here's an example. If a price is 61 cents, and the customer pays one dollar (which is equal to 100 cents), the clerk will need to give the customer 39 cents in change. The clerk starts with the quarters. He picks one up, giving him 25 cents out of the needed 39, but cannot select another quarter without exceeding 39 cents. So he keeps the quarter in his hand, and proceeds to the dimes. He can add one dime, giving him 35 cents, without exceeding 39 cents, and so taking the sole dime, he proceeds to the nickels. He can't take any nickels without going over, so he finally looks at the pennies. He needs to take four of them to make correct change, so he grabs them and hands a fistful of coins back to the customer that contains one quarter, one dime, no nickels, and four pennies.

Computer scientists call this process the *greedy algorithm*, but not because it has anything to do with money. In fact, this algorithm is useful for solving a variety of problems. At its simplest, the algorithm merely says, "for every decision, make the choice that will get you closest to your goal state." By always choosing to take the largest coin that you can without exceeding the amount, the greedy algorithm lets you make perfect change in the United States.

Problems with the Greedy Algorithm

Unfortunately, the greedy algorithm is not a very good general solution. There's a large class of problems it can't solve for the simple reason that sometimes always trying to get as close to your goal state as possible backfires, leaving you with a suboptimal finishing state.

Let me give an example using coins. While a greedy algorithm works for the U.S. coin system, it doesn't work for coin systems in general. Let's say you need to make 14 cents worth of change in a country where the coins are valued at 1, 7, and 10 cents. The greedy algorithm would have you first take a 10-cent coin, then ignore the 7-cent coins because taking one would exceed the desired amount. Finally, you would take four pennies. This gives a total of five coins' worth of change when you really should have given the customer back two 7-cent coins.

Brute Force

The obvious advantage of a coin system like the United States' is how easy it is for clerks to make change. A lot of the coin systems explored in this chapter won't necessarily have that property. Luckily, you can still always find the optimal change by running through all possible sets of coins that add up to the right amount and then picking the best. This is often referred to as a *brute force algorithm*. It won't be fast, but it will always get the job done. So while a human being might find some of these systems confusing, the simulation won't ever have problems making perfect change.

Would the United States ever switch to a system that made making change this hard, even if it meant people would end up hypothetically carrying less change? Definitely not. But it wouldn't actually be as crazy of an idea as it sounds. After all, most change is now made using computerized cash registers. It wouldn't be difficult for cash registers to instruct clerks which coins to return. In fact, many stores now use automatic change makers that remove the cashier from the process entirely.

Still, it'll never happen.

But let's ignore that for now. Since you can't rely on the greedy algorithm, you're going to implement a solution that relies on computational brute force.

Adding the min_by Method

You want to find the solution with the fewest possible coins, so begin by adding a method to the Enumerable module named min_by.

The Enumerable module is a special module that is mixed in (this means "has its methods added") to most common collection classes. This lets them all share common code and gives you a convenient place to add code you'd like all Ruby collections to support! Even though you'll probably only call min_by on arrays, by adding it to Enumerable, it's available anywhere you might need it.

Enumerable already provides a min method. The min method finds the minimum element in an enumerable instance. min_by is a related yet different operation. You want to find the element that is the smallest after the block is applied to it, as opposed to simply the smallest element. This is a common pattern in Ruby. Take sort and sort_by for example:

```
[5, -8, 3, 9].sort ➤ [-8, 3, 5, 9]
[5, -8, 3, 9].sort_by{|num| num.abs } ➤ [3, 5, -8, 9]
```

The relationship between min and min_by is similar:

```
[5, -8, 3, 9].min ➤ -8
[5, -8, 3, 9].min_by{|num| num.abs } ➤ 3
```

Here's one way to implement this method:

```
module Enumerable
  def min_by
    pairs = map{|x| [yield(x), x] }
    min_pair = pairs.min{|a, b| a.first <=> b.first }
    return min_pair.last
  end
end
```

The user must supply a block used to sort objects based on the result of calling the block on them. In this implementation, you build a list of pairs containing both the original value and the result of calling the block with the value. You then find the pair with the smallest result value, and return its original value.

This is a variation on the *decorate-sort-undecorate* pattern and is closely related to the Schwartzian Transform (which does sorting instead of minimization) of Perl fame. More important, though, it will help you make optimal change.

Putting It All Together

The ChangeMaker class will need to be passed in a list of denominations to use when making change. You'll assume it has a limitless supply of each of these coins. While cashiers occasionally run out of certain coins in the real world, these virtual businesses will make sure they always have enough coins on hand.

```ruby
class ChangeMaker
  def initialize(*coins)
    raise "ChangeMaker must have a coin of denomination 1" unless coins.include?(1)
    @coins = coins.sort
  end
end
```

The ChangeMaker constructor accepts a list of coins and stores them (sorted) in an instance variable. This is where you should enforce the rule that all coin systems must include a 1-cent coin. The actual change-making operation will be performed by a recursive method change.

```ruby
class ChangeMaker
  def change(amount)
    return [] if amount == 0

    possible = @coins.find_all{|coin| coin <= amount }
    best = possible.min_by{|coin| change(amount - coin).size }

    return [best, *change(amount - best)].sort
  end
end
```

The method change is called with an amount the cashier is supposed to return to the customer as change. Since you're using recursion (this method will call itself), you have two cases.

In the so-called "base case," the amount of change you need to return equals 0. When this happens, you'll return an empty list representing no coins. On the other hand, most of the time you're actually going to need to make change. This is the "recursive case."

First you exclude any coins that are larger than the desired amount. Trying to use them would cause you to give back too much change. Then, of the possible coins you could use, you figure out which one would require the least number of coins to finish the job (returning the amount of change required minus the value of the coin we could choose).

The whole process is repeated again and again, calling change with successively smaller amounts each time, until at least you reach the case where you are required to return 0 cents, at which point the base case is reached and you return no more coins. The collection of the best coins to pay is built up from each successive call until at least the original invocation returns the best possible change. Here's an example:

```
cm = ChangeMaker.new(1, 5, 10, 25)
cm.change(17) ➤ [1, 1, 5, 10]
cm2 = ChangeMaker.new(1, 7, 10)
cm2.change(14) ➤ [7, 7]
```

Excellent! It even handles coin systems where the greedy algorithm doesn't work.

So what's wrong? Well, on my machine, trying to make change for 25 cents takes over a minute. The times get much worse as the values get even a little larger. What's going on here?

The way this is written, you may need to calculate the best possible way to make change for any given value over and over again. When changing 25 cents, there are a number of ways to pay 15 cents, and when comparing them, each is required to figure out the best way to make change for the remaining 10 cents. These values are recalculated repeatedly in the recursive call tree. Luckily, there's an easy solution for this kind of problem called dynamic programming.

Dynamic Programming

Dynamic programming is a technique used to improve the performance of algorithms that solve the same subproblems repeatedly. The answers are saved the first time they are computed and then the result is immediately returned by future calls, thus avoiding costly recomputation. This process is called *memoization*.

You'll be using top-down dynamic programming, where the subproblems are solved when they are needed to solve the original problem, instead of ahead of time. To do this, you'll need to use memoization in your change method.

■**Tip** *Memoization* is one of those words you'll probably only hear computer programmers use. It is the proper name of the process by which function results are cached based on the arguments that produced them.

```ruby
class ChangeMaker
  def initialize(*coins)
    raise "ChangeMaker must have a coin of denomination 1" unless coins.include?(1)
    @coins = coins.sort
    @cache = {}
  end

  def change(amount)
    return @cache[amount] if @cache[amount]
    return [] if amount == 0

    possible = @coins.find_all{|coin| coin <= amount }
    best = possible.min_by{|coin| change(amount - coin).size }

    return @cache[amount] = [best, *change(amount - best)].sort
  end
end
```

I've added two lines and changed a third. The hash table stored in the instance variable named @cache will store the best way to make change for all amounts changed before. At the beginning of your change method, add a short circuit return to retrieve the answer from the cache if it exists. And at the end of the method, before you return any solution, make sure to save it in the cache. With this modification, your method makes change almost instantly.

```ruby
cm = ChangeMaker.new(1, 5, 10, 25)
cm.change(99) ➤ [1, 1, 1, 1, 10, 10, 25, 25, 25]
```

■**Caution** In coin systems where there are multiple optimal coin sets for a given value, the ChangeMaker will return one particular set every time. This means you can't use a ChangeMaker to check whether a given coin set is optimal simply by comparing it to the returned solution; instead you must check the size of the returned size against the size of your set.

The Customer

You've now got a random selection of purchase prices and an object to act as your cashier that always makes optimal change. But you still need to code a customer who can pay the cashier the optimal payment given what he has in his pocket.

If the goal is to minimize the amount of change the customer is lugging around, the customer should always give the cashier the combination of coins in his possession that will leave him with as few coins as possible remaining (including any change he receives) when the transaction is finished.

In real life, people don't always do this. Sometimes we're in too much of a hurry and sometimes we're just not smart enough to figure out exactly what we should give the cashier. Luckily, your simulated customer never has these problems. Here's the beginning of the Customer class:

```ruby
class Customer
  attr_reader :denoms, :coins

  def initialize(denoms, *coins)
    @coins  = coins.sort
    @denoms = denoms.sort

    @cm = ChangeMaker.new(*@denoms)
  end
end
```

The customer is passed a list of coin denominations, as well as a starting set of coins in the variable arguments slot. You'll create a new customer like this from now on:

```ruby
customer = Customer.new([1, 5, 10, 25], 1, 1, 1, 5, 25)
```

This customer is using the U.S. coin system and starts with three 1-cent coins, one 5-cent coin, and one 25-cent coin.

The customer has three instance variables. The first two hold the denominations and the coins that were passed to the constructor. You sort them before storing them for prettier printing. You also provide accessors for these variables. In the last instance variable, the Customer keeps a ChangeMaker object initialized with the appropriate denominations.

Unfortunately, the constructor in the preceding code doesn't do much in the way of error checking. A slightly more reliable version looks like this:

```ruby
class Customer
  def initialize(denoms, *coins)
    @coins  = coins.sort
    @denoms = denoms.sort

    coins.each{|denom| check_denom(denom) }

    @cm = ChangeMaker.new(*@denoms)
    check_optimal_start
  end
end
```

Why is this important? Well, obviously the first check is important because it keeps you from accidentally starting up in a bad state. It's the second check, though, that's more interesting. Without this code, there's the potential to initialize your customer in a nonoptimal configuration—for example with five 1-cent coins, instead of one 5-cent coin (a situation that should have never occurred given how good the customer is at paying). The following code implements these two checks:

```ruby
class Customer
  def check_denom(denom)
    raise "Bad denomination #{denom}" unless denoms.include?(denom)
  end

  def check_optimal_start
    optimal = @cm.change(amount)
    if coins.size != optimal.size
      raise "Bad starting state #{coins.inspect} should be #{optimal.inspect}"
    end
  end
end
```

To make the preceding code work, you'll need the amount helper. Here's its implementation along with the number method. The first totals the coins, while the second counts them.

```ruby
class Customer
  def amount
    coins.sum
  end

  def number
    coins.size
  end
end
```

Of course, amount in turn needs the sum method defined on Enumerable.

```ruby
module Enumerable
  def sum
    inject(0) {|a, b| a + b } rescue nil
  end
end
```

sum assumes the Enumerable contains numbers and adds them up. If anything goes wrong, it uses the rescue modifier to return nil.

As a convenience I'll also provide a class method on Customer to create a customer using the U.S. coin denominations.

```ruby
class Customer
  def self.us(*coins)
    self.new([1, 5, 10, 25], *coins)
  end
end
```

This method isn't for actual simulation, but it will be useful for testing your work. Although I haven't been talking about tests or writing them in this chapter, all of this code is unit tested. It's always a good idea to write tests while you write code. How else will you know if you wrote it right?

Using the previous class method, you can now create a new American Customer like this:

```ruby
customer = Customer.us(1, 1, 1, 5, 25)
```

In order to do proper testing, you're also going to need some basic Ruby methods for your customer object as well. You're going to want a == method and a to_s method at the very least. Without the ability to compare your objects or print them, testing and debugging can be difficult. The following two little methods will make life easier:

```ruby
class Customer
  def ==(other)
    return false unless other.kind_of?(Customer)
    return false unless coins == other.coins
    return false unless denoms == other.denoms
    return true
  end

  def to_s
    dollars = sprintf("$%.2f", amount.to_f/100)
    return "#{dollars} (#{coins.join(', ')})"
  end
end
```

The == method will consider a customer equal to another object only if the other object is also a Customer and has the same list of coins and denominations. For this reason, you're going to need to always keep the coins and denominations lists sorted. Here are some usage examples for both methods:

```
customer1 = Customer.us(1, 5)
customer2 = Customer.us(1, 10)
customer3 = Customer.new([1, 5, 10, 25], 1, 5)
customer4 = Customer.new([1, 3, 5, 7], 1, 5)

customer1 == customer1 ➤ true
customer1 == customer2 ➤ false
customer1 == customer3 ➤ true
customer1 == customer4 ➤ false

customer1.to_s ➤ "$0.06 (1, 5)"
customer2.to_s ➤ "$0.11 (1, 10)"
```

This brings us to the last and most important method. The pay! method is responsible for having the customer pay the clerk a certain amount. The hyper-intelligent customer will always give the clerk the amount that will result in him leaving the transaction with as few coins as possible in his pocket. This method combined with the ChangeMaker's change method are the heart of the simulation.

■Tip Why does the pay! method end with an exclamation point? It's not because we're excited (and we are)! We're following Ruby's convention of marking methods that change the state of an object with an exclamation point as a warning.

In order to write the pay! method, however, you're going to need to look at different configurations of the coins. Let's add another method named permutations (and its helper rest) to the Enumerable module.

```
module Enumerable
  def permutations
    return [[]] if empty?
    others = rest.permutations
    (others.map{|o| [first] + o} + others).uniq
  end

  def rest
    return [] if empty?
    self[1..-1]
  end
end
```

You'll be using the permutations method on ranges as well as arrays. The preceding version is a recursive solution. If the collection is empty, there is only one possible permutation, an empty collection. This is the base case, so you return it right away if permutations is called on an empty collection.

However, if the collection is not empty, you're going to recursively call permutations on a list of all of the elements except the first one. This is done using the rest method that has been added to Enumerable as well.

rest is typically used along with first. Between the two of them, they return all the elements in an enumerable. rest is often useful in recursive solutions and mimics the behavior of Lisp's cdr function when used on a cons list (I'll talk about this more in Chapter 9).

Before returning to the pay! method, you need a way to give and receive coins. Without the following code, your simulated customer would be paralyzed, halting the very engine of commerce itself.

```ruby
class Customer
  def take!(coin)
    coins.push coin
    coins.sort!
    return self
  end

  def give!(coin)
    # Be careful not to call delete() because it removes all instances of an
    # object, and we support having more than one of each coin. Use delete_at
    # instead.
    raise "Don't have #{coin} coin to give" unless coins.include?(coin)
    coins.delete_at(coins.index(coin))
    return self
  end
end
```

These methods are pretty straightforward (although, notice that the coins are kept in order). So let's finally return to the pay! method. It runs through all the combinations of coins the customer could give the cashier, using the permutations method, and selects the best using the min_by method. This is how the customer knows which coins are the best to give the clerk. It tries them all!

```ruby
class Customer
  def pay!(bill)
    give = coins.permutations.min_by do |perm|
      amount = (perm.sum - bill) % 100
      change = @cm.change(amount)
```

```
          number - perm.size + change.size
      end

      amount = (give.sum - bill) % 100
      get = @cm.change(amount)

      give.each {|d| give!(d) }
      get.each  {|d| take!(d) }
      return self
    end
end
```

Using the `rest` and `permutations` methods recurses and calculates what the permutations would be excluding the first element. But of course, you actually want the first element, too. Luckily, if you have a list of configurations, it's straightforward to find out what the new configurations are if you add one more coin. The answer is simply all of the old combinations as well as each old combination with the new coin added to them. So there are twice as many permutations when you're done. So you concatenate them and then call `uniq` at the end to avoid the duplicate permutations that can arise if a collection contains duplicate items. Unfortunately, this code is really slow.

Memoization

Solving for the optimal set of two coins (where one of them must be 1 cent!) took me 52 seconds with this implementation. But reusing the old memoization trick dropped the time to 15 seconds. When you increase the number of coins to three (still requiring a 1-cent coin), the nonmemoized version takes 18 minutes while the memoized version completes in around 8 minutes on my particular machine. You can memoize the code like this.

```
module Enumerable
  @@permutations_cache = {}

  def permutations
    return @@permutations_cache[self].dup if @@permutations_cache[self]
    return [[]] if empty?
    others = rest.permutations
    return (@@permutations_cache[self] = ➥
(others.map{|o| [first] + o} + others).uniq).dup
  end
end
```

You use the `@@permutations_cache` class variable (a confusing designation in this case because the class variable is being added to a module instead of a class) to store your results. You use a class variable this time instead of an instance variable because the input to the method is the `Enumerable` object itself. The class variable gives you a central place that is not unique to any particular instance where you can store all the precalculated answers.

The code now checks the cache for a result and returns it immediately if it exists. Well, actually, it returns a duplicated copy. The risk of returning something straight out of the cache is that someone could modify it and corrupt future results. A good way to get around this is to call `freeze` on the value stored in the cache. Another way is to call `dup` on the value stored in the cache to return a copy. Both ways ensure that your cached answers remain valid. Some quick tests I ran suggested that the strategy using `dup` was faster (surprisingly), so I used that technique. Unfortunately, there's a bug in this code. Any guesses?

Hash Problems

In my haste for better performance, I added a subtle bug to the code along with memoization. Hash tables are so darn fast because they compute a special hash index for each key object, and then use this index as a wrapped reference into a table of memory. In Ruby, these hash codes are generated by a method named `hash`. All objects inherit a simple `hash` method from the `Object` class and all the built-in classes provide class-specific implementations to instances. So when it's time to use an object as a hash key, the hash code for the object is calculated, the hash code is modulated so that it is between 0 and the number of slots in the hash table, and then the object is placed in that slot.

What happens if there's something else already in that slot? Well, there are a couple of ways to do it, but they all involve having a consistent rule about where to put the object instead. Some implementations might add a constant number to the hash code and try that slot instead. Others have a linked list at each slot of the table that they can hang additional objects off of. But the fact that multiple objects can have the same hash code leads to problems at lookup. It is no longer enough to solely use the key's hash code on storage or lookup. Instead, you must also check the equality of the lookup key against the key you used to store to the value. That means you'll need to keep that key object around somewhere in the hash table.

But this is all just background. Here's an example of two arrays that hash to the same value (111):

```
[8, 8, 8].hash ➤ 111
[1, 8, 8, 8, 8].hash ➤ 111
```

Luckily, though, because of the equality check performed on hash lookup, these two arrays won't interfere with each other when used as keys.

```
h = {}
h[[8, 8, 8]] = 1
h[[8, 8, 8]] ➤ 1
h[[1, 8, 8, 8, 8]] ➤ nil
h[[1, 8, 8, 8, 8]] = 2
h[[1, 8, 8, 8, 8]] ➤ 2
h[[8, 8, 8]] ➤ 1
```

But then why does the following happen?

```
h = {}
a = [8, 8, 8]
h[a] = 1
a.push 8
a.unshift 1
a ➤ [1, 8, 8, 8]
h[a] ➤ 1
```

Well, I made one of the cardinal mistakes of hash tables. I stored something with a key and then modified the key. Depending on the hash table implementation, this can have all sorts of interesting effects.

Here's what happens in Ruby. When you use an object as a key in Ruby, a reference to the original key is kept in the hash to be used for disambiguating collisions in the table. It is neither cloned nor frozen. If you ever accidentally modify the key to another state, hash lookups using keys equal to the modified state will retrieve the originally stored value, but only if the modified key hashes to the same hash code as it did in its original state. In fact, if you peer beneath the hood into Ruby's C code, you'll see that Ruby doesn't even bother calling the compare method if it's been passed two references to the same object:

```
#define EQUAL(table,x,y) ((x)==(y) || (*table->type->compare)((x),(y)) == 0)
```

The lesson learned here is don't mutate the keys you've used to store values in a hash. Unfortunately, if you make this mistake, the mechanics of the problem make symptoms intermittent and very difficult to debug.

So where's the bug in the preceding memoization code? permutations is called on the coin list, therefore you use the coin list as a key to your memoization hash. Unfortunately, the coin list changes throughout execution, giving rise to the strange behavior previously discussed. You can get around this by duplicating your keys before you use them to store objects in the hash. That way you won't accidentally change them. Here's the fixed solution:

```ruby
class Enumerable
  def permutations
    return @@permutations_cache[self].dup if @@permutations_cache[self]
    return [[]] if empty?
    others = rest.permutations
    return (@@permutations_cache[self.dup] = ➥
(others.map{|o| [first] + o} + others).uniq).dup
  end
end
```

■**Note** I'm duplicating both the keys used to store answers in the hash and the answers themselves. The first is to avoid the key modification problem just discussed. The second is to make sure no one accidentally changes any of the answers either. The problems are similar, but not quite the same.

Paying

So with the permutations method working, blazing fast, and now correct, the pay! method should work, too. Let's revisit the code:

```ruby
Class Customer
  def pay!(bill)
    give = coins.permutations.min_by do |perm|
      amount = (perm.sum - bill) % 100
      change = @cm.change(amount)
      number - perm.size + change.size
    end

    amount = (give.sum - bill) % 100
    get = @cm.change(amount)

    give.each {|d| give!(d) }
    get.each  {|d| take!(d) }
    return self
  end
end
```

The min_by invocation will return the set of coins the customer should give to the cashier to minimize the change in his pocket. Once you have this value, calculate the amount of change the cashier will give him in exchange, then have him give up the coins he's paying with and take the new ones. And that's all there really is to it. Here's an example of how to use the pay! method:

```
customer = Customer.us(1, 1, 5, 10, 25)
customer.pay!(15)
customer.coins ➤ [1, 1, 25]
customer.pay!(98)
customer.coins ➤ [1, 1, 1, 1, 25]
```

Everything seems to work, so let's put the pieces together and do some simulation.

The ChangeSimulator

The simulator itself is very small. I've put most of the intelligence into the Customer class and Enumerable's new permutations method. I'll initialize the ChangeSimulator with a price list and a list of coin denominations, as follows:

```
class ChangeSimulator
  def initialize(prices, *denoms)
    @prices   = prices
    @customer = Customer.new(denoms)
  end
end
```

Then I'll tell it how many purchases to run for, and it will return an average amount of change in the customer's pocket between each purchase.

```
class ChangeSimulator
  def run(length)
    sum = 0
    @prices.each(length) do |bill|
      @customer.pay!(bill)
      sum += @customer.number
    end
    return sum.to_f/length
  end
end
```

Now the simulator is ready for use.

So How Heavy Are Your Pockets?

Let's start by running a simulation to see how much change we'd be carrying around on average if we all made perfect change all the time using the American coin system. First you'll need your price list.

```
price_list = IO.readlines("prices.txt").map{|price| price.to_i }
prices = Prices.new(*price_list)
```

You're going to have to decide how long the simulation should run. You only have 253 purchases in your purchase list, but since they're randomly selected and the order of purchases affects the outcome, you'll want to run more purchases than that. The more purchases you run, the less variance you'll see between simulations. This is not a guarantee of real-world accuracy, of course, since you can't be sure that the data set or simulation accurately mimic the real world.

My computer is able to happily run 10,000 purchases in a short time, so let's start by simulating 10,000 purchases with the U.S. coin system.

```
sim = ChangeSimulator.new(prices, 1, 5, 10, 25)
puts sim.run(10000)
```

I ran this simulation a few times, and the average number of coins in the customer's pocket hovered at 4.7. I personally happen to have six coins in my pocket right now, for what it's worth. An interesting followup to the simulation would be to track your own average coin load for a month. The difference between your average and 4.7 could give you a sense of how close you come to making optimal change decisions at the register.

Replacing a Coin

Okay, let's make the next simulation a little more complicated. Now you're going to try to find the best replacement coin you could choose if you were given the chance to swap out one current U.S. coin. First you'll need to generate all the possible ways you could replace a coin. You need to leave the penny, but you can ditch the 5-, 10-, or 25-cent coin in exchange for any coin between 2 and 99 cents (including even the coin you have removed). If you found that the best move you could make was to replace one of your current coins with itself, it would mean your current system was optimal.

```
possibilities = []
us_denoms = [5, 10, 25]
us_denoms.size.times do |i|
  (2..99).each do |replacement|
```

```
    denoms     = us_denoms.dup
    denoms[i] = replacement

    possibilities << [1, *denoms]
  end
end
```

Once you've calculated all the possible configurations, search for the one that will minimize pocket weight. Of course, since you are now running almost 300 different simulations instead of just one, you can't afford to run as many purchases. I've dropped the number of purchases down to 1000, which makes things manageable (a run time of a few minutes):

```
winner = possibilities.min_by do |denoms|
  sim = ChangeSimulator.new(prices, *denoms)
  sim.run(1000)
end

puts "The winner is: #{winner.sort.inspect}"
```

I've run this a number of times and I always seem to get one of two answers. The most frequent result is to replace the 10-cent coin with an 18-cent coin. The less common answer is to replace the 25-cent coin with a 32-cent coin. Of course, I'd hate to see the looks on Americans' faces if they were ever forced to make change with 18- or 32-cent coins.

Adding a Coin

What if, though, instead of replacing a coin, you wanted to add one? The code doesn't have to change much. The main difference is that you'll be simulating with five coins. This slows you down because it means a larger set of possible ways to make change with each purchase.

```
winner = (2..99).min_by do |extra|
  sim = ChangeSimulator.new(prices, 1, 5, 10, 25, extra)
  sim.run(1000)
end
puts "The winner is: #{winner}"
```

Several simulations of this variety suggest that adding a 22-cent coin would be a good way to cut down on loose change. Other answers are possible as well.

Optimal Coins

If adding or swapping a coin seemed improbable, this next hypothetical is downright unbelievable. But let's say the U.S. government commissioned you to completely redo the U.S. coin system with no regard for ease of use, but instead with the goal of eliminating as much pocket change as possible. What should the new system look like?

The first question you need to ask is how many coins you get to use. After all, if you can have 99 of them, you can reduce the number of coins someone needs to carry down to one. On the other hand, trying to fit 99 coin trays into a cash register probably wouldn't work so well. Never mind figuring out how to make vending machines recognize all 99 coins. Luckily, you're limited to fairly small numbers of coins by the amount of permutations that can be simulated.

Remember, you'll need to always include a 1-cent coin. Also note that you've parameterized the simulation on the number of coins it's allowed to use, as well as the number of purchases to simulate. In order to make this possible, you'll need a variation on `permutations` named `permuations_of_size`. You could implement this method by post-filtering the permutations to remove permutations of the wrong size. But this will still have to produce all the combinations (an increasingly difficult task)!

Instead, let's implement it like this. To start with, this version uses iteration instead of recursion. It also ignores any combinations containing more elements than the specified limit. It is diligent about removing duplicates, and right before the very end, it removes any permutations without enough elements (it was important to keep them around until then, since they would be used to form combinations of the right size).

```ruby
module Enumerable
  def permutations_of_size(n)
    perms = [[]]
    each do |item|
      add = []
      perms.each do |prev|
        newone = prev + [item]
        add.push newone if newone.size <= n
      end
      perms.push(*add)
      # Adding perms.uniq! here enables us to process large values of coins
      # that are all the same without combinatorial explosion.
      perms.uniq!
    end
    return perms.find_all{|p| p.size == n }
  end
end
```

You can then use this to write a generic coin system solver. The following code finds the best two-coin system.

```
number = 2
purchases = 400
choices = (2..99).to_a.permutations_of_size(number - 1).map{|p| p.push(1) }

winner = choices.min_by do |denoms|
  sim = ChangeSimulator.new(prices, *denoms)
  sim.run(purchases)
end

puts "The winner is: #{winner.sort.inspect}"
```

As an aside, if you thought the combinatoric explosion was bad before, you're really in trouble now. The number of simulations being performing is now growing with the number of permutations that can be made using coins between 2 and 99 for n coins.

Two Coins

If you restrict yourself to systems that include a penny, there are only 98 two-coin systems. This means you can get away with a relatively large number of simulated purchases (though quite small compared to earlier simulations). For this number of simulations, I was able to run 400 purchases each while still keeping the simulation relatively fast. You'll find out quickly that if you only got two coins, you'd probably want an 11-cent coin to go along with the penny.

Three Coins

What about three-coin systems, though? I've kept the number of purchases at 400, even though this simulation takes significantly longer than the two-coin system. One simulation suggested that the optimal system would consist of a 1-cent, a 7-cent, and a 24-cent coin. Another suggested a 1-cent, a 13-cent, and an 18-cent coin. This simulation would benefit from several reruns with a much larger number of purchases.

Four Coins

At four coin denominations and 400 purchases each, the simulation took an entire weekend, clocking in at a little over 50 hours of simulation. But I did get an answer. It appears that if you were to replace the current four-coin system with a new one, you should have at least a passing look at [1, 3, 13, 31]. Of course, I didn't have the patience to run the simulation again to confirm the result.

This was the only occasion when permutations_by_size took any significant time. If you were consistently simulating problems with this large of a search space, it would probably be advisable to memoize permutations_by_size as well.

Beyond

Unfortunately, five- and six-coin systems lay outside my simulating power. It's frustrating but a common problem with simulation. One solution is to wait for faster machines. This helps, but never as much as you'd like because problems often grow exponentially in size.

Another solution, of course, is to find yourself a computer cluster. There's nothing quite like a few thousand computers to speed up your simulation. This technique is especially useful for simulations like this one where you have a large independent search space. Each machine can try running a different coin system and compare their best result when all machines are finished.

But what if you don't have a computer cluster? Well, you could check with your friends and see if they have one. But if that doesn't work out, you're probably going to have to come at the problem from a different angle.

What if you could avoid checking every possible configuration? At its core, this is a search problem. Up until now, the code has been using the brute force strategy and trying every configuration. This means you'll always find the optimal solution. But it also makes your larger simulations take forever. If you're constrained by processing power and need an answer, avoiding checking every possible solution makes a lot of sense.

One way to cut down the search space is to throw out possibilities ahead of time. From the results you've seen so far, you might be tempted to throw out all small coin systems that include a coin larger than 50 cents. None of the optimal systems has included a coin that large yet. Of course, there are no guarantees this heuristic would be a good one. After all, a coin system with 50 coins *must* have a coin worth 50 cents or more. In fact, coins larger than 50 cents probably appear long before you reach 50-coin systems.

Since culling the search space ahead of time requires a greater understanding of the problem than we have, we are lucky that there are algorithms available to dynamically decide which possibilities to explore next. These algorithms are designed to maximize value, but they can't guarantee you the optimal solution unless you have a way to cheaply test a given solution for optimality (we don't). But they can still often find an acceptable solution. Using an algorithm with an exotic name like *best first search*, *hill climbing*, and *simulated annealing* might be exactly what you need to get your simulation running in the time you have. I'll return to this question later in Chapter 7 using genetic algorithms.

Wizard Money

Okay, but if you're going to make up improbable currency schemes, why limit yourself to the mundane world of American currency? In J. K. Rowling's award-winning Harry Potter fiction series, wizards use a currency system based on *galleons*. Each galleon is worth 493 *knuts*. Wizards also use a second coin called a *sickle* that is worth 17 knuts, which also means that a galleon is worth 29 sickles. The classifications I've been using previously fall apart a little here.

So far I've been excluding dollars from the calculations. Since they are bills, I've accepted the fact that you can carry an almost unlimited supply (and get more when you need them) without weighing down your pockets.

Although as far as I can tell, Rowling never addressed this issue, so I'm going to have to assume wizards have some magical way to carry around large numbers of galleons (otherwise, they're walking around with sacks of gold all the time). This would mean all a wizard needs to worry about lugging around are his or her knuts and sickles.

Given this assumption, you have a two-coin system valued at 1 and 17 "cents" (knuts actually), accordingly. With a quick retooling, you can tweak your simulator to answer questions about Rowling's mythical world. The first step is to replace all occurrences of 100 in the code with 493. Like a good software engineer, I'll refactor the values into a constant named Unit:

```
Unit = 100
. . .
```

```
  def pay!(bill)
    give = coins.permutations.min_by do |perm|
      amount = (perm.sum - bill) % Unit
      change = @cm.change(amount)
      number - perm.size + change.size
    end

    amount = (give.sum - bill) % Unit
    . . .
```

Then I'll redefine Unit to 493.

```
Unit = 493
```

Since Rowling has not provided us with a very extensive list of wizard prices, I'm going to have to use random prices between 1 and 492. According to the following code, wizards are carrying on average around 22 knuts and sickles at all times.

```
prices = Prices.new(*1..(Unit - 1))
sim = ChangeSimulator.new(prices, 1, 17)
puts sim.run(10000)
```

That's way more than what average Americans would be carrying. So I'll ask the same questions about the wizard's system that I did about the U.S. coins. First of all, is there a better coin than a sickle the wizards could use (ignoring the fact that the whole 493 knuts to a galleon is probably an arbitrary number to begin with, unlike 100 which fits nicely into the base 10 system—unless, of course, wizards do math in base 493?

```
winner = (2..492).min_by do |denom|
  sim = ChangeSimulator.new(prices, 1, denom)
  sim.run(300)
end
puts winner
```

And the answer? The simulation suggests a 10-knut coin. But what if you got to add a coin to make the wizards' lives a little more bearable? The code looks almost identical.

```
winner = (2..492).min_by do |denom|
  sim = ChangeSimulator.new(prices, 1, 17, denom)
  sim.run(300)
end
puts winner
```

Apparently what they need is a 7-knut coin. Since the wizards seem to care so little for round numbers and are apparently capable of doing complex arithmetic in their heads, you might have better luck with them than with the U.S. government. Perhaps someone should write Ms. Rowling a letter?

In the Literature

I didn't mention it at the beginning of the chapter, but other researchers have looked at this problem before. Mathematician Jeffery Shallit apparently used a "Diophantine equation" (don't ask me, I don't know what that is either) to answer the same questions. One crucial difference in his investigation was that Shallit's assumed an equal distribution of all prices between 0 and 99 cents. A quick look at the prices.txt file shows that more than one third of all the prices were over 80 cents, with a full 15 percent equal to 99 cents. Despite that, what's startling is that Shallot recommends the exact same coin substitution as this simulation did. Both of these results suggest removing the 10-cent dime and adding a new 18-cent coin instead.

What about adding a coin? Well, the results differed. My simulation suggested adding a 22-cent coin, while Shallit suggested a 32-cent coin. Still, it's great to be able to compare results. After all, the whole point of simulation is to learn about the world around us, and science depends on corroborating evidence. And it's pretty cool that Ruby can be a tool for this discovery. For more information, see the following web sites:

www.discover.com/issues/oct-03/departments/featscienceof/

www.sciencenews.org/articles/20030510/mathtrek.asp

Summary

You've cobbled together an excellent framework for simulating pocket change and found tentative answers to real-world questions (and not so real-world questions). You've looked at change-making algorithms, as well as dynamic programming through memoization. And you've even explored some of the odder corner cases of the Ruby language.

However, you haven't even come close to exhausting the simulation possibilities of coins! For example, it would be interesting to see how taking the physical weights of the coins into account would changed the numbers. What if each coin had to be half again as heavy as the denomination before it? How many coins would be optimal then? What would their values be? And that's just coins. There's a whole world full of things waiting to be simulated, and Ruby is just the language to simulate them.

CHAPTER 5

■■■

Turn-Based Strategy in Ruby

He peered through the thick foliage, gun in his hand, his men at his back. He didn't want to be here. If only Lewis and Clark had returned from their damn expedition. Then the president wouldn't have sent him, Captain Nathaniel Adams of the U.S. Army, to find them.

He could be home right now, smoking his pipe and watching the evening roll in, instead of on this godforsaken mission into the heart of unexplored America, gun cocked, waiting for the next dinosaur attack.

Dinosaurs?!

Somehow the president had forgotten to mention that in the mission briefing. Lewis and Clark were probably velociraptor food somewhere between here and the Pacific. And if Adams didn't make it back alive, no one in Washington would ever learn the truth.

Trees snapped and the ground shook, breaking his reverie. Footsteps that heavy could only mean one thing.

T-Rex!

In this chapter, you'll be putting together a turn-based strategy game. Personally, I've always loved the genre, but the fact that you can do a solid job without fancy graphics makes it perfect for hobbyists. In fact, you'll be building the core engine for the game without any graphics at all. It'll be a text-based, turn-based strategy game, if you will. But don't worry, this project is designed so that you can easily drop a GUI on top. In fact, you'll build a graphical user interface for it in the very next chapter.

The game's story will follow a group of westward explorers (patterned on the Lewis and Clark expedition) in the young United States who discover that the center of the country is inhabited by dinosaurs.

A Strategy

Turn-based strategy games have their roots firmly in the world of board games. But since then, the genre has evolved heavily. At the games' most fundamental, players alternate taking turns. During their turns, players maneuver their characters or minions (often referred to as *units*) around a map, bringing them into conflict with other players' units. They may often claim resources or develop infrastructure on top of the map as well. I'll keep this game simple (almost more tactical than strategic), but by the end you'll have a working turn-based strategy game back end that supports multiple GUI front ends.

How do you decouple the game engine from the front end so completely, though? The key is to carefully define the sorts of operations the GUI is going to have to support, and then follow the Ruby way and build a loosely coupled, flexible system. Given this sort of foundation, you should be able to add new features simply by adopting new conventions on top of the existing infrastructure.

What are the ways a player interacts with a turn-based strategy game? First, the player observes the game. Typically this is done visually by looking at a map. However, it is fairly common for there to be textual descriptions involved as well. Second, the player must make a variety of choices typically regarding movement and actions of the units the player controls.

From this list, I've isolated three interactions: messages, map description, and choices. The first two are straightforward. Textual messages can be displayed in some kind of notification or added to a message log. Meanwhile, the map can be drawn using simple information about its layout. As long as everything that needs to be drawn has names, the user interface can use those names to pick a visual representation (perhaps find an image based on the name) or in the simple text-based example display the word itself.

This is an example of what I mean by *loosely coupled*. The game engine itself doesn't demand a piece of the map covered in forest be drawn in any particular way. Of course, you will need to tell the user interface how to draw a tree eventually. But this way keeps the game engine's code as simple as possible.

The last interaction, the ability to make choices, is the most complicated. You'll need a way to describe each option and present them to the user. The simple text-based front end will simply list a shorthand description of each option and let the user select one. But you'll architect things so that a user interface has the information it needs to present each type of decision in uniquely appropriate and intuitive ways. For example, when moving a unit, you might like the potential new locations to glow on the map. By clicking on one of the possible squares, the player selects a unit's destination. On the other hand, when selecting a weapon to attack with, a simple list of choices is probably more appropriate.

If you accept the same notion of loose coupling here, the game engine doesn't need to know how these choices will be presented. But it will need just enough information to let the interface present the choice in the best manner.

An Implementation

All of this sounds good, of course. But without a well-defined communication layer, how will the engine even talk to the user interface? Here's a general system of "representations" you can use. The game object will trigger these three interactions (message, draw, and choice) on the player objects. The player objects will be responsible for interacting with the user interface.

For the computer player classes, no interface is really required beyond the ability to make choices. For each interface type your game supports (only one is necessary, but you'll be building a text-based interface in this chapter, and then a Mac-only GUI in the next), you'll have a distinct player class that will handle the particulars of that interface. The player classes will be written in Ruby, but that doesn't mean the interfaces they talk to need to be! You could build a front end in C++ using OpenGL, Javascript using DHTML and AJAX, or Python using the PyGame framework.

How? You need to keep the requirements on the messages and descriptions minimal and only use four simple data structures (that all those programming languages support). The messages can consist of lists, strings, numbers, and nil. Lists are of course called *arrays* in Ruby, but the idea is the same. When talking about these representations, even outside of the code, I'll use Ruby syntax, but remember that these data structures are nearly universal and easily serialized.

As a simple example, textual messages to the interface are represented using a string. The representations for maps and choices are more complicated. You'll see them in detail later in this chapter in the sections "Representing a Map" and "Making Choices."

Now that you have a strategy for dividing work between the game engine and the game interface, let's make a list of what you'll need for the game engine. My list for the simplest game possible includes terrain classes, a Map class, unit classes, action classes, a Game class, a computer player class, and a human-controlled player class.

All these classes can live in a single file, perhaps named tbs.rb (although you might later want to separate out the generic infrastructure into a reusable file if you start building your own game). I'll start with the Terrain and Map classes.

Building the World Around Us

Most strategy game play is tightly linked to the map. The map not only describes what the world around the player looks like (in terms of terrain and distance); it also keeps track of any units (characters). As programmers, we must also be able to translate maps into a form the human players can understand (you'll be translating your maps into the special intermediate representation structures first, though).

The maps in this chapter will be represented with a two-dimensional grid. Each square will have a slot for a terrain type and for a unit. All squares should have a terrain type, but many squares won't be occupied by a unit at any particular time. Terrain objects tell the game whether a square is covered in forest, mountains, or perhaps part of a river.

Starting with Terrain

Let's think about the Terrain class first. At its simplest, different Terrain types need to be presented distinctly in the interface. A name should be sufficient for this. Some games use complicated Terrain bonuses and penalties, but I'll avoid this.

```
class Terrain
  attr_reader :name

  def initialize(name)
    @name = name
  end

  def rep
    [@name]
  end
end

forest = Terrain.new("Forest")
grass = Terrain.new("Grass")
mountains = Terrain.new("Mountains")
plains = Terrain.new("Plains")
water = Terrain.new("Water")
```

As you can see, a Terrain is really only distinguished by its name. But this is the first example of a representation. Notice how the rep method returns a list containing the terrain's name. I've only used the allowed types.

You'll be using these Terrain types to describe your map, and you'll also need to keep track of both the terrain at any given square and who (if anyone) is standing on it. I'll simplify life by only allowing one Unit to occupy a given square at a time. Even given the restriction that the maps must be rectangular, how are you going to store these two-dimensional grids of objects?

Implementing Maps with Matrices

In the Map class, you're going to need to store objects in a data structure indexed by x and y coordinates. You'd like to write code that looks like this:

```
map[x, y]
```

However, if you were doing this with a regular array, the previous expression would return the element at index x as well as the element at index y. Instead, you'd like to get back an object from a two-dimensional structure at the intersection of the x'th column and the y'th row. So you're going to need to build it. Let's call it a Matrix. It will be internally built using an instance of class Array that contains more instances of Array inside itself.

```ruby
class Matrix
  def initialize(cols, rows)
    @rows = rows
    @cols = cols
    @data = []
    rows.times do |y|
      @data[y] = Array.new(cols)
    end
  end

  def [](x, y)
    @data[y][x]
  end

  def []=(x, y, value)
    @data[y][x] = value
  end
end
```

The initialize method accepts the height and width of the two-dimensional array, stores the values, and then creates an Array instance of Array to fit the dimensions. The lookup method and set method then index into this structure. You could have used a raw Array instance of Array directly in the code, but encapsulating them like this allows you to abstract the code to create them and gives you a class to which to attach methods. Methods like what? Well, how about a method that returns all positions in the Matrix?

```ruby
class Matrix
  def all_positions
    (0...@rows).collect do |y|
      (0...@cols).collect do |x|
        [x, y]
      end
    end.inject([]) {|a, b| a.concat b}
  end
end
```

■**Tip** You're used to using the map method to transform Enumerable collections using a block. The name map comes from the Lisp programming language tradition. The Smalltalk programming language supports an identical operation. However, in Smalltalk, it's named collect. Out of kindness, Matz (the designer of Ruby) has provided us with both names for the same method in Ruby! In general, I've called it map throughout this book, but because you're dealing with actual maps in this chapter, I've made a conscious decision to spell the Enumerable map method as collect instead.

This method returns a list of coordinates pairs (each also in a list) that exist within the Matrix.

```
matrix = Matrix.new(2, 2)
matrix.all_positions => [[0, 0], [1, 0], [0, 1], [1, 1]]
```

Cartography 101

The Map class will contain two matrices in instance variables. One will hold Terrain instances. One will hold Unit instances. Both will require accessors.

```
class Map
  attr_reader :terrain, :units
end
```

Both matrices will be the same size. The @units Matrix will start unpopulated and units will be added using the place method).

```
class Map
  def place(x, y, unit)
    @units[x, y] = unit
    unit.x = x
    unit.y = y
  end

  def move(old_x, old_y, new_x, new_y)
    raise LocationOccuppiedError.new(new_x, new_y) if @units[new_x, new_y]
    @units[new_x, new_y] = @units[old_x, old_y]
    @units[old_x, old_y] = nil
  end
end

class LocationOccupiedError < Exception
end
```

I haven't talked about units yet, but trust for now that they have x and y accessors. The place method stores them in the @units matrix and then sets the unit's x and y fields. After the initial placement of a unit, the move method is used instead. This is the same move method that the units called earlier. It takes both the old and new x and y positions. It sets the object to its new location and then removes it from the old.

The LocationOccupiedError exception should never be raised (since you should only present movement choices for unoccupied locations to the player). But it's better to be safe than sorry.

So you've seen that the @units Matrix starts out empty. But what about the @terrain Matrix? It needs to populated.

Where Does Terrain Come From?

In a larger game, the game designers or the artists would create the maps. Typically a map editor program is built, which the designers use to lay out maps. When they are finished, the maps are often saved into a special file format designed for the game, which will be loaded into the structures the game engine uses.

But as amateurs, we don't have the manpower to do things that way. On the other hand, do you really want to write code like the following? (Not that this would work yet—you haven't written an initialize method.)

```
map = Map.new(20, 20)
map.terrain[0,0] = forest
map.terrain[1,0] = forest
map.terrain[2,0] = plains
```

Heck no! It's time to use an old game hacker's trick to avoid this. Consider the following:

```
gggggggggg
gggggggwww
gggggwwff
gggppppppp
ggppggwfpf
ggpgggwwff
```

What on earth is that? It all becomes clear once you have the key.

```
terrain_key = {
  "f" => forest,
  "g" => grass,
  "m" => mountains,
  "p" => plains,
  "w" => water,
}
```

Each letter in the string represents a `Terrain` type in a simple ASCII-encoded map. This leaves you with the interesting problem of turning a string or file containing the layout into a `Map`. The `initialize` method will do the heavy lifting!

```ruby
class Map
  def initialize(key, layout)
    rows = layout.split("\n")
    rows.collect! {|row| row.gsub(/\s+/, '').split(//) }

    y = rows.size
    x = rows[0].size

    @terrain = Matrix.new(x, y)
    @units  = Matrix.new(x, y)

    rows.each_with_index do |row, y|
      row.each_with_index do |glyph, x|
        @terrain[x, y] = key[glyph]
      end
    end
  end
end
```

You start with a terrain key and a layout string. Then you break the text into lines to get your rows. Ignore any white space. This is nice because it means you can have spaces at the beginning of the lines if you have maps embedded in your source code and want to tab indent them to the level of the surrounding code. Of course, there would be advantages to leaving the spaces alone, too. Then you could use them to represent a `Terrain` type, perhaps whatever the "normal" `Terrain` type of a `Map` was for cleaner layout. If you wanted to take that approach, you'd need to cut the `gsub` call that removes the spaces.

Anyway, you now have your two-dimensional array of character data. All that remains is to create the `Matrix` instances and insert the appropriate `Terrain` types based on the characters. The calls to `each_with_index` let you easily iterate through the arrays retrieving both the data stored in them and the locations it is stored at. This lets you easily copy it over to the `@terrain` `Matrix`, translating it through the terrain `key` on the way.

How about an example of all this in use?

```ruby
terrain_key = {
  "f" => forest,
  "g" => grass,
  "m" => mountains,
```

```
  "p" => plains,
  "w" => water,
}

map = Map.new terrain_key, <<-END
  gggggggggg
   gggggggwww
  gggggggwwff
  gggppppppp
  ggppggwfpf
  ggpgggwwff
END

map.terrain[0,0].name ➤ "Grass"
```

You're almost ready to finish up the Map class, but let's add a few helper methods first.

```
class Map
  def all_positions
    @terrain.all_positions
  end

  def within?(distance, x1, y1, x2, y2)
    (x1 - x2).abs + (y1 - y2).abs <= distance
  end

  def near_positions(distance, x, y)
    all_positions.find_all{|x2, y2| within?(distance, x, y, x2, y2) }
  end
end
```

The all_positions method just passes responsibility off to the Matrix class (whose all_positions method you've already looked at).

The within? method is a little more interesting. It calculates whether the *Manhattan distance* between two points is less than a certain number. Despite the fact that I've obviously included it in the preceding code, I honestly don't believe it belongs in the Map class! It uses none of the class's instance variables or methods and only operates on its parameters. This is always a clue that a method actually belongs to another class! In this case, however, because you are using unencapsulated x and y coordinates, there is no class to attach the method to. Since the Map class is related, attaching the method here is a satisfactory alternative. Finally, near_positions uses the other two methods to return a list of nearby locations.

█Note *Manhattan distance* is a funny term. It's an allusion to the fact that the blocks in Manhattan are all based on right angles. For example, if you need to travel diagonally, you'll need to make your trip in a series of movements that are at 90-degree angles to each other instead of simply following the shortest path at a 45-degree angle (as the crow flies).

Representing a Map

Brilliant! All you have left to do is to find a good representation for the Map. This will be passed to the player's interface via the player's draw method. Like the other representations, it can be made up of lists, strings, numbers, and nil. In the case of the Map, it needs to give enough information to distinguish among Unit instances and among Terrain instances and to figure out where they are located.

We'll use a very simple representation. It isn't set in stone, though, so if you feel like a different representation might fit your game better, all you'll need to do is to change this method and the draw methods in your player classes as well as any interfaces with the display (I'll talk about these shortly in the section titled "The Players").

Since a Map consists of information about Terrain and Unit instances, you'll return a list containing each in turn.

```
class Map
  def rep
    return [@terrain.rep, @units.rep]
  end
end
```

But to do this, you're going to need a rep method for the Matrix class as well. You'll just use a list of lists, and at each location that an object could reside, you'll include its representation.

```
class Matrix
  def rep
    @data.collect do |row|
      row.collect do |item|
        item.rep
      end
    end
  end
end
```

However, while you should always have a fully populated @terrain Matrix, you will definitely have empty spaces in the @units Matrix. These empty spots contain nil objects, and so nil must have representation. Luckily, all along nil has been an acceptable representation type. Using open classes, you can go ahead and make this work.

```ruby
class NilClass
  def rep
    nil
  end
end
```

That should do the trick. With the Map class done, let's think about the Unit class and its many subclasses.

Meeting Your Heroes

You'll need some classes to represent both the player's characters as well as the enemy dinosaurs. Despite their obvious differences, both will support the same basic actions, so you'll derive them from a common base class named Unit. You'll further subclass Unit into Human and Dinosaur in case each species has its own unique abilities. From there you'll make distinctions between human rank/profession and dinosaur species.

```ruby
class Unit; end

class Human < Unit; end
class Soldier < Human; end
class Doctor < Human; end

class Dinosaur < Unit; end
class VRaptor < Dinosaur; end
class TRex < Dinosaur; end
```

So what's common to all Unit classes?

The Universal Skeleton

To start with, all Unit classes have a name and a health counter.

```ruby
class Unit
  attr_reader :name, :health, :movement, :actions
  attr_accessor :x, :y
```

```ruby
  def initialize(player, name)
    @player = player
    @name = name
    @health = 10
    @movement = 2
    @actions = []
  end
end
```

You'll obviously initialize each Unit with its own name. You'll also bestow a default of ten health points, a standard movement rate of two squares, and an empty list of actions (these values can be overwritten in the subclasses). You'll also provide accessors to x and y coordinates (which are left blank by default; remember that the Map#place method sets them). However, the Unit initializer also accepts a player object.

I haven't talked about players yet, but for now it's enough to know that they represent either a human or a computer that controls a team of units. Player objects also provide access to the Game object through the game method. Once you have a reference to the Game, you can script anything you need. For example, to get access to the map, you would write the following.

```ruby
@player.game.map
```

Since the units have health points (and this is a combat game), you'll want a way for units to be injured as well. The following additions make that possible as well as opening the door for subclasses to perform special behavior upon death.

```ruby
class Unit
  def hurt(damage)
    return if dead?
    @health -= damage
    die if dead?
  end

  def dead?
    return @health <= 0
  end

  def alive?
    return ! dead?
  end
```

```ruby
  def die
    player.game.message_all("#{name} died.")
  end
end
```

Units are considered dead if they have 0 or fewer hit points. Units that are dead can't take any more damage, and when they first drop to 0 or lower, the die method is called.

Units also can tell that another unit is an enemy if it is controlled by another player, or that a unit is a friend if it is controlled by the same player.

```ruby
class Unit
  def enemy?(other)
    (other != nil) && (player != other.player)
  end

  def friend?(other)
    (other != nil) && (player == other.player)
  end
end
```

Units also keep track of whether they've already acted this turn.

```ruby
class Unit
  def done?; @done; end
  def done; @done = true; end
  def new_turn; @done = false; end
end
```

Beyond living and dying, perhaps the most important thing units do is move. The move method will take absolute coordinates to make things easy.

```ruby
class Unit
  def move(x, y)
    @player.game.map.move(@x, @y, x, y)
    @x = x
    @y = y
  end
end
```

All the hard work is actually done by the Map class. But it's worth noting that you pass both the old and new coordinates into the map's move method, and, afterward, update the unit's internally stored location. Keeping copies of the x and y coordinates around in the Unit instances makes it easy for range-limited actions to figure out where the unit performing them is standing. You could wrap methods on the map to avoid storing x and y within the units, but the cost is low and it simplifies your code.

Stubbing Out Undefined Classes

As you can see, the code is very interdependent (maps contain references to units and units contain references to players that contain references to maps). Interdependence like this makes incremental construction painful and should, in general, be avoided when possible.

Because you haven't written your Game classes or classes to represent your players, you can't run the preceding code. However, if you're willing to "stub out" the missing classes with a bare minimum of functionality, you can at least try out some of the code.

```ruby
class FakeGame
  attr_accessor :map
end

class FakePlayer
  attr_accessor :game
end
```

This is enough to create a fake player and game to use with your units. Now you can try out the move method.

```ruby
player = FakePlayer.new
player.game = FakeGame.new
player.game.map = Map.new(terrain_key, layout)
dixie = Unit.new(player, "Dixie")
player.game.map.place(dixie, 0, 0)
dixie.move(1, 0)
```

This technique is used a lot when building complex systems. Just don't forget to write the rest of the code later!

Now that your units are equipped with basic functionality and you've stubbed out the dependent classes, let's take a minute to nail down unit representations.

Representing Units

As you'll remember, representations are limited to lists, strings, numbers, and nil. Almost all of your representations will use at least one list (since it's your only container type). You'll also almost always list the distinguishing type of the representation in the first position of the list. This is not to be confused with the more general type. You're describing a Unit instance here, yet the first item in your array will be the kind of unit, not the word "Unit" itself. The user interface will know this representation is for a unit simply because of when and where it receives the representation (in this case as part of the map drawing). Here's the code:

```
class Unit
  def rep
    [self.class.shortname, name]
  end
end

class Class
  def shortname
    name().gsub(/^.*:/, '')
  end
end
```

As you can see, the rep method uses a new method added to Class. The method returns the name of the class it is called on, but unlike the name method on class, it strips any module prefixes out. So, calling shortname on the Dinosaur class returns "Dinosaur" even if Dinosaur is inside the DinoWars module. For example, consider the full representation for a T-Rex named Johan.

```
trex = TRex.new(player, "Johan")
trex.rep ➤ ["TRex", "Johan"]
```

The first string is his type, the second is his name.

Making Choices

There are more features to add to your Unit class. But they all resolve around this notion of letting the player make choices. For example, your units have a move method, but it's not enough to be able to move. The units also need to be able to present a list of movement choices. You should only present movement choices that are reachable given a unit's movement rate, and it should only include valid coordinates on the map (you can't move past the borders). The representations for these movement choices will look like the following:

```
["Move", 2, 3]
["Move", 3, 2]
```

The numbers are the x coordinate followed by the y coordinate. In order to support this, however, you need a class to represent choices that will bind these representations to the actions that accompany them.

```
class Choice
  attr_reader :rep
  def initialize(*rep, &action)
    @rep, @action = rep, action
  end

  def call(*args, &proc)
    @action.call(*args, &proc)
  end
end
```

Instances of the Choice class are created with a representation and an action. The representation can be accessed through the rep method, and the action can be triggered with the call method (call isn't the most intuitive name, but it's the standard Ruby invocation method name, so you might as well use it). Here's an example:

```
x, y = 0, 1
choice = Choice.new("Move", x, y) { unit.move(x, y) }
choice.rep ➤ ["Move", 0, 1]
choice.call
```

You can assume the representations are all contained within a list, so you can just pass the parameters into the new method, and they will be grouped automatically. You can also use the special * prefix operator to inject a prebuilt list as the representation. You'll also define a constant Choice named DONE.

```
DONE = Choice.new("Done")
```

You'll use DONE to represent the player's desire to avoid a choice or finish making choices. The DONE Choice has no action to be invoked, but since it is available as a constant, code can easily compare the selected choice against it. See the section titled "The Players" for more information.

Finding Possible Moves

Let's put the information about what moves are valid together with these Choice objects inside the Unit class.

```ruby
class Unit
  def move_choices
    map = @player.game.map
    all = map.all_positions
    near = all.find_all {|x, y| map.within?(@movement, @x, @y, x, y) }
    valid = near.find_all {|x, y| map.units[x, y].nil? }
    return valid.collect do |x, y|
      Choice.new("Move", x, y) { self.move(x, y) }
    end
  end
end
```

The move_choices method uses the all_positions convenience method to generate a list of coordinate pairs that exist on the map. The method then limits the list to the positions that are within movement distance and have no one else standing on them. This list is then used to build a set of choices that if selected and invoked would perform the appropriate movement.

Choosing Among Actions

The last piece of code missing from the Unit class handles actions. Each Unit type will have a list of actions it can take after it moves (tradition limits each unit to moving and then performing one action). The user will select one of the unit's actions, and then potentially select among the possible ways to take that action. Here's how the list of action choices is generated:

```ruby
class Unit
  def action_choices
    return actions.collect do |action|
      Choice.new(*action.rep) { action }
    end
  end
end
```

Notice how the * prefix operator's job is to flatten the representation returned by action.rep into a parameter list for Choice.new. Okay, now let's look closer at the Action class.

Taking Action

The Action class is relatively simple compared to the Unit class. Specific actions will be subclasses of the Action class. Each subclass of the Action class will have its own representation available via the rep method. Each will also have a method that will produce a list of instances of the class that represent the possible ways the action could be taken. These instances will have their own representations and a call method that can be invoked to actually perform the actions.

It's pretty easy for instances of subclasses of the Action class to support the same interface as a Choice object (rep and call), so you'll be able to avoid wrapping them in Choice objects when you need the player to select between them. But the subclasses themselves won't implement the interface, only their instances.

Because the generate method requires parameters before it can produce its instances, you can't just rename it to call. Here are the class methods that Action supports.

```
class Action
  def self.rep
    ["Action", self.class.shortname]
  end
  def self.range(unit); 1; end
  def self.target?(unit, other); unit.enemy?(other); end

  # Default Action generator assumes action is something you
  # do to the enemy standing next to you. This behavior will
  # overriden in many subclasses.
  def self.generate(unit, game)
    map = game.map
    near = map.near_positions(range(unit), unit.x, unit.y)
    targets = near.find_all{|x, y| target?(unit, map.units[x, y]) }
    return targets.collect{|x, y| self.new(unit, game, x, y) }
  end
end
```

See how the generate method takes the current unit and the master Game object? These can be used to figure out exactly which ways to execute this action are possible. Let's look at the instance methods of Action. Following are the methods that will be called on the results returned from the generate class method.

```
class Action
  attr_reader :unit, :game
  def initialize(unit, game, x, y)
    @unit = unit
    @game = game
```

```
    @x = x
    @y = y
  end

  def call
    raise NotImplementedError
  end

  def target
    game.map.units[@x, @y]
  end

  def rep
    [self.class.shortname, @x, @y]
  end
end
```

The parameters passed into the `generate` class method will also be passed into to the instance objects it creates so that they can perform any manipulations they need to actually perform the action. Additionally, an x and y coordinate is passed in to represent the location of the action that could be performed. This information is important to have around so you can pass it to the interface so that it can present a spatial selection mechanism. The representation will contain the name of the action and the location it will occur at. Action types that don't have a location should probably use the location of the acting unit.

Since the generic `Action` superclass should never have its `call` method invoked, you should stub it out and raise a `NotImplementedError`.

To make this all a little more concrete, let's implement some `Action` subclasses. For example, consider the `Bite` action we will give to our dinosaurs and the `Shoot` and `FirstAid` actions we give the humans.

```
class Attack < Action
  def damage_caused(unit); raise NotImplementedError; end
  def past_tense; raise NotImplementedError; end

  def call
    amount = damage_caused()
    game.message_all("#{unit.name} #{past_tense} #{target.name} for ➥
#{amount} damage.")
    target.hurt(amount)
  end
end
```

```ruby
class Bite < Attack
  def damage_caused; @unit.teeth; end
  def past_tense; "bit"; end
end

class Shoot < Attack
  def self.range(unit); unit.range; end
  def damage_caused; @unit.caliber; end
  def past_tense; "shot"; end
end

class FirstAid < Action
  def self.target?(unit, other); unit.friend?(other); end
  def call
    target.hurt(-unit.heal)
    game.message_all("#{unit.name} healed #{target.name} for #{unit.heal} health.")
  end
end
```

The representation for a Bite instance looks like this.

```ruby
["Bite", 0, 1]
```

Wiring these up to our Unit classes is easy.

```ruby
class Human < Unit
  attr_reader :caliber, :range
  def initialize(*args)
    super(*args)
    @actions << Shoot
    @caliber = 4
    @range = 3
  end
end

class Doctor < Human
  attr_reader :heal
  def initialize(*args)
    super(*args)
    @actions << FirstAid
    @heal = 2
  end
end
```

```ruby
class Dinosaur < Unit
  attr_reader :teeth
  def initialize(*args)
    super(*args)
    @actions << Bite
    @teeth = 2
  end
end

class TRex < Unit
  def initialize(*args)
    @teeth = 5
  end
end
```

If you wanted to have a weapon system where each weapon did a different amount of damage, or even potentially a random amount of damage, you could rewrite the `call` method like this:

```ruby
def call
  enemy = game.map.units[x, y]
  damage = unit.weapon.damage
  enemy.hurt(damage)
  game.message_all("#{unit.name} attacked #{enemy.name} for #{damage} damage.")
end
```

With this understanding, let's see what you have to do to get the game up and running!

The Players

I'm going to take a flexible approach to players in the game. I'll start by creating a base player class that provides the required infrastructure, and then each different kind of player can subclass and fill in the interesting bits. These subclasses of `BasePlayer` will replace the `FakePlayer` class. I'll write one class for human players and one class for computer players. In the next chapter, I'll write a full GUI for the human player, but for now the interface will be strictly command line.

```ruby
class BasePlayer
  attr_reader :name
  attr_accessor :game
```

```ruby
  def initialize(name)
    @name  = name
    @units = []
  end

  def message(string); raise NotImplementedError; end
  def draw(map); raise NotImplementedError; end
  def do_choose; raise NotImplementedError; end
end
```

At the minimum, each player needs a name and a reference to the master Game object. You'll also need to keep track of a player's units. The game instance variable is not set in the constructor because it is set via the accessor defined in the preceding code when a player is added to a game with add_player.

However, you'll also expect the subclasses to provide message, draw, and do_choose methods (I've stubbed them out in the base class by raising NotImplementedError exceptions). For the most part, the rest of the methods in BasePlayer will work just fine if the subclasses make sure to provide these three.

What kind of functionality are you going to provide them, though? For one, you'd like to be able to assign units to a player. The class should have a simple add_unit method for that and provide a method to check if a player still has units left alive (so the game can tell when a player has been defeated). The clear_units method will empty the list of units, the new_turn method resets the units themselves, and the unit_choices method returns all units that aren't marked done.

```ruby
class BasePlayer
  def add_unit(unit); @units.push unit; end
  def clear_units; @units = []; end
  def units_left?; @units.any?{|unit| unit.alive? }; end
  def new_turn; @units.each{|unit| unit.new_turn }; end
  def done; @game.message_all("Level finished"); end

  def unit_choices
    not_done = @units.find_all{|unit| unit.alive? && ! unit.done? }
    return not_done.map do |unit|
      Choice.new("Unit", unit.x, unit.y) { unit }
    end
  end
end
```

Implementing the various choice methods will be the majority of the code. Since all of these methods are in BasePlayer, they still don't talk to any particular front end. However, you can use the do_choose method, which will be implemented in the subclasses to get a choice back from the user. The method choose is mostly a thin wrapper on do_choose.

```ruby
class BasePlayer
  def choose(choices, &block)
    do_choose(choices, &block) if choices?(choices)
  end

  def choices?(choices)
    ! (choices.empty? || (choices.size == 1 && choices[0] == DONE) )
  end
end
```

Notice how do_choose is only called if choices? returns true. The choices? method specifically checks to make sure you aren't presenting DONE as the only option. In that case, you shouldn't bother the user. However, this is not the same as having only one choice. If the user has a non-DONE option, you should still let the user select it so that he knows what's happening.

On top of the choose and the choices? methods, you can build the choose_all method, the choose_all_or_done method, and the choose_or_done method.

```ruby
class BasePlayer
  def choose_all(choices, &block)
    while choices?(choices)
      choose(choices) do |choice|
        block.call(choice)
        choices.delete(choice)
      end
    end
  end

  def choose_all_or_done(choices, &block)
    choices_or_done = choices.dup
    choices_or_done.push DONE
    choose_all(choices_or_done, &block)
  end

  def choose_or_done(choices, &block)
    choices_or_done = choices.dup
    choices_or_done.push DONE
    choose(choices_or_done, &block)
  end
end
```

The `choose_all` method should keep looping until there are no meaningful choices left (either none at all, or only a DONE choice). For each selected choice, the method removes the choice from the list and then restarts the loop. A `break` statement inside the invoked block will terminate the loop if reached. This is how the early exits on DONE are achieved.

Additionally, you'd like the convenience methods that automatically added DONE to the choices like we used earlier. The list is duplicated first, just in case it was going to be reused again. This way you won't modify the original. Everything else happens inside the subclasses of `BasePlayer`.

The Artificial Intelligence Doesn't Seem So Intelligent

What's the simplest computer player you could code? It doesn't get much simpler than this:

```ruby
class DumbComputer < BasePlayer
  def message(string)
  end

  def draw(map)
  end

  def do_choose(choices)
    yield choices[0]
  end
end
```

That's right! The `message` and `draw` methods don't even do anything. An empty `message` method will probably be standard for computer players, since they can't understand human language and have little use for the niceties of the messages the game sends out. They certainly don't need to be fed bits of the story or alerted when characters die (after all, they can see the data structures—they don't need to be told in words). The same goes for the `draw` method. The drawing data could theoretically be used by the computer player to figure where units are on the map, but in fact, the AI has a much better means of inspecting the world.

Since the computer player class inherits from the `BasePlayer` class, it has direct access to the `Map` class through the `map` instance method. It can use this to "see" the map in a much simpler fashion. A computer player could hypothetically cheat using this access (for example, removing its opponents from the board), but since you'll be coding the computer players yourself, it's not a big deal.

So what's the DumbComputer class's do_choose method do? Some advanced AI algorithm? Machine learning? Nope. You'll just always select the first choice of the options presented. You couldn't possibly ship this with a real game, but it's good enough to start testing. If you go on to write your own game, putting together a reasonable AI will be one of the challenges you face. On the other hand, an AI that moves toward its enemies and attacks any it can reach will get you a long way.

Writing a Command-Line Player

Okay, the DumbComputer player almost shouldn't count it was so quick. The command-line player class will provide a better example of a well-implemented player class. Since this client forgoes fancy graphics for a simple command-line interface, implementing the message method is as simple as printing the text.

```ruby
require 'pp'
class CLIPlayer < BasePlayer
  def message(string)
    puts string
  end

  def draw(map)
    puts "Terrain:"
    pp map.terrain.rep
    puts "Units:"
    pp map.units.rep
  end
end
```

Drawing the map is a little more interesting. You could potentially draw an ASCII representation where each square was one letter representing the terrain type or the unit standing there. However, for simplicity, I'll just use the standard "pretty print" module to dump the terrain and units. This is reasonably human-readable. The do_choose method is the most interesting of the three methods.

```ruby
class CLIPlayer
  def do_choose(choices)
    mapping = rep_mapping(choices)
```

```ruby
      choice = nil

      until choice
        puts "Choose: "
        puts mapping.keys

        print "Input: "
        choice_key = STDIN.gets
        choice = mapping[choice_key]

        puts "Bad choice" unless choice
      end

      yield choice
    end

    def rep_mapping(data)
      mapping = {}
      data.each do |datum|
        mapping[datum.rep.inspect] = datum
      end
      return mapping
    end
  end
end
```

do_choose first calls a helper method that builds a mapping between the textual representations of choices and the choices themselves. This method is called rep_mapping and builds a hash table from versions of the representations of the choices converted into strings.

The do_choose method then prints all the representations from the mapping and waits for command-line input. This input is then indexed into rep_mapping to retrieve the choice the user selected. If the input is bad, the process is repeated. Finally, when a choice is selected, do_choose invokes its code block on the selected choice, which brings us to the Game class.

The Game

The Game class is going to control your turn-based strategy game. For each specific game, you'll subclass this base class. Most of the basic functionality remains in the base class, but each subclassed game will be responsible for naming itself and for defining how a turn progresses (which turns out to vary dramatically across games).

The base Game class will keep track of lists of maps and players, as well as an index into each of the lists pointing to the current map and the player whose turn it is currently. Game replaces the previously defined FakeGame class.

```ruby
class Game
  attr_reader :players

  def initialize
    @maps = []
    @on_start = []
    @players = []

    @map_index = 0
    @player_index = 0
    @done = false
  end

  def map; @maps[@map_index]; end
  def player; @players[@player_index]; end
  def next_map; @map_index += 1; end
  def next_player; @player_index = (@player_index + 1) % @players.size; end
  def start_map; @on_start[@map_index].call(map) if @on_start[@map_index]; end
end
```

The methods map and player return the current objects, and next_map and next_player advance the indexes. As you rotate through the players, you expect to return to the beginning again, so make sure to modulo the index by the total number of players. You don't need to worry about this for the maps because, when all the maps have been played, you'd like the game to end.

Because Ruby arrays return nil if indexed past their last element, letting the map index keep increasing is no problem, since calls to the map method will return nil no matter how high the index gets (even though you'll probably only call it once, at most, before noticing you're done).

Maps and players can be added to a game instance using the add_map and add_player methods. The game's add_player method also stores the game in the player's game attribute. The add_map method also takes an optional block to be triggered using the start_map method in the preceding code. The game's turn method will be able to invoke this callback for the current map using the start method. This is useful for dynamically creating enemies for maps and laying out the units.

```ruby
class Game
  def add_map(map, &on_start)
    @maps.push map
    @on_start.push on_start
  end

  def add_player(player)
    @players.push player
    player.game = self
  end
end
```

You also need a done method that notifies each player that the level is over and a done? method to check if the @done variable has been set.

```ruby
class Game
  def done
    players.each{|player| player.done }
    @done = true
  end

  def done?; @done; end
end
```

There are two more important methods to implement before you reach the run method. In particular, you want methods to force all players to redraw their displays or display a message.

```ruby
class Game
  def draw_all
    @players.each {|player| player.draw(map) }
  end

  def message_all(text)
    @players.each {|player| player.message(text) }
  end
end
```

These methods just pass the messages on to the players, and the run method you've been waiting for isn't any more complicated.

```ruby
class Game
  def run
    message_all("Welcome to #{name}!")

    while true
      break unless map

      start_map
      until done?
        turn(player())
        next_player()
      end

      next_map
    end

    message_all("Thanks for playing.")
  end
end
```

Aha! That's because all the hard work is done inside the turn method (a method our subclasses must provide). The name method will also be implemented there.

```ruby
class Game
  def turn
    raise NotImplementedError
  end

  def name
    raise NotImplementedError
  end
end
```

But all of this is useless without a defined turn method, so it's time to subclass Game and write one!

```ruby
class DinoWars < Game
  def name
    return "DinoWars: Westward Ho!"
  end

  def turn(player)
    player.new_turn
```

```ruby
    draw_all()

    player.choose_all_or_done(player.unit_choices) do |choice|
      break if choice == DONE
      unit = choice.call

      draw_all()

      player.choose(unit.move_choices) do |move|
        move.call
      end

      draw_all()

      player.choose_or_done(unit.action_choices) do |choice|
        break if choice == DONE
        action = choice.call

        player.choose(action.generate(unit, self)) do |action_instance|
          action_instance.call
        end
      end

      unit.done

      draw_all()
    end

    done() unless players().find_all{|player| player.units_left?}.size > 1
  end
end
```

Whoa. That's a big method. Let's have a closer look and see what rules I've defined for the game. It looks like the first thing to do is notify the current player object that it's his turn. This gives the player class a chance to notify his units in turn and perform any appropriate actions (for example, health recovery or poison damage).

■**Caution** While there is no fossil record that suggests the existence of venom-spitting dinosaurs, a video game is a work of fiction. These dinosaurs can damn well spit poison if you want them to. Approach with care.

The first part of a turn consists of selecting a unit from the list of units that haven't acted yet. We use a method named choose_all_or_done to make this choice. choose_all is unusual because, unlike other choices, the options aren't exclusive. You can expect the player to give each unit instructions one at a time. Of course, the player isn't required to give every unit a command, that's why you use the or_done version, which adds the DONE choice to the list, allowing you to stop early. This method will continue looping until you've selected each unit and had it perform an action or else selected DONE.

You can see in the following code that if the choice was DONE, you break out of the choice loop. Otherwise, we can invoke Choice to get a reference to the data it represents (the Unit).

```
break if choice == DONE
unit = choice.call
```

Next the player must move the unit. You first have all players redrawn using the draw_all method. Then you present the player with a list of movement choices for the unit. You call the regular choose method this time, since the unit can only move to a single one of the valid movement spaces. Don't bother including the DONE choice this time, since you'll make sure one of the movement choices is the square the unit is currently standing on. When a movement choice has been selected, you perform the move using the choice's call method.

Now it's time for the player to select an action type the unit will perform. You'll present a list of actions the unit has to the player, using the choose_or_done method. This method allows only one selection, but also automatically adds the DONE choice.

```
player.choose_or_done(unit.action_choices) do |action|
  break if action == DONE
  player.choose(action.generate(unit, game)) do |action_instance|
    action_instance.call
  end
end
```

If the player chooses no action, you break from the choice; otherwise, you'll need to generate the list of ways the action could be taken. Pass in both the Unit instance and the Game instance to the generation. The player must then choose from these ways to take the action (DONE is not an option here). The call method invokes whatever final action was selected. Finally, the unit is marked as done and redrawn one final time.

```
unit.done
draw_all()
```

The only other important note is the end game condition at the bottom of the turn method. Since the termination conditions vary depending on the game, relying on the turn method to decide when the map is done is a great way to put control in the hands of the game designer (you!). This DinoWars class together with some maps, units, and, of course, the player classes all come together to make up the game.

Putting It All Together

Let's put everything together now into a real game. Let's use the DinoWars game class and the Map instances and Unit subclasses we've already defined. You start by constructing your Game instance and your players.

```
game = DinoWars.new

human = CLIPlayer.new("Human")
computer = DumbComputer.new("Computer")

game.add_player(human)
game.add_player(computer)
```

Then we add the human player's units (which will persist across Map instances).

```
nathan = Soldier.new(human, "Nathan")
vik = Soldier.new(human, "Vik")
winston = Doctor.new(human, "Winston")

human.add_unit(nathan)
human.add_unit(vik)
human.add_unit(winston)
```

Assuming that the map you defined before has been named map1, you can script the placement of the good guys and the creation of the bad guys in the add_map method callback.

```
game.add_map(map1) do |map|
  map.place(3, 0, nathan)
  map.place(4, 0, vik)
  map.place(5, 0, winston)

  vr1 = VRaptor.new(computer, 'Velociraptor 1')
  vr2 = VRaptor.new(computer, 'Velociraptor 2')
  vr3 = VRaptor.new(computer, 'Velociraptor 3')
```

```
  computer.clear_units
  computer.add_unit(vr1)
  computer.add_unit(vr2)
  computer.add_unit(vr3)

  map.place(0, 5, vr1)
  map.place(1, 5, vr2)
  map.place(2, 5, vr3)
end
```

Finally, all you need to do is run the game.

```
game.run
```

Here's a sample of the interactions from the game.

```
Choose: ["Unit", 5, 0] ["Unit", 3, 0] ["Unit", 4, 0] ["DONE"]
Input: ["Unit", 4, 0]
---
Choose: ["Move", 4, 1] ["Move", 2, 0] ["Move", 5, 1] ["Move", 6, 0] ➡
["Move", 4, 2] ["Move", 3, 1]
Input: ["Move", 4, 2]
---
Choose: ["Unit", 5, 0] ["Unit", 3, 0] ["DONE"]
Input: ["DONE"]
---
Choose: ["Unit", 5, 0] ["Unit", 4, 2] ["Unit", 3, 0] ["DONE"]
Input: ["Unit", 4, 2]
---
Choose: ["Move", 4, 1] ["Move", 2, 2] ["Move", 4, 0] ["Move", 5, 3] ➡
["Move", 5, 2] ["Move", 5, 1] ["Move", 4, 4] ["Move", 3, 3] ["Move", 4, 3] ➡
["Move", 3, 2] ["Move", 3, 1]
Input: ["Move", 2, 2]
---
Choose: ["DONE"] ["Action", "Shoot"]
Input: ["Action", "Shoot"]
---
Choose: ["Shoot", 2, 3] ["Shoot", 0, 3] ["Shoot", 1, 3]
Input: ["Shoot", 2, 3]
---
Vik shot Velociraptor 3 for 3 damage.
Choose: ["Unit", 5, 0] ["Unit", 3, 0] ["DONE"]
```

And those are the basics.

Summary

In this chapter, you built a functional and extensible engine for a turn-based strategy game. It supports all the basic conventions of strategy games including maps, units, special abilities, a combat system, and even computer opponents. In the process, you experimented with a loosely coupled system (using the representation format). You also built several complex subclass hierarchies to accurately model the differences among units and actions. And hopefully you thought of some game ideas of your own you'd like to play with in the future!

I'll spend the next chapter discussing how to get an attractive GUI on the game. But a lot of improvements can still be made to the engine and gameplay. Some gameplay changes would require very little new engine support for example, designing new maps, adding new unit types, or actions can all be done immediately.

Other gameplay improvements will require new support code in the engine. A weapon and item system, for example, would require an `Item` class, unit support for inventories, a means to acquire items, and major changes to the combat system. Or, for example, an experience or leveling system would require a complete overhaul of the `Unit` class.

And finally, there are also just simple improvements to the engine that could improve the total excitement of the game. For example, sound effects could easily be integrated by adding a `play_sound_all` method that worked just like the `message_all` method. Rich interfaces would be able to use the information passed in to select a sound effect, while simple interfaces like the AI and command-line system could ignore them.

And, of course, the single best increase in gameplay would come from an improved AI system. The good news is, this simple decoupled system gives you a lot of flexibility to experiment. For example, try modifying the `DumbComputer` player to check the list of selections for `"Move"` choices. The computer can then use the coordinates in those choices as well as its access to the map to find the move choice that puts it closest to an enemy unit. Suddenly, the dinosaurs have the ability to chase the player's units! It's that simple. After all, building a complicated game can be complicated. But building a simple game? Not hard at all, thanks to Ruby.

> *As the smoke cleared, Captain Adams took stock of the battlefield. At least they'd be eating dino steaks tonight, he thought grimly. But at what cost in ammunition and bandages?*
>
> *"Medic!" Vik called weakly from high grass. As Winston dashed out to help him, Nathan idly wondered if they'd live to see the west coast. Or would they spend the rest of their lives lost in the dizzying jungle, fighting for their very lives, waging DinoWars!*

CHAPTER 6

▪▪▪

RubyCocoa

Ruby plays nice everywhere. From Windows to Mac to Linux, you can almost always find a way to do what you want (or need). And most of the time, you can do it in a cross-platform manner. Cross-platform is wonderful, but there's one big exception. User interfaces deserve to be native.

There are good multiplatform widget libraries out there, but even with the best, your users will be able to tell. And while users can't see your novel algorithms or your beautiful class hierarchy, they'll spend every moment using your interface. Good design can minimize the cost of a separate, native user interface for each platform. The core of your application is cross-platform, but a set of native interfaces exists to wrap it.

There's a lot to be learned from any of the big interface toolkits for Ruby. But in this chapter I'll focus on RubyCocoa, the Ruby bindings to Apple's premier application and GUI framework for Mac OS X.

But RubyCocoa is more than just bindings for the Cocoa Application Kit. It provides a complete interface layer between Ruby and the Objective-C runtime (Objective-C is the programming language Cocoa is written in), which is pretty cool. Interestingly, Ruby and Objective-C were both influenced by Smalltalk. You'll be able to see some of the similarities as you go.

Let's put RubyCocoa to use and build a RubyCocoa interface for last chapter's turn-based strategy game!

The Very Basics

I'm told that Mac OS X 10.5 may very well ship RubyCocoa (this book is going to press just before Leopard is released). Otherwise, you can get RubyCocoa from `http://rubycocoa.sourceforge.net/` or by using the excellent DarwinPorts tool (`sudo port -d selfupdate; sudo port install rb-cocoa`). To make sure it's installed properly and working, try this in irb:

```
require 'osx/cocoa'
```

Depending on your installation, Ruby may have trouble finding the RubyCocoa install. When this happened to me on my PPC Mac using MacPorts, I was able to fix the problem by locating the installed files and manually adding them to the Ruby library search path by putting the following at the top of my Ruby code. You probably won't need to add any lines like this.

```
$: << '/opt/local/lib/ruby/vendor_ruby/1.8'
$: << '/opt/local/lib/ruby/vendor_ruby/1.8/powerpc-darwin8.2.0'
```

As long as you can get this working for your development, don't worry too much. I'll cover the process by which you can bundle your Ruby applications into full OS X applications later. You'll bundle RubyCocoa inside the application, so your users won't ever have to worry about things like search paths.

Opening a Window

There's no example quite like Hello World, so let's start by opening a window (see Figure 6-1). You can set the window's title accordingly.

■**Tip** You'll be running a lot of the code in this chapter from the command line. To stop your program, simply hit Ctrl+C on the command line. You may need to hit it twice.

```
require 'osx/cocoa'

app = OSX::NSApplication.sharedApplication

window = OSX::NSWindow.alloc.initWithContentRect_styleMask_backing_defer([0, 0, ➥
500, 500], OSX::NSTitledWindowMask + OSX::NSClosableWindowMask, ➥
OSX::NSBackingStoreBuffered, true)
window.setTitleWithRepresentedFilename('Hello')
window.makeKeyAndOrderFront(nil)

OSX.NSApp.run
```

This simple example actually has a lot of complexity, so I'll take it line by line, starting with the `require` at the top. You'll see that `require 'osx/cocoa'` is at the top of every RubyCocoa project. It hooks you up to the Objective-C runtime and dynamically generates the Ruby interface into the Cocoa classes. These classes, as well as all other exposed functionality, are available through the OSX module.

Figure 6-1. *Hello World, RubyCocoa style*

But you're still not quite ready to start using Cocoa yet. You first need to retrieve your application object. Calling the class method `sharedApplication` of `NSApplication` returns the singleton object that represents the current application. It also connects to the OS X windowing environment.

So far, so good, right? But what's up with line 3? It starts out like standard Ruby, using the `NSWindow` class from the `OSX` module. But what is this `alloc` method? And why is `initWithContentRect_styleMask_backing_defer` named so weirdly?

Learning Objective-C Basics

It's time to do a quick overview of Objective-C and Cocoa. Unlike Ruby, versions of Objective-C prior to 2.0 are not garbage collected. This means memory is managed manually. In other words, every time you create an object, you must at some later point explicitly delete it. This can be tricky to keep track of, which is why most languages are garbage collected these days. The garbage collector does the work for you. With that said, if you've only ever managed memory in C (using `malloc` and `free`), you're in for a surprise. Life with Objective-C is a definite step forward.

Allocation is performed using a class method (object-oriented—how about that for a C-based language?) named `alloc`. Memory can be explicitly freed using `dealloc`. But

Objective-C objects also support manual reference counting. When you're done using an object, you can call the `release` method to decrease its reference count. If you'd like to hang on to an object (for example, in an add method of a collection class), you can call `retain`, which will increment the reference count.

If the reference count ever hits 0, the object is deallocated. Here are some examples (written in real Objective-C, so you can get a look at the syntax—which turns out to be important).

```
NSString *string = [[NSString alloc] initWithCString: "Hello World"];
[string retain];
[string release];
[string release];
```

Reading this code, you should understand two things. First of all, messages are "sent" (read: methods are called) inside square brackets. Just as important, they are written in Smalltalk style. The method name is separated from the object by a space. Parameters are always passed in keyword style. And just as in Smalltalk, the keywords are part of the method name. Consider the following method call:

```
[mutable_array insertObject: an_object atIndex: 7]
```

Its name is `insertObject:atIndex:`. This is very different from Ruby, although both approaches have their benefits. And the difference will cause some hiccups as the two languages interact.

For now, notice the pattern of `alloc` and `init`. You'll see this throughout Cocoa code. In Ruby, the class method `new` automatically calls `initialize` for you. In Cocoa, it's a two-step process. One nice thing about this is that a class can provide multiple initializers.

Calling Objective-C from Ruby

The previous string example uses an initializer that takes a C-style string and uses it to initialize the newly allocated `NSString`. It only has one keyword argument. How would you write the previous code in Ruby?

```
NSString.alloc.initWithString("foo")
```

It's not quite the same (since you don't have a C-style string sitting around), but you can see the similarities. And no-argument methods are straightforward too, as you can see from the previous call to `alloc`.

It's the multi-argument methods that are complicated. Thankfully, RubyCocoa provides a couple of different ways to call these methods. One of these approaches is bound to resonate with your sense of style.

Using `insertObject:atIndex:` as an example, consider the following Ruby code.

```
mutable_array.insertObject_atIndex_(an_object, 7)
mutable_array.insertObject_atIndex(an_object, 7)
mutable_array.insertObject(an_object, :atIndex, 7)
```

All three do the same thing. The first convention replaces colon (:) with underscore (_). This rule is straightforward and consistent. But man is it ugly!

■Note PyObjC, the Python to Objective-C bridge, provides method names in this format only. They believe the weirdness of the names is worth the consistency. Hard to say if we Rubyists should follow their example or not.

The second example will be the preferred one in this chapter. It simply omits any trailing underscores. This aids readability, and, while it potentially hinders dispatch (consider a no-argument and a one-argument method of the same name), these situations are extremely rare and can be resolved by inspecting the arguments.

The last example is the closest stylistically to Objective-C. It uses Ruby symbols to mimic Objective-C syntax. This syntax reads well, but will be deprecated in RubyCocoa 1.0, so should be avoided.

In your own objects, you'll use Ruby-style naming for method names on objects that inherit from Ruby objects, but you'll use Objective-C method names (but translated using the conventions mentioned previously) for methods on objects that inherit from Objective-C objects.

Applications and Windows

With that out of the way, let's flip back to the Hello World example.

```
require 'osx/cocoa'

app = OSX::NSApplication.sharedApplication

window = OSX::NSWindow.alloc.initWithContentRect_styleMask_backing_defer([0, 0, ➥
500, 500], OSX::NSTitledWindowMask + OSX::NSClosableWindowMask, ➥
OSX::NSBackingStoreBuffered, true)
window.setTitleWithRepresentedFilename('Hello')
window.makeKeyAndOrderFront(nil)

OSX.NSApp.run
```

The invocations upon OSX::NSWindow should make more sense now. You first allocate a new window, then initialize it with the sophisticated initWithContentRect:styleMask: backing:defer: method. Put this method aside for the moment, and let's move on. The next method call sets the window's title (putting the Hello in Hello World). And the method call after it makes sure the window appears as the application's key window. The last line is worth mentioning. This is the line that starts up the Cocoa part of the application (which handles the event loop, and so forth).

Note that NSApp is not a constant here, but actually a method call. NSApp returns the current application. You could also have run the following and reused your old reference to the application object.

```
app.run
```

That would have been just as effective, but OSX.NSApp.run is nice because it can be called from anywhere.

Okay, back to the window initializer. styleMask isn't too complicated, it's a simple set of constants that identify different features the window can have. You add together the ones you want and pass them in. backing is another argument that defines how the window is buffered, and passing in true for defer only determines when the window is first drawn and can be ignored.

But let's not forget this first argument ContentRect. Cocoa includes a C structure named NSRect that defines an x and y coordinate plus a width and height. RubyCocoa allows you to use an NSRect class, or simply an array of four items. Here's how you'd use the class version of NSRect:

```
window_rect = OSX::NSRect.new(0, 0, 500, 500)
```

Okay, enough examples. Let's dive into the turn-based strategy game front end.

Building a Turn-Based Strategy Game

You're going to reuse the engine from the previous chapter, so there's no need to worry about game logic. All you need to do is implement the user interface methods discussed in the last chapter. You'll need to provide a draw method, a message method, and the ability to make choices. But no more ugly text clients. This is your chance to make things look good.

Building a Player Using Cocoa

Let's start by refactoring the Hello World example into a CocoaPlayer class that opens a window. You'll need to load the tbs.rb file from the previous chapter. I've provided a slightly modified version that has all its setup code inside a method named run_dino. This method does all of the same setup, including creating a new game, except instead of creating a human player, it uses the one passed in as an argument. At the end it returns the newly created game object.

This method makes it easy to load and configure the game, but avoids starting play immediately. You should be able to perform this refactoring yourself, or you just grab the modified version in this chapter's source code bundle. The CocoaPlayer class will be a subclass of that project's BasePlayer class.

```ruby
require 'tbs'
require 'osx/cocoa'

class CocoaPlayer < BasePlayer
  DEFAULT_WIDTH = 500
  DEFAULT_HEIGHT = 500

  def initialize(name)
    super(name)

    app = OSX::NSApplication.sharedApplication
    app.setMainMenu(OSX::NSMenu.alloc.init)

    @window = OSX::NSWindow.alloc.initWithContentRect_styleMask_backing_defer([0, 0,➡
500, 500], OSX::NSTitledWindowMask + OSX::NSClosableWindowMask, ➡
OSX::NSBackingStoreBuffered, true)
    @window.setTitleWithRepresentedFilename('Turn Based Strategy')
    @window.makeKeyAndOrderFront(nil)

    return self
  end
end
```

Returning self at the end of init is important because variables are often assigned from the product of initializer methods. You also create an NSMenu, even though you won't be using it for a very long time.

To prove that you have a player, even if it is not complete, you can add the following methods:

```ruby
class CocoaPlayer
  def message(text)
    puts text
  end
```

```
  def draw(map)
    puts map.inspect
  end

  def do_choose(choices)
    handle_events while true
  end
end
```

These are the basic methods you're required to add to a player class. But I need to talk about the handle_events method for a minute. The do_choose method is supposed to wait for the human player to make a choice, so looping forever is a reasonable response, considering the code isn't ready for that yet. But if the method just loops, the Cocoa interface will freeze (since Ruby has full control of the master thread).

It would be wonderful if you could use Ruby's green threads to get around this problem. Then you run the game engine in a separate thread. Unfortunately, using Ruby threads along with RubyCocoa can lead to strange behavior and even crash occasionally. Instead, you can do something a little deviant and dispatch the queued up Cocoa events yourself. This is sort of bad form, but it works very well in this case. Here's the implementation of handle_events:

```
class CocoaPlayer
  def next_event(app)
    return app.nextEventMatchingMask_untilDate_inMode_dequeue(
      OSX::NSAnyEventMask,
      nil,
      OSX.NSDefaultRunLoopMode,
      true)
  end

  def handle_events
    app = OSX::NSApplication.sharedApplication
    while event = next_event(app)
      app.sendEvent(event)
    end
  end
end
```

With that in place, you should be able to pass your player into a game instance and see the initial welcome message like this:

```
class ApplicationGameDelegate < OSX::NSObject
  def initWithGame(game)
    init
    @game = game
    self
  end

  def applicationDidFinishLaunching(sender)
    @game.run
  end
end

human = CocoaPlayer.new("Human")
game = run_dino(human)
delegate = ApplicationGameDelegate.alloc.initWithGame(game)
OSX::NSApplication.sharedApplication.setDelegate(delegate)
OSX.NSApp.run
```

NSApplication is designed so that subclassing isn't required. Instead, you create a delegate that will handle selective messages for the application. The ApplicationGameDelegate is very simple. When the application finishes launching, it starts the game. All you need to do is run the app and everything starts.

Of course, so far you haven't really implemented any of the methods the BasePlayer abstract class expects.

An Odd Way to Do Things

Before you go too much farther, you should be aware that this is an unusual way to write a Cocoa application (even beyond dispatching events yourself). To start with, I'm ignoring the excellent Interface Builder tool and constructing the GUIs programmatically in order to minimize the scope of this chapter and keep it focused on Ruby.

Equally unusual is the way I'm having you run the code. Cocoa applications are almost always distributed as an application bundle. The bundle contains not only the binary code, but also any libraries, resources, and metadata required. One result of this is that you can double-click these bundles, and the application will start. It will have a Dock icon and only allow one instance to be running.

You've done none of this so far (although you will before you finish). The results are a little weird. As you've seen, you have no application menu or Dock icon. If you hit Control-C in the terminal, the application terminates. All in all, very unnatural for a Cocoa application. This approach is simple, however, and makes debugging easier, since there is no need to rebuild the application after modifying it.

Okay, how do you go about putting something inside your window? You'll need to use something called a *view*. Let's talk about views, controls, and cells.

Understanding Views, Controls, and Cells

Cocoa can be confusing at times, and understanding the difference between NSViews, NSControls, and NSCells isn't easy.

An NSView is an abstract class that supports the ability to draw and receive input. Like other GUI canvas classes, it allows the programmer to programmatically draw on its surface. Windows have a setContentView method that takes a view and associates it with the window. This is how the contents of your windows get drawn.

■**Tip** An *abstract* class is a class that is not meant to be instantiated and used directly, but is intended to be subclassed for code reuse purposes. So when you subclass NSView, you get all of its graphics management code for free, but you still need to tell it what to draw.

View objects are very useful, but you wouldn't necessarily like to implement every part of your user interface library with them. Because they are so sophisticated, they are expensive objects (in terms of memory and CPU used). As a result, Cocoa was designed with the notion of *controls* and *cells*. NSControl is a subclass of NSView (though it is also abstract and not meant to be used without further subclassing). Its main addition is the logic necessary to interact with cells. Cells are not views. They do not manage a canvas like views do, but they do know how to draw themselves upon a view.

So, NSButtonControl is a subclass of NSControl, and NSButtonCell is a subclass of NSCell. Whenever you create an NSButton, you also get an NSButtonCell (see Figure 6-2). This raises the following question: if for every element in your interface, you have both an NSControl (which is a subclass of NSView, with all its overhead) and an NSCell, how is this helping?

As always, the savings come when you buy in bulk. Picture for a moment a row of buttons. Do they all really need their own canvas? Or could they share a view? Or better yet, picture a file list like the Finder presents. There's a lot of potential savings there, if you can share the same view. There are a couple of control classes just for this purpose. The most common is probably NSMatrix, which I'll talk about more later when I use it and some NSButtonCell subclasses to build a button bar for making choices.

But first, let's get the messages showing up in the window instead of printing on the command line.

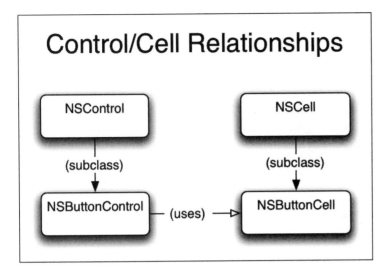

Figure 6-2. *Controls and cells*

Adding a View

A new `CocoaPlayer` can be created with the following code:

```
human = CocoaPlayer.new("Human")
OSX.NSApp.run
```

Notice how you don't start the `NSApplication` inside the `CocoaPlayer`, but wait until after it is created. This is a more flexible approach, since you can initialize multiple Cocoa objects before you start the application.

Let's also move the creation of the `NSWindow` into its own method to make the initialize method a little easier to read.

```
class CocoaPlayer < BasePlayer
  DEFAULT_WIDTH = 500
  DEFAULT_HEIGHT = 500

  def initialize(name)
    super(name)

    app = OSX::NSApplication.sharedApplication
    app.setMainMenu(OSX::NSMenu.alloc.init)
```

```
    @window = create_window
    return self
  end

  def create_window(view=nil)
    window = OSX::NSWindow.alloc.initWithContentRect_styleMask_backing_defer(
      [0, 0, DEFAULT_WIDTH, DEFAULT_HEIGHT],
      OSX::NSTitledWindowMask + OSX::NSClosableWindowMask,
      OSX::NSBackingStoreBuffered,
      true)
    window.setTitleWithRepresentedFilename('Turn Based Strategy')
    window.makeKeyAndOrderFront(nil)
    window.setContentView(view)
    return window
  end
end
```

You've added a view parameter that defaults to nil and then set the window's content view to it. As is, this code should give the same results as before.

But now let's add a view. Let's call it TBSView.

```
class TBSView < OSX::NSView
  def drawRect(rect)
    color = OSX::NSColor.colorWithDeviceRed_green_blue_alpha(0.0, 1.0, 0.0, 1.0)
    color.set
    OSX::NSBezierPath.fillRect(rect)
  end
end
```

You won't be explicitly calling drawRect, but every time the windowing system needs to redraw, it will call drawRect for you. If you want the view to redraw, you can call setNeedsDisplay(true), and it will be redrawn at the earliest convenient point.

Inside the drawRect method, you create an instance of NSColor. You pass in values between 0 and 1 for red, green, blue, and the level of transparency. But setting green to 1, while setting red and blue to 0, you'll end up with a completely green view (see Figure 6-3). And by setting the alpha value to 1.0, this example will be completely opaque.

So let's change the CocoaPlayer's initialize method a little.

```
class CocoaPlayer
  def initialize(name)
    super(name)

    app = OSX::NSApplication.sharedApplication
    app.setMainMenu(OSX::NSMenu.alloc.init)

    @view = TBSView.alloc.init
    @window = create_window(@view)
    return self
  end
end
```

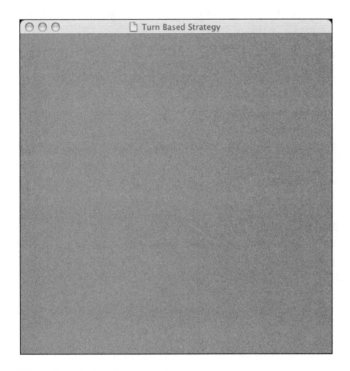

Figure 6-3. *A simple green view*

Let's pretend that what's shown in Figure 6-3 is the grass of the playing field for now and work on getting some of the player methods working better.

Displaying Messages

You'll be using the simple NSTextView, which is a type of view. Here's a create_messages method that builds the message box for you:

```
class CocoaPlayer
  def create_messages(y, width)
    position = OSX::NSRect.new(0, y, width, MESSAGE_HEIGHT)
    messages = OSX::NSTextView.alloc.initWithFrame(position)
    return messages
  end
end
```

It's positioned at the top of your window. You don't make it too tall because it should only need to hold a couple of lines of text. Then you'll add it to your TBSView as a subview. The initialize method should now look like this:

```
class CocoaPlayer
  MESSAGE_HEIGHT = 30

  def initialize(name)
    super(name)

    app = OSX::NSApplication.sharedApplication
    app.setMainMenu(OSX::NSMenu.alloc.init)

    @view = TBSView.alloc.init
    @window = create_window(@view)

    messages_y = @view.frame.height - MESSAGE_HEIGHT
    @messages = create_messages(messages_y, @view.frame.width)
    @view.addSubview(@messages)

    return self
  end
end
```

The whole point of the message box is to send messages, though, so let's update the message method. You can see the results in Figure 6-4.

```
class CocoaPlayer
  def message(text)
    @messages.setString(text)
  end
end
```

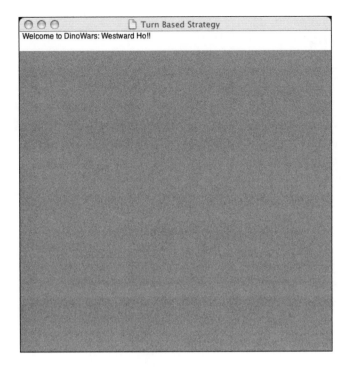

Figure 6-4. *The newly added message box*

Creating a Row of NSButtonCells

The first step will be to make a create_button_bar method, just like the create_window method. For now, you'll make a label and a button and put them into your 2 × 1 matrix.

```
class CocoaPlayer
  def create_button_bar(x, y, width)
    label = OSX::NSTextFieldCell.alloc.init
    label.setStringValue("Actions:")

    button = OSX::NSButtonCell.alloc.init
    button.setTitle("Test")
    button.setBezelStyle(OSX::NSRoundedBezelStyle)

    height = button.cellSize.height

    matrix = OSX::NSMatrix.alloc.initWithFrame([x, y, width, height])
    matrix.renewRows_columns(1, 2)
    matrix.putCell_atRow_column(label, 0, 0)
```

```
      matrix.putCell_atRow_column(button, 0, 1)
      matrix.setCellSize(button.cellSize)
      return matrix
    end
end
```

The label and the button require no explanation, except to point out that OSX::NSRoundedBezelStyle is the default style you're used to for Cocoa buttons. Not setting a bezel style gives you a bland grayish button reminiscent of Microsoft Windows.

The matrix is interesting. You've passed in x and y coordinates as well as a width. (The button bar shouldn't extend out of the window, after all!) However, you wait until inside the create_button_bar method to calculate the height. You'll base the height on the height of a button so that you can make sure it fits.

It's also important to note that NSMatrix uses row major ordering, meaning the first index represents the vertical position, while the second represents the horizontal position. Finally, set the matrix to use the button's dimensions as its cell size. You'll have to do some work to find the largest-sized button in the bar later, but for now this is enough.

With a few quick changes to the initialize method, the button bar is up and working.

```
class CocoaPlayer
  def initialize
    . . .
    @view = TBSView.alloc.init
    @window = create_window(@view)

    messages_y = @view.frame.height - MESSAGE_HEIGHT
    @messages = create_messages(messages_y, @view.frame.width)
    @view.addSubview(@messages)

    @bar  = create_button_bar(0, 0, DEFAULT_WIDTH)
    @view.addSubview(@bar)
    return self
  end
end
```

Adding it to the master view as a subview causes it to draw itself inside the main view. Position it at the bottom left (see Figure 6-5).

Try clicking the button. See how it works, even though it doesn't do anything?

Okay, it's time to start making things a little more object-oriented.

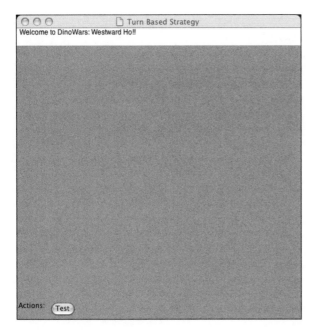

Figure 6-5. *Adding the button bar*

The Choice Bar

Since the button bar will behave rather differently than a standard NSMatrix, it makes sense to create a subclass to do exactly what you want. Since you'll be presenting choices to the user, why not call it a ChoiceBar? The ChoiceBar will support the following operations: clear, add, and setup. Clearing the ChoiceBar removes all buttons (used when the choice has been made). The add method appends a button with a label and a callback to the ChoiceBar. And setup lets the ChoiceBar know you're done adding buttons and that it should resize itself appropriately.

Here's the skeleton of the ChoiceBar class. (Limiting it to a max number of choices lets you tell it how many it will have at setup time with the renewRows_columns method and avoids some of the trickiness of changing it at run time.)

```
class ChoiceBar < OSX::NSMatrix
  MAX = 5

  def initAt(point)
    initWithFrame(OSX::NSRect.new(point.x, point.y, 1, 1))
    renewRows_columns(1, MAX)
    clear
    self
  end
```

```
  def clear
    @buttons = []
    setup
  end

  def add(label, &callback)
    button = OSX::NSButtonCell.alloc.init
    button.setTitle(label)
    button.setBezelStyle(OSX::NSRoundedBezelStyle)
    button.setRepresentedObject(callback)
    button.setTarget(self)
    button.setAction(:clicked)
    @buttons.push(button)
  end

  def clicked(me)
    callback = selectedCell.representedObject
    callback.call unless callback.nil?
  end
end
```

The initAt method calls the superclass's initializer with the specified coordinates and 1-by-1 dimensions. You can then call clear, which always resets your button list to empty, a perfect starting value. It then calls setup to appropriately size things. I'll talk about that more in just a bit.

The add method is no more complicated. It creates your button, saves the callback in the special representedObject slot for NSButtonCell, and instructs this cell to send messages back to the ChoiceBar.

You don't want to automatically invoke setup from add like you do with clear. This is because you'll usually be adding several buttons at a time to the ChoiceBar and resizing it for each of them would be a waste. Instead, just always call setup after you've finished adding buttons.

The clicked method will handle any mouse clicks on the buttons. Because the argument passed into clicked is the ChoiceBar itself (not the NSButtonCell), you'll need to use the selectedCell method to figure out which cell was clicked on.

So what does setup look like? It's a little hairy.

```
class ChoiceBar
  def setup
    MAX.times do |i|
```

```
      putCell_atRow_column(nil, 0, i)
    end

    @buttons.each_with_index do |button, i|
      putCell_atRow_column(button, 0, i)
    end

    if @buttons.size == 0
      setFrameSize(OSX::NSSize.new(1, 1))
    else
      size = @buttons.sort_by{|b| b.cellSize.width }.last.cellSize
      setFrameSize(OSX::NSSize.new(size.width * @buttons.size, size.height))
      setCellSize(size)
    end
    setNeedsDisplay(true)
    sv = superview
    sv.setNeedsDisplay(true) unless sv.nil?
  end
end
```

The first line just sets the NSMatrix subclass's dimension to be one cell high and as many cells wide as required. You then place each ButtonCell in the appropriate location in the NSMatrix subclass.

The last chunk of code sets the appropriate cell and frame dimensions for your NSMatrix subclass. If it doesn't have any buttons, it can go back to the old 1-by-1 dimensions and not worry about the cell size. If you have buttons, though, the code first needs to find the size of the biggest button. Then it'll use that as its cell size and to calculate the total size of the frame.

All you need to do to start using the ChoiceBar is replace the following line in your CocoaTBS#initialize method

```
@bar = create_button_bar(0, 0, DEFAULT_WIDTH)
```

with this line:

```
@bar = ChoiceBar.alloc.initAt(OSX::NSPoint.new(0, 0))
```

You can also delete the create_button_bar method.

Now put ChoiceBar aside for the moment. It's time to switch over to working on drawing the map. But your ChoiceBar will be waiting for you as soon as you're ready to start implementing do_choose.

Drawing the Map

It's time to finally implement the draw method. This will replace the long-standing green background to your TBSView object.

The map is a two-dimensional grid. Since locations share common tile images, you'll need to decouple the visual representation of a particular location from its general type. Each location must have a terrain type, may have a unit located on it, and may also be highlighted. Here's a crack at representing all that:

```ruby
class Location
  attr_accessor :col, :row, :terrain, :unit, :highlight, :on_click
  def initialize(col, row, drawer)
    @col, @row, @drawer = col, row, drawer
  end

  def draw
    @drawer.terrain(col, row, terrain) unless terrain.nil?
    @drawer.unit(col, row, unit) unless unit.nil?
    @drawer.highlight(col, row, highlight) unless highlight.nil?
  end

  def clear
    @on_click = nil
    @highlight = nil
  end
end
```

Each Location is initialized with its own column and row coordinates and a Drawer object. The Drawer object knows how to actually draw each tile, provided you give it a location for the tile, as well as an identifier for which tile is requested. You can use strings for the identifiers.

What does the Drawer look like? The Drawer just handles retrieving the right tile object and then invoking draw on it.

```ruby
class Drawer
  def initialize(terrain, units, highlights)
    @terrain, @units, @highlights = terrain, units, highlights
  end

  def terrain(col, row, type); draw(col, row, @terrain[type]); end
  def unit(col, row, type); draw(col, row, @units[type]); end
  def highlight(col, row, type); draw(col, row, @highlights[type]); end
```

```
  def draw(col, row, tile)
    tile.draw(col, row) unless tile.nil?
  end
end
```

Let's start by using NSColors to draw the tiles. Here's the super simple ColorTile:

```
class ColorTile
  attr_reader :width, :height
  def initialize(width, height, r, g, b, a=1.0)
    @width, @height = width, height
    @color = OSX::NSColor.colorWithDeviceRed_green_blue_alpha(r, g, b, a)
  end

  def draw(col, row)
    x = col * @width
    y = row * @height
    area = OSX::NSRect.new(x, y, @width, @height)
    @color.set
    OSX::NSBezierPath.fillRect(area)
  end
end
```

This is almost ready to go, but you've reached the point where CocoaPlayer is losing its orthogonality. The images and colors used really depend on the specific game being played. You could pass in lists of tiles when you create the player, but as you go on, the number of customizations will keep getting larger.

Instead, let's create a subclass of CocoaPlayer named DinoCocoaPlayer. Any game-specific code or data can go into DinoCocoaPlayer. A lot of that data can be easily stored in class constants. Unfortunately, code in CocoaPlayer won't be able to see constants belonging to the subclass, even when the subclass inherits the code. This is a pain, but you can get around it with the following little dance. Add the following methods:

```
class CocoaPlayer
  def cols; self.class.const_get(:COLS); end
  def rows; self.class.const_get(:ROWS); end
  def terrain_tiles; self.class.const_get(:TERRAIN); end
  def unit_tiles; self.class.const_get(:UNITS); end
  def highlight_tiles; self.class.const_get(:HIGHLIGHTS); end
end
```

The methods retrieve the actual player class and then request the constants from that. Admittedly, you could have asked the child to implement methods instead of using class constants, but I think this strategy makes the subclasses read cleaner. With the refactoring and the addition of the tile maps, the DinoCocoaPlayer now looks like this:

```
class DinoCocoaPlayer < CocoaPlayer
  COLS = 10
  ROWS = 6
  W = 50
  H = 50
  TERRAIN = {
    'Blank'  => ColorTile.new(W, H, 0.5, 0.5, 0.5),
    'Grass'  => ColorTile.new(W, H, 0.0, 1.0, 0.0),
    'Water'  => ColorTile.new(W, H, 0.0, 0.0, 1.0),
    'Forest' => ColorTile.new(W, H, 0.0, 0.8, 0.3),
    'Plains' => ColorTile.new(W, H, 0.8, 0.8, 0.8),
  }
  BLACK_BLOB = ColorTile.new(W, H, 0, 0, 0)
  UNITS = {
    'Captain' => BLACK_BLOB,
    'Doctor'  => BLACK_BLOB,
    'Soldier' => BLACK_BLOB,
    'VRaptor' => BLACK_BLOB,
  }
  HIGHLIGHTS = {
    'Unit'  => ColorTile.new(W, H, 0.8, 0.4, 0.0, 0.5),
    'Shoot' => ColorTile.new(W, H, 1.0, 0.0, 0.0, 0.5),
    'Move'  => ColorTile.new(W, H, 0.1, 0.1, 1.0, 0.5),
  }
end
```

For now, the interface just uses black blobs to represent the units. However, in order to actually store the locations of terrains and units, you'll need to build a grid of locations. You can use the Matrix class from the last chapter and slip this code in at the top of the initialize method before the Cocoa setup.

See how Drawer uses the methods that retrieve the constants? The Drawer is then passed into each Location.

```
class CocoaPlayer
  def initialize(name)
    super(name)
```

```
    @drawer = Drawer.new(terrain_tiles, unit_tiles, highlight_tiles)
    @grid = Matrix.new(cols, rows)
    @grid.each_position do |col, row|
      @grid[col, row] = Location.new(col, row, @drawer)
    end

    some_tile = terrain_tiles.values.first
    window_width = cols * some_tile.width
    window_height = rows * some_tile.height

    app = OSX::NSApplication.sharedApplication
    app.setMainMenu(OSX::NSMenu.alloc.init)

    @view = TBSView.alloc.initGrid(@grid)
    @window = create_window(window_width, window_height, @view)
    . . .
  end
end
```

The code also grabs a random terrain tile and uses it, plus the newly added `cols` and `rows` arguments to calculate the appropriate width and height for the window. The `create_window` method uses these values to size the window, like this:

```
class CocoaPlayer
  def create_window(width, height, view=nil)
    position = OSX::NSRect.new(0, 0, width, height)
    window = OSX::NSWindow.alloc.initWithContentRect_styleMask_backing_defer(
      position,
      OSX::NSTitledWindowMask + OSX::NSClosableWindowMask,
      OSX::NSBackingStoreBuffered,
      true)
    . . .
  end
end
```

But you've still got to write `drawRect`.

```
class TBSView
  def initWithGrid(grid)
    init
    @grid = grid
    self
  end
```

```
  def drawRect(rect)
    @grid.all_positions.reverse.each do |x, y|
      @grid[x, y].draw
    end
  end
end
```

It's great to have `drawRect` implemented, but unfortunately the grid `Location` objects are still empty. The `CocoaPlayer`'s `draw` method needs to populate them.

```
class CocoaPlayer
  def draw(map)
    map.terrain.all_positions.each do |x, y|
      terrain = map.terrain[x, y]
      terrain_type = terrain.rep.first
      @grid[x, y].terrain = terrain_type
    end
    map.units.all_positions.each do |x, y|
      unit = map.units[x, y]
      unit_type = unit.nil? ? nil : unit.rep.first
      @grid[x, y].unit = unit_type
    end
    @view.setNeedsDisplay(true)
  end
end
```

You use the first element of each terrain type's `rep` to tag the appropriate drawing type. At the end, you use `setNeedsDisplay` to let the view know it should redraw as soon as possible. Ready to try out your new `CocoaPlayer`? Check it out in Figure 6-6!

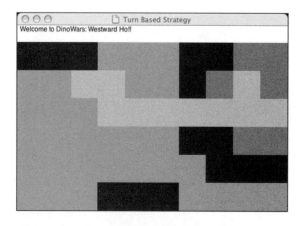

Figure 6-6. *A first look at the map*

Making Choices

The user interface may seem hung at this point, but what's actually going on behind the scenes is that the game is waiting for you to make a move. But there's not really any way to tell yet! It's time to look at the choice code.

All of the inherited choice-related methods from BasePlayer depend on do_choose being implemented. This method is passed in a list of choice objects as well as a code block. One of the choices must be selected and then passed in as a parameter to the invoked code block. Each of the Choice objects has a rep method, as you may remember, that provides the relevant information about the choice in a nice platform-independent representation of lists, strings, and numbers.

I should point out that player object cannot be truly decoupled from the game design. Theoretically, you could just present a list of buttons for every action. This is great for deciding whether to attack or defend, but clicking on the button labeled "Unit 3 4" to select the unit at location 3, 4 is a horrible interface. You want your users to be able to just click on the unit!

So there's a need to present choices by alternate means. Additionally, you can't even depend on all choice instances in a given decision using the same presentation. In turn-based strategy games, it is quite common to be presented with the choice to select a unit or do nothing. The unit selection should happen via the map, but ending the turn should be accomplished with a Done button.

The only distinguishing feature about each Choice object is its rep. So you're going to use the first item in the rep to figure out how to present each choice. The default can fall back on the button bar, but you should let each type of choice have its own presentation.

```ruby
class CocoaPlayer
  def do_choose(choices)
    choices.each do |choice|
      choice_rep = choice.rep
      choice_type = choice_rep.first
      ideal = "present_#{choice_type.downcase}_choice"
      if respond_to?(ideal)
        send(ideal, choice_rep, *choice_rep.rest)
      else
        present_choice(choice_rep)
      end
    end
    start_choice
    . . . # Code to be resumed shortly
end
```

As you can see, do_choose loops through the choices, converting them into their rep methods. It then checks to see if the ideal presentation method exists for them in the form of present_TYPE_choice. If it finds one, it calls it; otherwise, it falls back on the default present_choice method. Not that the full rep of the Choice object is passed in as well as the unpacked arguments into the present_TYPE_choice methods. This is for convenience. Calling make_choice will eventually require the full rep, so keeping that around is handy. But passing in the rest of the rep (without the type) as flattened arguments lets you name them and use them easily inside the presentation methods, as you'll see shortly.

Don't forget the definition of the rest method from previous chapters:

```ruby
module Enumerable
  def rest
    self[1..-1]
  end
end
```

It's time to finish the do_choose method. The old infinite loop that dispatched events should now be changed to wait for @choosen_rep to be set.

```ruby
class CocoaPlayer
    . . . # Code resumed
    start_choice

    while @choosen_rep.nil?
      handle_events
    end

    choosen_rep = @choosen_rep
    @choosen_rep = nil
    end_choice

    choices.each do |choice|
      choice_rep = choice.rep
      return yield choice if choice_rep == choosen_rep
    end

    raise "Somehow a bad choice was selected"
  end
end
```

The start_choice invocation triggers any code that needs to be run before the choice is made (you'll use it to set up and resize the button bar). The end_choice code performs any teardown that needs to happen (you'll use it to clear the button bar, highlighted squares, and registered choice callbacks). Nestled between those two method calls is the meat.

Once @choosen_rep is set, it copies the choice out of the instance variable into a temporary variable, and then resets the instance variable. This gets everything ready for the method to be called again.

Next the method needs to use the rep to figure out which Choice it came from, and then finally call the supplied block with that selected Choice object. If somehow the rep is not found in the choices, you'll throw a string exception (since this would be a highly aberrant situation and it doesn't make sense to rescue the exception).

Here are the related methods:

```ruby
class CocoaPlayer
  def make_choice(choosen_rep)
    @choosen_rep = choosen_rep
  end

  def start_choice
    @bar.setup
  end

  def end_choice
    @bar.clear
    @grid.all_positions.each do |col, row|
      @grid[col, row].clear
    end
  end

  def present_choice(rep)
    @bar.add(rep.join(" ")) { make_choice(rep) }
  end
end
```

The make_choice method is just a nicer face on setting @choosen_rep. The start_choice and end_choice methods set up and tear down, respectively. And the generic present_choice method simply uses the button bar combined make_choice. Still, with this code, you should actually be able to play the game now! You can see the choices being presented in Figure 6-7.

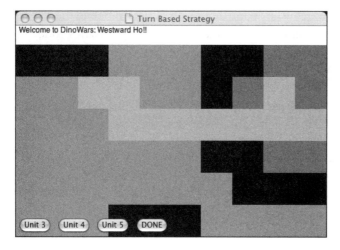

Figure 6-7. *Presenting choices as buttons*

Selecting Units from the Map

With a working game, you're in a good place to start identifying potential improvements. For example, wouldn't it be nice to be able to select units by just clicking on them?

Highlighting Map Locations

You've got most of the code required for visual unit selection already. Let's start by defining a convenience method in the CocoaPlayer class that you can use to set a Location instance's highlight.

```ruby
class CocoaPlayer
  def highlight(x, y, type)
    @grid[x, y].highlight = type
  end
end
```

Let's also create three present_TYPE_choice methods. They will call highlight, but you will still use present_choice to make the actual selection for the moment.

```ruby
class DinoCocoaPlayer
  def present_unit_choice(rep, x, y)
    highlight(x, y, 'unit')
    present_choice(rep)
  end
```

```
def present_move_choice(rep, x, y)
  highlight(x, y, 'Move')
  present_choice(rep)
end

def present_shoot_choice(rep, x, y)
  highlight(x, y, 'Shoot')
  present_choice(rep)
end

def present_firstaid_choice(rep, x, y)
  present_shoot_choice(rep, x, y)
end
end
```

You can see the effects of highlighting on the lightened black unit squares in Figure 6-8.

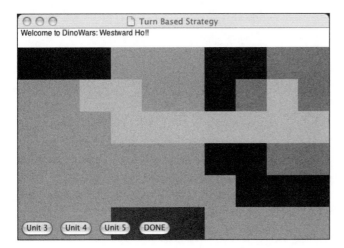

Figure 6-8. *The bottom three black unit blobs have been lightened by highlighting. The action buttons are still being used for decisions, though.*

Handling Clicks

It's not enough to just highlight the squares, though. You need to catch mouse clicks on squares and trigger the appropriate callbacks. Luckily, you already wired the Location objects to support an on_click attribute. With the addition of a simple on_click method, you can start storing useful callbacks in that attribute.

```ruby
class CocoaPlayer
  def on_click(x, y, &callback)
    @grid[x, y].on_click = callback
  end
end
```

So how do you receive the mouse click notification? You need to implement the `mouseDown(event)` method on `TBSView` to receive its clicks. But since you're going to want to hand the clicks back to the `CocoaPlayer` (which has access to the grid and can trigger the right `on_click` callback), `TBSView` will need a reference to `CocoaPlayer`. Change the initializer to pass the `CocoaPlayer` in.

```ruby
class TBSView < OSX::NSView
  def initWithGrid_mouseResponder(grid, responder)
    init
    @grid = grid
    @responder = responder
    self
  end

  def mouseDown(event)
    @responder.mouseDown(event)
  end
end
```

This means the `CocoaPlayer` now initializes the `TBSView` like this:

```ruby
@view = TBSView.alloc.initWithGrid_mouseResponder(@grid, self)
```

You'll also need a `mouseDown` method for `CocoaPlayer`. In order to translate window coordinates into map grid locations, the constructor will need to be changed to save the width and height of the tiles.

```ruby
class CocoaPlayer
  def initialize(name)
    . . .
    some_tile = terrain_tiles.values.first
    @tile_width = some_tile.width
    @tile_height = some_tile.height
    . . .
  end
```

```ruby
def xy_to_colrow(x, y)
  col = (x / @tile_width).to_i
  row = (y / @tile_height).to_i
  return col, row
end

def mouseDown(event)
  click = event.locationInWindow
  col, row = xy_to_colrow(click.x, click.y)
  if col < cols && row < rows
    callback = @grid[col, row].on_click
    callback.call unless callback.nil?
  end
end
end
```

In order to calculate the column and row that were clicked on, you need to not only divide the click's x and y by the width and height, but you also need to convert the resulting values into integers so they can be used as indexes. Since the view starts right at the bottom of the window (the choice bar hovers above it), the math works out perfectly, as long as you make sure the click isn't greater than the maximum column and row (if the user clicks somewhere in your message box, for example).

Your present_TYPE_choice methods should now resemble the following code. You can see the results in Figure 6-9.

```ruby
class DinoCocoaPlayer
  def present_unit_choice(rep, x, y)
    highlight(x, y, 'Unit')
    on_click(x, y) { make_choice(rep) }
  end

  def present_move_choice(rep, x, y)
    highlight(x, y, 'Move')
    on_click(x, y) { make_choice(rep) }
  end

  def present_shoot_choice(rep, x, y)
    highlight(x, y, 'Shoot')
    on_click(x, y) { make_choice(rep) }
  end
end
```

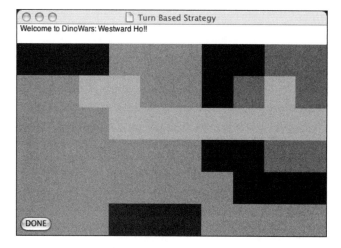

Figure 6-9. *You can click directly on units now, so there's no need for any button choices, except for Done.*

Using Image Tiles

You've got a playable strategy game now. There's only one problem. It's ugly! If you were part of a real game production team, the artists would be cranking out top-notch tilesets. But since you don't have that luxury, you're going to need to scavenge, even if this means the tileset doesn't quite match the game.

PlanetCute to the Rescue

You'll be using Danc's freely available PlanetCute tileset. Danc released the tileset to help developers prototype games more easily. This game was aiming for Dinosaur Western, and this is a more of a Chibi-space look—but beggars can't be choosers.

■**Note** The PlanetCute tileset is available for download at www.lostgarden.com/2007/05/dancs-miraculously-flexible-game.html.

The tileset is made of PNG images using alpha transparency. Lucky for us, Cocoa's NSImage can handle them with no problem. The one weirdness (actually a virtue) of these tiles is that they depict three-dimensional blocks. This makes them great for prototyping because you can build complex multilevel environments. You won't be using them like that, but the tiles look incredible no matter what. Unfortunately, though, this means that each tile is actually larger than the square it fills.

That's right. The part of the tile that a unit would stand on doesn't start until about 26 pixels or so up. This has two important implications. First of all, the mouse click to grid coordinate translation code will need to be adjusted. I'll talk about that later in the section titled "Fixing the Weirdness." Additionally, suddenly the drawing order of tiles becomes important. Since tiles hang down below themselves, if you draw the "front" tiles first, the overhangs from the back tiles will draw partially on top of them. So you'll need to draw in reverse order as well.

Switching from Colors to Images

You'll deal with the challenges of the new tile size eventually, but let's start by coding up an ImageTile class to replace ColorTile.

```ruby
class ImageTile
  attr_reader :image, :height, :width

  def initialize(filename)
    @filename = filename
    @image  = OSX::NSImage.alloc.initByReferencingFile(filename)
    @width  = @image.size.width
    @height = @image.size.height
  end

  def source
    OSX::NSRect.new(0, 0, @width, @height)
  end

  def destination(col, row)
    OSX::NSRect.new(col * @width, row * @height, @width, @height)
  end

  def draw(col, row)
    image.drawInRect_fromRect_operation_fraction(destination(col, row),
                                                 source,
                                                 OSX::NSCompositeSourceAtop, 1.0)
  end
end
```

You can use NSImage to load the actual image. The height and width are derived from the image's height and width. You're responsible for making sure your images all have the same size. The source and destination methods are just convenience methods to calculate the parameters for the drawing method. The source is the entire image, and the destination is the appropriate coordinates in the TBSView.

Adding Image-Based Tilesets to DinoCocoaPlayer

Here's the adjusted DinoCocoaPlayer class using the awesome PlanetCute art.

```
class DinoCocoaPlayer
  TERRAIN = {
    'Grass'  => ImageTile.new('PlanetCute/Grass Block.png'),
    'Water'  => ImageTile.new('PlanetCute/Water Block.png'),
    'Forest' => ImageTile.new('PlanetCute/???.png'),
    'Plains' => ImageTile.new('PlanetCute/Stone Block.png'),
  }
  UNITS = {
    'Captain' => ImageTile.new('PlanetCute/Character Boy.png'),
    'Doctor'  => ImageTile.new('PlanetCute/Character Pink Girl.png'),
    'Soldier' => ImageTile.new('PlanetCute/Character Horn Girl.png'),
    'VRaptor' => ImageTile.new('PlanetCute/Enemy Bug.png'),
  }
  W = TERRAIN.values.first.width
  H = TERRAIN.values.first.height
  HIGHLIGHTS = {
    'Unit'  => ColorTile.new(W, H, 0.8, 0.4, 0.0, 0.5),
    'Shoot' => ColorTile.new(W, H, 1.0, 0.0, 0.0, 0.5),
    'Move'  => ColorTile.new(W, H, 0.1, 0.1, 1.0, 0.5),
  }
end
```

Most of the images loaded work pretty well, but there isn't an obvious image for the forest tiles. Putting in an invalid filename like ???.png will give you a blank image, so that's fine for now. Of course, the characters don't look much like cowboys, and that bug isn't a very realistic raptor (see Figure 6-10). I think this is probably what separates us amateur game developers from the pros.

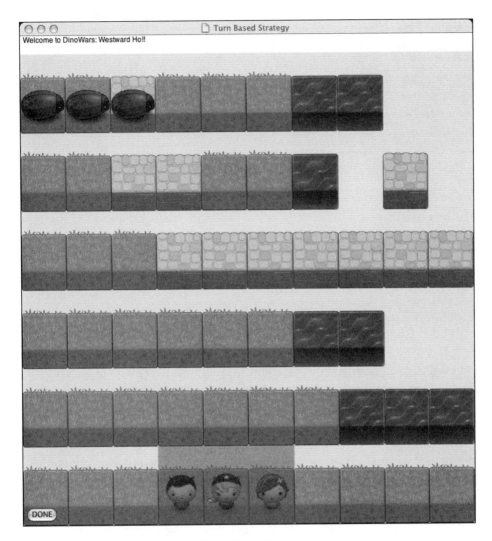

Figure 6-10. *DinoWars using the PlanetCute tileset*

Fixing the Weirdness

Okay, there are two problems that I see. First of all, you're missing a forest tile. If you
browse the tileset, there is a tree tile, but it's missing a background. You can fix this with
a new tile class.

```
class MergedTile
  def initialize(*tiles)
    @tiles = tiles
  end
```

```ruby
  def draw(col, row)
    @tiles.each{|tile| tile.draw(col, row) }
  end

  def height; @tiles.first.height; end
  def width;  @tiles.first.width; end
end
```

With this merged tile class, you can implement the forest tile like this:

```ruby
class DinoCocoaPlayer
  TERRAIN = {
    'Grass' => ImageTile.new('PlanetCute/Grass Block.png'),
    'Water' => ImageTile.new('PlanetCute/Water Block.png'),
    'Forest' => MergedTile.new(ImageTile.new('PlanetCute/Grass Block.png'), ➥
ImageTile.new('PlanetCute/Tree Ugly.png')),
    'Plains' => ImageTile.new('PlanetCute/Stone Block.png'),
  }
end
```

The forest tile looks good, as shown in Figure 6-11. But the next problem is a little more serious. There are clearly some spacing issues.

As I mentioned previously, the tiles' images not only extend below the space where units stand, they also extend beyond it (although luckily their backgrounds are transparent).You can start by tweaking the ImageTile to eliminate the padding. You're going to have to decouple the image's height and width used for calculating its drawing boundaries from its height and width used for placement. You can do this in a subclass:

```ruby
CUTE_TERRAIN_SHORTEN_Y = 66

class CuteTile < ImageTile
  def height; @height - CUTE_TERRAIN_SHORTEN_Y; end
  def destination(col, row)
    OSX::NSRect.new(col * @width, row * height, @width, @height)
  end
end
```

You'll then need to replace all your ImageTile.new terrain instances with CuteTile.new. You can see the results in Figure 6-12.

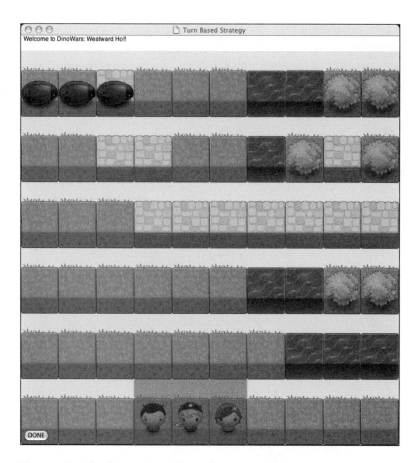

Figure 6-11. *The forest tile replaces the previously blank squares.*

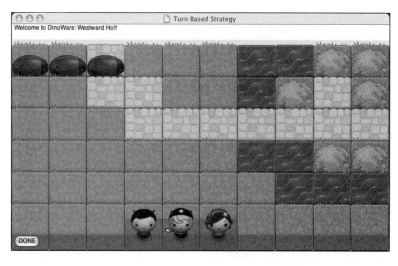

Figure 6-12. *With the terrain spacing problem solved, the map is starting to look great.*

This is a huge step forward, but another part of the offset problem is visible now. The units and highlights are resting too low, and the top of the uppermost row of tiles is cut off (along with the enemy sprites that are standing there). You can fix this with more tile classes modifications. (Although beware: mouse clicks are still expected in the old locations, which won't be obvious right now.)

```
CUTE_TILE_OFFSET_Y = 28

class CuteUnitTile < CuteTile
  def destination(col, row)
    OSX::NSRect.new(col * @width, row * height + CUTE_TILE_OFFSET_Y, ➥
@width, @height)
  end
end

class CuteColorTile < ColorTile
  def draw(col, row)
    x = col * @width
    y = row * @height
    area = OSX::NSRect.new(x, y + CUTE_TILE_OFFSET_Y, @width, @height)
    @color.set
    OSX::NSBezierPath.fillRect(area)
  end
end
```

Don't forget to change the unit instances of ImageTile to CuteUnitTile. Also change your ColorTile instances to CuteColorTile instances.

Now's probably a good time to change the drawing order between units and highlights (see Figure 6-13). While it made sense when you were using opaque blocks to put the semi-transparent highlight at the very top, it doesn't look as good as it used to when you were using images.

Changing Location's draw method makes things look better, as you can see in Figure 6-13.

```
class Location
  def draw
    @drawer.terrain(col, row, terrain) unless terrain.nil?
    @drawer.highlight(col, row, highlight) unless highlight.nil?
    @drawer.unit(col, row, unit) unless unit.nil?
  end
end
```

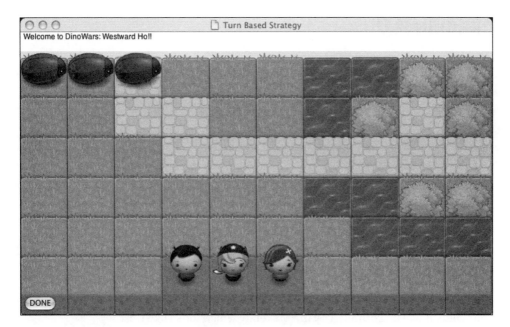

Figure 6-13. *Highlights are now drawn over the terrain, but under the units.*

All that's left is to add the required padding to the total window size and fix the mouse down handling. Mouse handling is easy. Check this out:

```
class DinoCocoaPlayer
  def xy_to_colrow(x, y)
    col = (x / @tile_width).to_i
    row = ((y - CUTE_TILE_OFFSET_Y ) / @tile_height).to_i
    return col, row
  end
end
```

And adding some extra padding? Piece of cake.

```
class DinoCocoaPlayer
  def create_window(width, height, view=nil)
    super(width, height + CUTE_TILE_OFFSET_Y + 10, view)
  end
end
```

Packaging It Up

Now that you've built an entire Cocoa app running just from the command line, let's bundle it together as a real Cocoa application bundle. You'll use a Makefile based on the Hakoiri-Musume RubyCocoa example written by Masatoshi SEKI san. The install should have placed this project at /Developer/Examples/RubyCocoa/Hakoiri-Musume. In fact, you'll use variants on the Makefile, the main.m Objective-C file, and the Info.plist.tmpl property list. main.m must be changed to run your Ruby code.

```
#import <RubyCocoa/RBRuntime.h>

int main(int argc, const char* argv[])
{
  return RBApplicationMain("cocoa.rb", argc, argv);
}
```

This file provides the binary stub necessary to load the RubyCocoa environment and run your code. It will be compiled by the Makefile, which looks like this:

```
# -*-makefile-*-

APPNAME = DinoWars
BUNDLEID = rubyapp.$(APPNAME)

RUBYSRCS = cocoa.rb tbs.rb
OBJS = main.o
LIBS = -lobjc -framework RubyCocoa

TARGET = $(APPNAME).app
CFLAGS = -Wall

SED_CMD_0 = -e "s/%%%APPNAME%%%/$(APPNAME)/"
SED_CMD_1 = -e "s/%%%BUNDLEID%%%/$(BUNDLEID)/"


$(TARGET): $(OBJS) $(RUBYSRCS)
        $(CC) $(OBJS) $(LIBS)
        -/bin/rm -rf $(APPNAME).app
        mkdir $(APPNAME).app
        mkdir $(APPNAME).app/Contents
        mkdir $(APPNAME).app/Contents/MacOS
```

```
        mkdir $(APPNAME).app/Contents/Resources
        mv a.out $(APPNAME).app/Contents/MacOS/$(APPNAME)
        sed $(SED_CMD_0) $(SED_CMD_1) Info.plist.tmpl > $(APPNAME).app/Contents/➥
Info.plist
        echo -n "APPL????" > $(APPNAME).app/Contents/PkgInfo
        cp -p $(RUBYSRCS) $(APPNAME).app/Contents/Resources/
        cp -r PlanetCute $(APPNAME).app/Contents/Resources/


clean:
        -/bin/rm -rf $(APPNAME).app *.o a.out *~ core
```

As you can see, the APPNAME is set to DinoWars, RUBYSRCS includes your two Ruby files, and additionally, the PlanetCute tiles are copied into the Resources directory. Among other things, the Info.plist.tmpl gets filled in with the APPNAME. Before the template substitution, it looks like this:

```
<?xml version="1.0" encoding="UTF-8"?>
<!DOCTYPE plist SYSTEM "file://localhost/System/Library/DTDs/PropertyList.dtd">
<plist version="0.9">
<dict>
        <key>CFBundleExecutable</key>
        <string>%%%APPNAME%%%</string>
        <key>CFBundleIdentifier</key>
        <string>%%%BUNDLEID%%%</string>
        <key>CFBundlePackageType</key>
        <string>APPL</string>
        <key>CFBundleSignature</key>
        <string>????</string>
</dict>
</plist>
```

The Info.plist describes the application to Mac OS X.

You're now ready to run Make! Make will build a DinoWar.app bundle that you can double-click (or launch with open Dinowar.app in the same directory). But, uh oh! Nothing happens!

Unfortunately, you can no longer use the current working directory to find your tileset. This means your window's calculated size is negative. You'll need to make a quick change to the ImageTile class to get around this. The new initializer looks like the following code and uses a special Cocoa function to get access to the Resources directory inside the bundle. Writing it this way allows you to continue to run from the command line when you wish but also work as a bundle.

```ruby
class ImageTile
  def initialize(filename)
    if ! File.exist?(filename)
      path = OSX::NSBundle.mainBundle.resourcePath.fileSystemRepresentation
      filename = File.join(path, filename)
    end

    @filename = filename
    @image   = OSX::NSImage.alloc.initByReferencingFile(filename)
    @width   = @image.size.width
    @height  = @image.size.height
  end
end
```

You probably also want to give the application a menu item to let users quit! Replace
the line in CocoaPlayer's initializer that reads app.setMainMenu(OSX::NSMenu.alloc.init)
with a call to create_menu. The new method looks like this:

```ruby
class CocoaPlayer
  def create_menu
    app = OSX::NSApplication.sharedApplication
    main_menu = OSX::NSMenu.alloc.initWithTitle("MainMenu")

    app_item = main_menu.addItemWithTitle_action_keyEquivalent("Apple", nil, "")
    app_menu = OSX::NSMenu.alloc.initWithTitle("Apple")
    app_item.setSubmenu(app_menu)

    quit_item = app_menu.addItemWithTitle_action_keyEquivalent("Quit DinoWars", ➥
:terminate_, "q")
    quit_item.setTarget(app)

    app.setAppleMenu(app_menu)
    app.setMainMenu(main_menu)
  end
end
```

And with your users able to quit, you've created your first Cocoa application!

Summary

Whether it's games or business applications, a native user interface will always help woo your users. And RubyCocoa makes native interfaces easy for Ruby on the Mac. You should have enough under your belt now to continue working on the game engine or building user interfaces of your own.

A great next step would be to explore some of the many wonderful resources for RubyCocoa online at `http://rubycocoa.sourceforge.net/doc/` or `www.rubycocoa.com/`. This has been a relatively unorthodox look at RubyCocoa. I've avoided using some of the excellent Cocoa development tools like Xcode and Interface Builder. So there's still plenty more to learn if you're interested. (You can read more about Cocoa in general at `www.cocoadev.com`.)

And next time you're thinking about writing a Ruby application, think about giving it a native user interface. The results can be stunning.

CHAPTER 7

■■■

Genetic Algorithms in Ruby

In Chapter 2, you simulated the average weight of pocket change given different coin systems. In order to find the best denominations of coins (given a specific sample of prices), the code did a brute force search of all possible configurations you were interested in. But it become apparent that, as the coin set grew larger, the time required became exponentially longer with each additional possible coin.

This happens all the time in optimization problems. Trying every possibility is only a feasible strategy for the smallest of search spaces. Happily, there are a variety of algorithms and strategies for exploring large solution spaces. Many of these algorithms take advantage of the fact that good solutions often resemble the best solutions. Searching for solutions similar to your best solutions may reveal better ones still. Of course, these strategies can get trapped in locally optimum solutions, missing even better solutions. It's a delicate balance, but many of these algorithms take steps to prevent this kind of shortsightedness. Some of these strategies have exciting names like *hill climbing*, *simulated annealing*, and *ant colony optimization*.

But you'll be focusing in one particular strategy that's received a lot of popular press since its inception. *Genetic algorithms* are based on the observed process of biological evolution. Solutions are randomly generated and then pitted against each other. The most promising solutions are kept for the next round where they will "reproduce" in order to produce new solutions, which then compete in the next round. Capturing the essence of this biological process makes genetic algorithms a fascinating topic for beginners and experts alike. It's easy to be awed as you watch evolution play out before your very eyes.

In this chapter, you'll put together a flexible system for building genetic algorithms. Then you'll return to the coin simulation and use genetic algorithms to explore some of the larger variants of the problem (like the optimal 4- and 5-coin variants). With any luck, you'll get some interesting insights into evolution along the way.

Simulating Evolution

So what, exactly, does a genetic algorithm look like? To start with, you need an initial population. You can think of it as having four phases: *initialization*, *selection*, *recombination*, and *termination* (although the selection and recombination phases are executed multiple times). However, in order to start, you'll need to be able to generate an initial population. You can think of the population as the life-forms in our ecosystem (although, to be accurate, the population is really these life-forms' genetic material). Which brings us to an interesting question: what would this collection of genetic material (genome) look like inside a computer?

In many biological systems genetic information is stored using deoxyribonucleic acid (DNA). DNA is built from four nucleotides named adenine (A), cytosine (C), guanine (G), and thymine (T). In the right light, DNA starts to look a lot like a number in base four. So why shouldn't you just represent the genetic information using numbers? Most computers store numbers as base two (binary) numbers, but there's no fundamental difference between base two and base four systems (just simple practical differences).

Given that, there are four main phases in a genetic algorithm. During *initialization*, the population of genomes is usually generated randomly, although it is possible to intelligently select a starting population. Be careful, though, if you try to prime your system like that. It's possible to exclude the best solutions if you focus your starting population on the wrong features. Because you'll be using numbers to represent genetic information, Ruby's built-in random number generation will be all you need to construct the initial population.

Then it's time for *selection*. In some ways, this step models the natural selection process seen in real ecosystems. Instead of being a simple label attached to the genomes that survive, the very definition of fitness is bent on the goal of finding your optimal solution. Selection then occurs based on that metric. Inferior solutions will be removed from the pool before reproduction occurs. This can be done across the board, but an even better idea is to let chance have some say. Pruning all unsuccessful solutions might prevent the very best solutions from being discovered later.

Next, during *recombination*, a new population is produced from the survivors of selection. Just like biological sexual reproduction, the recombination stage of a genetic algorithm creates children from the combined genetic material of their two parents. The process that merges portions from each of their genomes is called *crossover*, and it is vitally important. Crossover is the mechanism that allows two parents to produce a child with strengths from both of them. Of course, not all crosses produce better solutions. Luckily, the next round of selection will probabilistically cull these less-successful offspring. During recombination, *mutation* (the random changing of genetic material) is usually modeled as well. Mutation adds an element of variability (just as in biological systems) and helps produce entirely new solutions.

This sequence of steps can be repeated indefinitely, so you'll have to impose a *termination* condition. In many cases, you'll want to halt the algorithm after you've hit your desired number of iterations. But if you know something about your problem space, you can simply keep running until you've found an answer that you consider an acceptable solution. In the coin example, you might run for an hour and keep the best result, or you might keep searching until the code found a solution superior to a previous best effort (or it finished exploring the search space and couldn't find one).

Implementing the Algorithm

You'll start by implementing the algorithm itself, encapsulated inside the GeneticAlgorithm class. It might help to think of the GeneticAlgorithm class as an ecosystem, which also describes the rules of existence for the genetic material.

Probably two of the most important parameters for the algorithm (besides the details of the genomes themselves) are the population size (how many genomes compete in each round) and the selection size (how many genomes survive each round). The initialize method represents the initialization phase of the algorithm.

```ruby
class GeneticAlgorithm
  attr_reader :population

  def initialize(population_size, selection_size)
    @population     = (0...population_size).map{|i| yield i }
    @selection_size = selection_size
  end
end
```

Notice how each genome is created using a block provided to the initialize method. The selection size is stored for later use. You'll need some helper methods to implement the iterations of the algorithm, so let's start by defining them.

```ruby
class GeneticAlgorithm
  def fittest(n=@selection_size)
    @population.sort_by{|member| member.fitness }[-n..-1]
  end
end

module Enumerable
  def random
    self[rand(size)]
  end
end
```

The method named `fittest` selects the n fittest members of the population, using the `fitness` method on each genome and the previously specified selection size. If no number n is specified, it uses `@selection_size` by default.

The second helper method is named `random`. By defining it in the `Enumerable` module, all collections that mix in `Enumerable` will automatically get the `random` method. The `random` method uses the `rand` method from the set of `Kernel` methods (functions) to generate a random index between 0 and the number of elements in the collection, and then return the element at that location. Here's an example:

```
[1, 2, 3].random ➤ 3
[1, 2, 3].random ➤ 2
```

But how do the actual algorithmic iterations work?

Running the Iterations

During each step in the selection phase, the algorithm selects a group containing the fittest members of your population using your helper method. Then, in the recombination phase, it rebuilds the population to its full size by repeatedly selecting random members of the survivors and asking them to reproduce using some form of crossover. The details of the reproduction are up to the survivor, but it passes in the list of all survivors (including itself!) so that you can implement any sort of genetic product you choose. This actually means reproduction can involve more than two genomes, although you'll stick to the simplest models of crossover in this chapter.

Restricting the `GeneticAlgorithm` class's knowledge about the intimate details of genome reproduction means you won't need to alter the class's code if you change the underlying representation of the genomes (a subject you'll be looking at in the next section).

I'll call the method `step`, since it steps the algorithm forward one round by running the selection and recombination phases.

```ruby
class GeneticAlgorithm
  def step
    survivors = fittest
    @population = (0...@population.size).map do |i|
      parent = survivors.random
      parent.reproduce(survivors)
    end
  end
end
```

And that's it. You'll add a `run` method for convenience that takes a number of iterations to run, and then returns the fittest member of the final population. Running for a fixed number of iterations like this is the simplest form of condition for the termination phase, but more sophisticated heuristics based on the quality of the population can be used instead.

```ruby
class GeneticAlgorithm
  def run(steps)
    steps.times { step }
    return fittest(1).first
  end
end
```

All that's left is a simple genome to run the algorithm on, and you can test it out. After that, you'll figure out what you need to run a real example, and then get your coin problem up and running.

What's Required to Be a Genome?

Looking at the previous code, the requirements on your genomes are minimal. Each must have a `fitness` method that returns a comparable value that they can be sorted by. They also need a `reproduce` method that takes a list of population members and returns a new member.

Let's try to design the simplest possible genome to test the algorithm before you dive into the full complexities of designing encodings and reproduction algorithms. This class exists solely to exercise the `GeneticAlgorithm` class.

The `fitness` method is supposed to calculate its value from the genome's genetic material. In the coin problem, you'll need to run a simulation, and the fitness will be the average number of coins your customers need to carry (actually, the inverse of the number of coins, since you select for larger numbers but want to minimize the number of coins).

To test the algorithm here, though, the genome will just return the very number you're using to encode the genetic information. This causes the genetic algorithm to select genomes that are encoded as the largest binary numbers (that have 1s instead of 0s in the most significant bits).

```ruby
class DummyGenome
  attr_reader :fitness

  def initialize(information)
    @fitness = information
  end

  def reproduce(mates)
    return self
  end
end
```

The reproduce method is also simplified. It returns a reference to the instance it is called on. This lets you test your algorithm without implementing a mechanism for combining parent genomes (crossover). These simplifications let you test out the GeneticAlgorithm class.

```
ga = GeneticAlgorithm.new(10, 4) { DummyGenome.new(rand(8)) }
ga.run(10) ➤ 6
```

You create a population of ten DummyGenome instances, four of which will be selected with each iteration. You'll run the algorithm for ten iterations on a starting population consisting of DummyGenome instances assigned an arbitrary fitness value between 0 and 7.

The end result? 6. Why not 7? Remember, your genome fitness values were assigned arbitrarily. In this case, it appears that no 7s were in the initial population. Which brings us back to the issue of genetic algorithms. In order to run the GeneticAlgorithm class on anything more than test objects, you're going to need to implement a proper genome.

But let's make one small improvement to the GeneticAlgorithm class before you call it complete.

Remembering Winning Solutions

Consider the situation where the initial population has an extremely fit genome. It's currently possible for successive iterations to lose or destroy this genome. You can avoid this by always remembering the best genome the algorithm has seen yet.

```
class GeneticAlgorithm
  def remember_best
    current = fittest(1).first
    @best = current if @best.nil? || current.fitness > @best.fitness
  end
end
```

You then integrate this code into the initialize and step methods, and make sure to return @best from the run method.

```
class GeneticAlgorithm
  def initialize(population_size, selection_size)
    @population = (0...population_size).map{|i| yield i }
    @selection_size = selection_size
    remember_best
  end

  def step
    survivors = fittest
```

```ruby
    @population = (0...@population.size).map do |i|
      parent = survivors.random
      parent.reproduce(survivors)
    end
    remember_best
    return @best
  end
end

  def run(steps)
    steps.times { step }
    return @best
  end
end
```

Now, even if the algorithm runs in a bad direction, it'll never accidentally make things worse than the initial state. Of course, you certainly expect your algorithms to produce better solutions than the starting state. But this buys you some freedom in the selection process (you can take bigger risks and not worry about conserving good solutions). It also means you don't need to worry as much about crossover and mutation's ability to erase your solutions.

Okay, back to thinking about bit fields and ways you might encode your problem domain.

Thinking About Encodings

You could implement your bit strings in a few ways. The simplest conceptually is probably a list of boolean values. But you're going to encode them as integers. The two approaches work in a similar fashion, but it's more common to encode the genome as integers. This also gives you a chance to explore some of the features of Ruby integers.

Using Integers As Bit Strings

The Integer class already provides some good features for you. One nice aspect of Ruby's integers is that they already support bitwise indexing using the standard [ ] accessing method.

```ruby
5[0] ➤ 1
5[1] ➤ 0
5[2] ➤ 1
5[3] ➤ 0
```

The number 5 is represented by the following bits (from the most significant to the least significant): 101. At the zeroth index (the rightmost digit), you see that the first bit is 1. The second is 0, the third is 1, and all indexes beyond that (3, etc.) are 0. This gets you part way to what you need, but you still need a way to combine two integers.

Playing with Crossover

It's time to start thinking about crossover. Remember that crossover is the process by which two genomes produce a new genome. Happily, while crossover strategies need to be implemented specifically for each underlying genome representation, they are general purpose. So as long as a given problem (say the test code or the coin problem) can be encoded for the genome implementation, the crossover methods you've implemented will work seamlessly.

Since you're combining bits, you might naively try to use Ruby's bitwise operations. For example, bitwise "and" (spelled & in Ruby) produces a new number that only has 1s for bits, where both input bits were also 1. Bitwise "or" (spelled | in Ruby) results in a new number with 1s for bits, where either or both input bits were 1. Where both input bits have a 0, the resulting bit is 0. Bitwise "exclusive or" (spelled ^ in Ruby) results in a new number with a 0 for any bit where the two source bits are the same, and 1 for any bit where the source bits are different.

```
0b0100 & 0b1100 == 0b0100 ➤ True
4 & 12 == 4 ➤ True
0b0101 & 0b1100 == 0b1101 ➤ True
5 & 12 == 13 ➤ True
0b0100 ^ 0b1100 == 0b1000 ➤ True
4 ^ 12 == 8 ➤ True
```

Unfortunately, each of these approaches is flawed. By their very definitions, bitwise "and" tends to produce numbers with fewer 1s, and bitwise "or" tends to produce numbers with more 1s. Since these genomes represent real solutions in your problem domain, this kind of bias would be disastrous. Imagine if the reproduction step of the coin solver genetic algorithm kept repeatedly producing certain inferior genomes because of a bias like this!

"Exclusive or" is better because it at least tends to preserve the bit ratios (although because a number combined using bitwise "exclusive or" with itself produces 0, there's a potential to accidentally converge on an all 0 population). The real problem is that these solutions are too deterministic. Instead of looking to standard bitwise operations for inspiration, let's switch back to biology for inspiration. For example, in sexual reproduction, a process called *chromosomal crossover* is used to synthesize new genetic combinations from a given parent's set of chromosomes. An offspring is provided with one of these new genomes from each parent.

In the biological case, crossover is literal. Parts of one genome literally replace the corresponding parts of other genomes and vice versa (although unaligned crossovers are possible and can cause serious problems). Of course, our genomes aren't diploid (they don't have two sets of genetic material), but that doesn't mean you can't use the notion of chromosomal crossover to combine genomes. The fact that this strategy is such a good fit (and is almost always used) is the reason that the phase of the algorithm where genetic material is combined is usually referred to simply as crossover.

Modeling Crossover

Since you're using integers to model your numbers, you'll probably want to attach your crossover methods to them somehow. Since you're only producing one new set of genetic material, you can actually afford to think of the problem not as "swapping" strings of bits, but as selecting strings of bits in turn from alternating parent genomes.

You'll start with the `uniform_crossover` method. Using uniform crossover, each bit has equal probability of coming from either parent. In order to implement this, you're going to need to know how many bits are needed to represent a given number and you'll also need a means of converting a list of bits back into a number.

```ruby
module Enumerable
  def bits_to_int
    (0...size).inject(0){|total, i| total + (self[i] * 2**i) }
  end
end

class Integer
  def bit_size
    raise "bit_size only valid for positive integers" if self < 0
    to_s(2).size
  end
end
```

`bits_to_size` uses one of my favorite Ruby tricks. You create a `Range` object between 0 and the number of items, then take advantage of the fact that the `Range` class supports `Enumerable` methods, and then use the result as a big list of indexes. You call `inject` to transform the indexes into the binary values each value would represent if that bit was part of a binary coded number. An `inject_with_index` method could have avoided the need to do this, but implementing a version that supplies indexes for every method in `Enumerable` would get boring pretty quickly, while the preceding example works with no fuss. Oh, and it goes without saying that the results are undefined if you call `bits_to_int` on a list that contains values other than 0 or 1.

As for `bit_size`, well, you're cheating here! In order to find out how many bits are required to encode a number, you'll use the feature of `Integer#to_s`, which lets you specify an output base. Then you just need to count up the characters. Of course, this is a slow and complicated way to do things (for example, it only works for positive integers as the raised exception should indicate).

The right way to do this would be to use a base two logarithm method. Unfortunately, even though Matz okayed the addition of a `log2` method to Ruby, the method hasn't made it into a released version of Ruby. (See `http://blade.nagaokaut.ac.jp/cgi-bin/scat.rb/ruby/ruby-talk/191465` for more information.)

You could implement it using `log` or `log10`, but using `to_s` works well enough. Note that I've given myself permission to use a string exception here, since the method's means of calculating `log2` is convoluted enough that it won't find its way into larger circulation.

Uniform Crossover

Given those helpers, here's the `uniform_crossover` method.

```ruby
class Integer
  def uniform_crossover(other)
    max_bit_size = [self.bit_size, other.bit_size].max
    decision = rand(2**max_bit_size)
    crossover_when(other) {|i| decision[i] == 0 }
  end
end
```

You first figure out which integer has the largest bit size. You then generate a random number large enough to hold the same number of bits as the largest of the two integers. The actual crossover is performed by the `crossover_when` method.

The idea is that you'll pass in a block that will be called with the index of the current bit. If the block returns true, you'll switch which source you're currently reading bits from. You'll keep reading bits from that source until the next time the block returns true.

```ruby
class Integer
  def crossover_when(other)
    max_bit_size = [self.bit_size, other.bit_size].max
    one, two = self, other
    result = (0...max_bit_size).inject(0) do |total, i|
      one, two = two, one if yield(i)
      total + (2**i * one.to_i[i])
    end
    return result
  end
end
```

You can get away with using the notion of "switching" because the probability of a switch each time is always 50 percent, so in the end it's no different than randomly selecting a source for each bit. But the real reason you've implemented it this way is to make it easier to implement another kind of crossover.

So far you've been using uniform crossover where each bit can be randomly selected from either parent. What if, instead, you took whole chunks of bits from one parent or the other?

Point Crossovers

Point crossovers only switch sources a few times during crossover. This lets larger chunks from previous genomes continue to exist in their descendants. The chance of "good" structures being utterly destroyed during crossover is lowered by this kind of crossover.

```ruby
class Integer
  def point_crossover(other, n)
    possible_points = (0...bit_size).to_a
    points = []
    n.times { points.push(possible_points.delete_at(rand(possible_points.size))) }
    crossover_when(other){|i| points.include?(i) }
  end

  def one_point_crossover(other)
    point_crossover(other, 1)
  end

  def two_point_crossover(other)
    point_crossover(other, 2)
  end
end
```

You implement point crossover by generating a list of all possible crossover points. You then select as many of them as requested. You implement this selection in such a way that no point can be chosen more than once (because you remove them from the list after selection). You then call the crossover_when method with a block that will return true only if the given index was one of your selected points, thus triggering a crossover.

Since one- and two-point crossovers are relatively common, you might as well give them convenience methods. However, while proper crossover will ensure that good genomes are combined to (hopefully) produce new genomes, crossover can't introduce every desired variation. Consider a population where all the genomes contain a 0 in the first bit. Just using crossover, there's no way for that bit to ever get set to 1. You need to fix this before you can successfully run a real simulation.

Using Mutation

To help encourage diversity, you're going to need mutation. *Mutation* (which occurs in real biology all the time) is the random altering of genetic values. You'd like to just keep grafting methods onto the `Integer` class to do all the hard work.

```ruby
class Integer
  def mutate(prob)
    decision = rand(2**bit_size)
    mutated = (0...bit_size).map{|i| decision[i] == 0 ? self[i] : self[i] ^ 1}
    mutated.bits_to_int
  end
end
```

Considering the following, as it seems to work:

```
5.mutate(0.25) ➤ 5
5.mutate(0.25) ➤ 1
5.mutate(0.25) ➤ 5
5.mutate(0.25) ➤ 7
```

Unfortunately, there's a problem. `bit_size` returns the number of bits needed to encode the number. Unfortunately, this is not actually the same as the size of your conceptual bit space. For example, if you've decided that your genome value uses 3 bits (and can therefore encode up to a 7), you'd like `bit_size` to return 3. But if you call it on a number like 1, you'll only get a bit size returned of 1. After all, you can code the number 1 in 1 bit with no problem.

But if the code thinks the size is only 1, the top two bits will never mutate! So you're going to need to start explicitly tagging bit fields with their length so that bit size can return the intended value. Having to set this at the instance level would be a pain, so let's look at what you need to do to create a subclass of `Integer` with a predefined number of bits. You won't actually enforce a limit; you'll just use the number to return the right number of bits from `bit_size`. In the process, you're going to encounter some weird stuff about the `Integer` class.

Subclassing Integer

Unfortunately, while you can subclass `Integer`, you may not get the results you expect. Because `Integer` is layered on the "value class" `Fixnum`, there's no way to construct a new instance explicitly. All references to a given integer actually refer to the same underlying instance. In that context, initializing a "new" Integer doesn't make sense.

```
class MyInt < Integer
end
```

```
MyInt.new ➤ NoMethodError: undefined method 'new' for MyInt:Class
MyInt.allocate ➤ NoMethodError: undefined method 'allocate' for MyInt:Class
```

Instead, you'll need to use delegation. *Delegation* is when one object wraps another object and passes method calls through to the wrapped object. This lets the delegate implement methods of its own but also forward some method calls straight on to the proxied object. Ruby even gives you some tools to make this process automatic. Using the delegate library and its DelegateClass makes the process nearly transparent (it almost looks just like subclassing!).

```
require 'delegate'
class BitInt < DelegateClass(Integer)
  def bit_size
    self.class::BIT_SIZE
  end
end
```

```
bi = BitInt.new(5)
bi + 4 ➤ 8
bi.bit_size ➤ NameError: uninitialized constant BitInt::BIT_SIZE
```

Hmm, but bit_size still doesn't work, and you need integers tagged with sizes to get mutation to work! You've made the bit_size method read from a class constant, a class constant you've left undefined.

Subclassing BitInt

In order to set BIT_SIZE, you'll want to subclass BitInt. It's lot of inheritance, but doing it this way means that you can have multiple BitInt subclasses that each have different bit sizes.

```
class BitInt8 < BitInt
  BIT_SIZE = 8
end
```

Of course why can't it be even simpler? Check out this class method:

```ruby
class BitInt
  def self.sized(bits)
    subclass = Class.new(self)
    subclass.const_set(:BIT_SIZE, bits)
    return subclass
  end
end
```

sized is a class method. It uses the optional parameter to Class.new to create subclasses of the class it's called on. Then it uses the const_set method to declare BIT_SIZE and returns the subclass. Now all you need to write is this:

```ruby
BitInt8 = BitInt.sized(8)
```

While you're at it, you might want to add some checking to BitInt's initialization.

```ruby
class BitIntAbuseError; end

class BitInt
  def initialize(value)
    raise BitIntAbuseError.new("Please subclass BitInt!") if self.class == BitInt
    raise BitIntAbuseError.new("BitInt values must be positive") if value < 0
    super(value)
  end
end
```

The constructor raises an exception if the value is negative or if someone is trying to directly instantiate BigInt without subclassing first. This trick lets you encapsulate the process of creating new subclasses and keeps the code readable. If you settle on a fixed size encoding for a given genome, you can simply declare a new subclass using the sized class method. And because this functionality is exposed as a method, you can also write code that easily creates subclasses on the fly to represent differently sized data.

Wrapping BitInt Return Values

There's only one problem left. Because it's a delegate, methods delegated to Integer return Integer values. You'll need to wrap any results you'd like to return in instances of BitInt subclasses explicitly. This matters most for any method that will be used during reproduction to make a new genome (like crossover methods and your newly defined mutate).

Ideally, you'd only need to wrap `crossover_when` because it generates the new instance. But here's where delegation can bite you if you're not careful. Because `crossover_when` is called from inside the `Integer` class, redefining it in the delegate won't affect calls that originate from inside `Integer`. So you'll need to wrap each individual crossover method plus `mutate`.

```
class BitInt
  def uniform_crossover(other); self.class.new(super(other)); end
  def one_point_crossover(other); self.class.new(super(other)); end
  def two_point_crossover(other); self.class.new(super(other)); end
  def point_crossover(other, n); self.class.new(super(other, n)); end
  def mutate(prob); self.class.new(super(prob)); end
end
```

With a generic skeleton for running genetic algorithms and a delegate for `Integer` that supports crossover and mutation for genome representation, you're ready to return to the problem from Chapter 4.

Making Change . . . Again!

Since you've already got an interesting problem and simulator, let's return to the change-making simulation from Chapter 4. Here's the problem again (in case you've been skipping around, which, of course, is encouraged!): prices being what they are and assuming cashiers make optimal change, what is the average number of coins someone will end up carrying if he pays intelligently? You explored the possible coins you could add or replace existing coins with to reduce that number.

I've included a copy of the source from Chapter 4 in this chapter's source code bundle. Remember the simulator was called like this:

```
purchases = 400
coins = [1, 5, 10, 25]
price_list = IO.readlines("prices.txt").map{|price| price.to_i }
prices = Prices.new(*price_list)
sim = ChangeSimulator.new(prices, *coins)
sim.run(purchases)
```

You're going to need to encode the coin list in the genome, but you're also going to need to pass around most of those parameters. The situation is actually a lot like `BigInt`. You'd like to parameterize a subclass of the `ChangeGenome`. Since you're inheriting from

BitInt anyway, let's wrap up the parameterization in another method that does the subclassing for you.

```ruby
class ChangeGenome < BitInt
  def self.given(prices, purchases, number_of_coins, bits_per_coin)
    bits = (number_of_coins - 1) * bits_per_coin
    subclass = self.sized(bits)
    subclass.const_set(:PRICES, prices)
    subclass.const_set(:PURCHASES, purchases)
    subclass.const_set(:NUMBER_OF_COINS, number_of_coins - 1)
    subclass.const_set(:BITS_PER_COIN, bits_per_coin)
    return subclass
  end
end
```

Notice how it automatically calculates the number of bits you want as the number of coins (minus the mandatory 1-cent coin) times the number of bits you'd like to use per coin for encoding.

Choosing an Encoding

Picking a bits_per_coin value will be tricky. You'd really like to encode a range from 2 to 99, but unfortunately that's not an option. Using 6 bits gets you 64 distinct values. Using 7 bits gets you 128. For now, stick with 6 bits, since that will cover coins from 2 to 65, which shouldn't get in your way (good systems with very large coins are rare).

You can reuse the old reproduce method.

```ruby
class ChangeGenome
  def reproduce(mates)
    mate = mates.random
    return uniform_crossover(mate).mutate(0.25)
  end

  def fitness
    sim = ChangeSimulator.new(self.class::PRICES, *denoms)
    return 1.0/sim.run(self.class::PURCHASES)
  end
end
```

But this is your first real fitness method. And in order to use the simulator, you need to turn the bit string into a list of coin denominations.

■**Tip** Notice how you divide 1.0 by the simulation result. Remember that the simulator returns the average number of coins the simulated person would have in his pockets at any given time. If you didn't take the reciprocal of the number, you'd be solving for the coin system that causes the heaviest pockets.

It calls the denoms method, which unpacks the denominations from your genome and returns a simple ordered list of coins (including the required 1-cent coin). I've defined some helper methods to retrieve constants from the appropriate class as well.

```ruby
class ChangeGenome
  def num
    self.class::NUMBER_OF_COINS
  end

  def bpc
    self.class::BITS_PER_COIN
  end

  def denoms
    coins = [1] + (0...num).map do |i|
      starting = i * bpc
      ending = (i + 1) * bpc
      value = unpack(starting, ending) + 2
    end
    coins.sort
  end
end
```

You calculate indexes where the bits for any particular coin's representation begin, and then use a method named unpack to extract the number (normalized to start at 2) from the appropriate bits. The unpack method looks very similar to other bit-to-number conversions you've done.

```ruby
class ChangeGenome
  def unpack(starting, ending)
    num = ending - starting
    (0...num).inject(0) do |total, i|
      total + (self[starting + i] * (2**i))
    end
  end
end
```

And just for convenience, let's add a class method to create a random ChangeGenome with the appropriate bits.

```ruby
class ChangeGenome
  def self.new_random
    bits = self::NUMBER_OF_COINS * self::BITS_PER_COIN
    return new(rand(2**bits))
  end
end
```

The method first calculates the bits, then create a new genome. This is enough to run the first simulation, so shall we?

Running the Simulation

Here's the basic code:

```ruby
require 'change'

number = 3
purchases = 400
bpc = 6

price_list = IO.readlines("prices.txt").map{|price| price.to_i }
prices = Prices.new(*price_list)

ChangeGenomeNumber = ChangeGenome.given(prices, purchases, number, bpc)
ga = GeneticAlgorithm.new(10, 7) { ChangeGenomeNumber.new_random }
puts ga.run(20).denoms.inspect ➤ [1, 7, 17]
```

Excellent. One quick fix stands out immediately. Caching your previous results for a given set of coins prevents you from needlessly rerunning costly simulations. Admittedly, the first result isn't guaranteed to be "representative," but you only ran simulations once for each combination during your brute force exploration, so this is not a new inaccuracy.

So here's how you'll memoize the fitness method. You'll start by creating a class constant named CACHE during subclassing and add a helper method to access it. Class constants are often useful because each subclass can have its own separate constant, unlike class variables (written as @@cache), which are shared down the inheritance tree.

```ruby
class ChangeGenome
  def self.given(prices, purchases, number_of_coins, bits_per_coin)
    bits = (number_of_coins - 1) * bits_per_coin
    subclass = self.sized(bits)
```

```ruby
    subclass.const_set(:PRICES, prices)
    subclass.const_set(:PURCHASES, purchases)
    subclass.const_set(:NUMBER_OF_COINS, number_of_coins - 1)
    subclass.const_set(:BITS_PER_COIN, bits_per_coin)
    subclass.const_set(:CACHE, {})
    return subclass
  end

  def cache
    self.class::CACHE
  end
end
```

You can then tweak the `fitness` method to use the cache:

```ruby
class ChangeGenome
  def fitness
    coins = denoms
    if ! cache.key?(coins)
      sim = ChangeSimulator.new(self.class::PRICES, *coins)
      cache[coins] = 1/sim.run(self.class::PURCHASES)
    end
    return cache[coins]
  end
end
```

Running 400 purchases on a size 10 population and size 7 survivor population using a 6-bit per coin genome with 3 coins for a total of 20 iterations took 1 minute 41 seconds without caching. With caching, that time is down to 41 seconds on my laptop. Not a bad little speed boost!

Looking at the Results

All of the following results were obtained running 400 purchases per simulation, 6 bits per coin, a population of 20, and a survivor population of 15.

In the previous chapter, you fully explored the optimal three-coin problem. There were no guarantees that you'd found the "one true answer," since you randomized the price list for each simulation. But to provide an easy comparison, I reran the brute force check on the three-coin problem. It took 36 minutes and selected a coin set (1, 14, and 22) with an average pocket weight of 4.98. Meanwhile, the simple 50-round genetic algorithm selected a coin set (1, 15, and 19) with an average pocket weight of 5.06. But it took only 17 seconds to run!

In addition, the five-coin simulation (which was too intensive to be run before) can now be explored within a reasonable time. In 50 iterations, it comes up with an average pocket weight of 3.31 for the coins 1, 4, 11, 16, and 49. This took 3 minutes 15 seconds. For comparison, I rewrote the brute force search to only generate permutations as needed and let it run for the same length of time. This partial brute force search selected 1, 2, 4, 19, and 30 with the larger average weight of 3.50.

Take these results with a grain of salt, since randomizing the price list sometimes prevents them from being directly comparable. But hopefully they explain why genetic algorithms can be so useful!

Adding Further Improvements

There's a lot you can still do to tweak your algorithm. Here are some more tricks you can try.

Dealing with Invalid Genomes

You'd really like to resolve the problem of invalid genomes. It's frustrating to be able to solve the coin problem only for denominations valued up to 65. If you used a 7-bit encoding, you'd have 128 possible encodings, but you'd only need 98 of them (2 through 99).

In order to get around the problem, you'd need a policy about what to do when an invalid genome is generated. For example, you could allow invalid genomes, but then assign them a fitness of 0. Another option might be to discard them at generation time, repeating reproduction until a valid genome is generated. Or you could attempt to correct the genome and convert it into a valid encoding.

Unfortunately, each of these strategies risks subtly skewing your results. Penalizing the offspring of any particular sort of genome (in particular the genomes that are valid themselves but are very close to invalid genomes) will risk diverting exploration of the nearby space. This is why you stuck with a 6-bit range earlier. Since the numeric range produced should be sufficient, you can avoid these biases. But if you really needed to solve for the coin denominations all the way between 2 and 99, you'd have to deal with the problems associated with using all 7 bits and risk possible skew.

Letting Parents Live On

One interesting variant allows parents to live on to the next generation. This preserves some of the best genomes for future rounds of reproduction, thus exploring the space around them more thoroughly. Adding this kind of multigenerational survival to your algorithm is easy.

Here's a straightforward modification to the step method:

```ruby
class GeneticAlgorithm
  def step
    survivors = fittest
    num_old = @population.size / 2
    num_new = @population.size - num_old
    population_old = (0...num_old).map{ survivors.random }
    population_new = (0...num_new).map do |i|
      parent = survivors.random
      parent.reproduce(survivors)
    end
    @population = population_old + population_new
    remember_best
    return @best
  end
end
```

In the preceding code, half of each new population is directly from the previous generation and half belong to the new generation.

Experimenting with Gray Code

So far I've taken the binary number system for granted. I haven't really discussed what using the standard unsigned binary encoding really means. The simple binary encoding is not the only game in town. There are other ways to encode numbers as bits.

One of these systems, named Gray code, has some very interesting properties. Gray code is built around the notion that you should never need to flip more than one bit to raise or lower a number by one. You can implement this several ways in practice, but it's often done using the rule that to increase a number, you toggle the bit farthest "right" (talking about least and most significant bits is deceptive with Gray code) that will produce a yet unused representation.

I'll talk about why this single-bit adjacency is good for genetic algorithms in a minute. But first some examples. Here are the first seven numbers in Gray code as previously described. The left bit is the least significant in the following Gray code numbers:

Decimal	Binary	Gray Code
0	000	000
1	001	001
2	010	011
3	011	010
4	100	110
5	101	111
6	110	101
7	111	100

Weird, huh? So why is Gray code so interesting for genetic algorithms? One problem with traditional binary encodings is that there are certain numerical barriers between values. In order to convert a 3 into a 4 in two's complement, you must flip three bits.

Because you never need to flip more than one Gray code bit to reach the next consecutive integer, Gray code makes it easier for genetic algorithms to walk toward better solutions. But there are side effects as well. Gray code also enables mutation to change numbers dramatically. In two's complement, the largest number you can convert 000 into with a single flip is 100 (also known as 4). But with Gray codes, you can turn 000 into 100, which represents 7!

There's been a lot of research into using Gray codes with genetic algorithms. What would you need to do to try out Gray codes? Start by subclassing the venerable BitInt:

```ruby
class GrayBitInt < BitInt
  def from_gray
    bits = [0]
    indices = (0...bit_size).to_a.reverse
    indices.each{|i| bits.unshift((self[i] + bits.first) % 2) }
    bits.bits_to_int
  end
end
```

The only new method is the from_gray method. The algorithm is a little bit tricky, but basically each bit (starting from the leftmost, known as the most significant in two's complement) is the sum (modulo 2) of that bit in the raw representation and the previously converted bit (use 0 for the previously converted bit on the first iteration).

Let's calculate the bits for 10. You start with the leftmost bit 1. You add it to 0 (since this is the first iteration), and mod it by 2 (to produce a value that is 1 or 0). Thus the first bit is 1. You then take the next bit (0) and add it to the previous result bit (1). You mod by 2 and get 1. Thus your binary two's complement representation is 11, also known in decimal as 3.

The code does this exact operation, but with a few tricks. You initialize your list of final bits starting with a 0. You'll insert bits at the beginning of the list as you go, so this is essentially a right padded 0, which will have no effect on the final outcome. It makes looking at the previous result bit simple, though.

You then generate a list of all the indexes (in reverse) for the bits. Each is added to the result of the previous, modded by 2 (just as in your algorithm), and then you use the Ruby array's unshift method to insert the new bit at the beginning of your bit list. At the very end, the bits are turned back into an integer and returned.

All you need to do to put this to work is to subclass GrayBitInt and call from_gray on each genome before you unpack the value for fitness computation. Reproduction, crossover, and mutation should all happen with the original encoding.

```ruby
class ChangeGenome < GrayBitInt
  def unpack(starting, ending)
    value = from_gray
    num = ending - starting
    (0...num).inject(0) do |total, i|
      total + (value[starting + i] * (2**i))
    end
  end
end
```

That's all that's needed. Of course, encodings are not the only area that need improvement.

Roulette Selection

A genetic algorithm doesn't simulate biological evolution; it merely takes inspiration from it. The algorithmic definition of fitness underscores this distinction. In real evolution, fitness is an emergent property of the system. However, even though it's not a direct translation doesn't mean you shouldn't look to real evolution for improvements. One problem so far is that you've been deterministically selecting the best candidates in each round. In real life, there is significantly more chance in the selection/survival process. By culling all of the least-fit genomes in each round, you're robbing the algorithm of a major source of diversity that might ultimately provide even better solutions.

Roulette selection is a popular remedy. Picture, if you will, a roulette wheel. Assign each genome to a portion of the wheel sized in proportion to the genome's fitness. Now, you spin the wheel, but instead of a marble or a pointer, consider the case where you have an arbitrary number of pointers in the center. The distance between each pointer is equidistant, so they all point outward like star or the spokes of a wheel. Thus every spin selects a whole batch of evenly spaced genomes. And, of course, the probability of selection is directly linked to a given genome's fitness (as represented by its size).

Following is an implementation of roulette selection. It uses two helper methods. The shuffle method randomly reorders a list of elements and helps avoid any ordering bias.

```ruby
module Enumerable
  def shuffle
    sort_by { rand }
  end

  def weighted_ranges
    total = 0.0
    ranges = map do |item|
      value = yield(item)
      start = total
```

```
          total += value
          [start, value, item]
        end
        return total, ranges
    end
end
```

The `weighted_ranges` method uses the supplied block to calculate the value of each element. Then it assembles a list of triples. Each triple contains the start of an item's position in the ring, its length, and the item itself. When it's done, `total` conveniently contains the size of the wheel's circumference.

```
module Enumerable
  def roulette(n, &block)
    total, ranges = weighted_ranges(&block)

    pointer = rand * total
    interval = total / n

    selected = []
    while true
      ranges.each do |start, length, item|
        if start <= pointer && pointer < start + length
          selected.push(item)
          pointer = (pointer + interval) % total
        end
        return selected unless selected.size < n
      end
    end
  end
end
```

The `roulette` method uses the calculated ranges and picks a starting point around the ring (`pointer`). Then it calculates the spacing between this pointer and all the other virtual pointers you'll consider to exist evenly spaced around the center of your ring.

And finally, it loops as many times as it needs to through this list of ranges and values until it finds the right one that matches the pointer. Then it increments the pointer by the interval and finds the next selection. When it's built the full list, it returns it. Here's an example:

```
[1, 2, 3, 4, 5, 6, 7].roulette(2){|x| x}
```

Notice that you needed to supply a block for value computation. And here's the modification you'd need to use it in the GeneticAlgorithm class:

```ruby
class ChangeGenome
  def fittest(n=@selection_size)
    @population.roulette(@selection_size){|genome| genome.fitness }
  end
end
```

See how easy it was to integrate that into your system? One of the interesting things about genetic algorithms is the sheer diversity of improvements or customizations you can make.

Summary

In this chapter, you implemented a harness for running genetic algorithms. You also explored how to use Ruby integers to implement a genome class. You looked at various means of implementing crossover and how to encode your problem domain in a genome. Best of all, you put the genetic algorithm to use on the change problem from Chapter 4 and compared the solutions to the results of a brute force search.

However, you've barely scratched the surface of genetic algorithms. If you'd like to learn more, there are a number of good papers available on the Internet. A good place to start is Darrell Whitley's survey of genetic algorithms titled "A Genetic Algorithm Tutorial." You can find the paper online at his web site: www.cs.colostate.edu/~genitor/Pubs.html.

There are still a ton of tweaks left, including everything from tracking and preventing incest to simply avoiding the introduction of duplicates. You can fiddle with your algorithm for hours, but, of course, don't forget: the whole point is problem solving!

CHAPTER 8

■■■■

Implementing Lisp in Ruby

All the hip hackers seem to be talking about Lisp these days. Not a lot of them are using Lisp, but they're definitely talking about it. Why? Well, there are a lot of reasons. Despite its age (it was invented by John McCarthy in 1958!), most Lisp implementations have all the features that programmers demand of modern languages, like garbage collection and closures. But Lisp also has a powerful homoiconic syntax that makes macros, code generation, and metaprogramming incredibly easy. Of course, it's no silver bullet, but learning Lisp can be a great educational experience.

■**Note** *Homoiconic* means that a language's syntax is represented by that language's basic data structures. For example, Lisp's syntax consists of symbols and lists.

It's a rite of passage to implement your own Lisp interpreter. A lot of the language's intricacies only become apparent once you get under the hood. The exercise is typically done in Lisp itself, but unless it is your primary language, you're not necessarily going to get everything out of the exercise that you can. Since you're reading this book, chances are you know Ruby pretty well. So I'm going to go ahead and buck tradition by implementing Lisp in Ruby.

In this chapter, you'll explore how to implement the standard Lisp data types, manage variables and environments, implement the intertwined `eval` and `apply` functions, supply special forms to the language, learn about s-expressions, write the basic Lisp primitive functions, build support for closures and macros, and even make it easy for Ruby and Lisp to interoperate!

If it sounds like a lot, don't worry! You'll take it one step at a time. And when you're done, you'll have your own Lisp—not to mention a window into the world of programming language implementation.

Learning Lisp

If you haven't had a chance to learn Lisp yet, you've got a lot of fun ahead of you. Learning Lisp probably won't change your life, but it sure is interesting. If you need somewhere to start, I recommend beginning with a dialect named Scheme. Lisp comes in a few flavors these days, the most popular of which are named Common Lisp and Scheme. In turn, each of these language variants has a variety of implementations you can download and run on your computer.

Probably the most interesting book about Lisp is titled *Structure and Interpretation of Computer Programs, Second Edition,* by Harold Abelson and Gerald Jay Sussman (MIT, 1996), shortened in hacker pop-culture to SICP. Another interesting book is *Practical Common Lisp* by Peter Seibel (Apress, 2005), which tackles the Common Lisp dialect in a project-oriented manner (similar to this book). However, both are large books, so I've included a guide to Lisp (see the sidebar titled "Lisp Basics") at the end of the chapter.

If you're quite familiar with Lisp, just keep reading. Otherwise, you should flip to the overview of the language. Without some basic Lisp knowledge, this chapter might be hard going!

Choosing Your Lisp Data Types

A working Lisp interpreter doesn't really require that many data types. You're going to need symbols, conses (constructs), and functions at the minimum. You'll probably also want numbers and strings. It's possible to implement numbers and strings only using symbols and conses, but since you have nice Ruby implementations available, just steal those. You can reuse Ruby's symbols, as well, but you're going to need to implement conses yourself.

■**Note**   Quick refresher about symbols. A symbol is an archetypal representation of some text. Ruby symbol literals are prefixed by a colon and are immutable. For example, while the string `"foo"` is a string that happens to contain the word "foo," the symbol `:foo` actually represents the word "foo."

Building Cons Cells

A *cons cell* (sometimes just called a *cons*) is just a pair of values as illustrated in Figure 8-1. You can get the first element of a cons using the `car` function. You can get the other element of a cons using the `cdr` function. Cons cells are created with a function named `cons`.

Note So what's up with the strange names? cons is just an abbreviation for "construct." But car and cdr are a little weirder. They're named for the assembly instructions that were used to retrieve the first and second half of a machine word on the IBM 704, the machine Lisp was originally designed for. car stands for Contents of Address of Register and cdr stands for Contents of Decrement of Register.

Building a Cons class in Ruby is pretty easy.

```
class Cons
  attr_reader :car, :cdr
  def initialize(car, cdr)
    @car, @cdr = car, cdr
  end
end
```

Here are some usage examples:

```
c = Cons.new(1, 2)
c.car ➤ 1
c.cdr ➤ 2
```

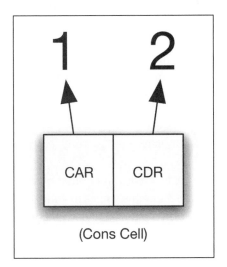

Figure 8-1. *A cons cell points to two values.*

```
d = Cons.new(1, Cons.new(2, Cons.new(3, :nil)))
d.car ➤ 1
d.cdr ➤ #<Cons:0x32e810 @cdr=#<Cons:0x32e824 @cdr=:nil, @car=3>, @car=2>
d.cdr.car ➤ 2
d.cdr.cdr.cdr ➤ :nil
```

Look closely at Figure 8-2. A list in Lisp is nothing more than a sequence of conses, each contained in its predecessor's `cdr` and ending with the symbol `nil`, as in the preceding code sample. So `d` is a list containing the numbers 1, 2, and 3.

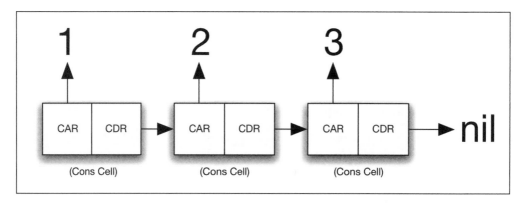

Figure 8-2. *A list containing the numbers 1, 2, and 3 built from cons cells and terminated with a nil value*

The cons structure is the backbone of any Lisp implementation, and your interpreter will be no exception. Before you're done, you'll need to add some additional methods to your Ruby cons object, but let's move on for now.

Saving Values in the Environment

Most programming languages are built around the notion of an environment that binds symbolic names to values. In Lisp, you'll just use symbols to name the values in your environment. While symbols are prefixed with a colon in Ruby, a plain bare word is considered a symbol in Lisp.

A Lisp implementation works by getting the value of (or evaluating) an expression. I'll talk more about this in the section titled "eval." But there are different rules for evaluating different types. When symbols are evaluated, though, the value stored in the environment under that symbol name is returned. If there's no value stored under that name, it is considered an error.

```
(define a 1)
a ➤ 1
```

To support this notion of environments and bindings, you're going to need to have a Ruby environment class. You'll need to be able to define bindings, set bindings, and lookup bindings. All the keys in this structure will be symbols.

At first it seems like you might just be able to get away with using a hash table, but there's one more feature to support. You're going to be implementing a form of scoping known as *lexical* scoping. Lexical scoping means that variable references retrieve their values from the nearest lexically enclosing block in the source code where the variable is defined. In order to do this right, you need the ability to chain your environments. An example might help:

```
(define var 1)
(define f (lambda (x) var))
(f 2) ➤ 1
```

So the environment of f is going to be chained to the root environment (see Figure 8-3). When a lookup fails in f's environment, the root environment will be checked as well. Technically, only the values in the root environment at the time they were defined should be accessible, but I'll talk more about that in the section titled "Saving the Environment."

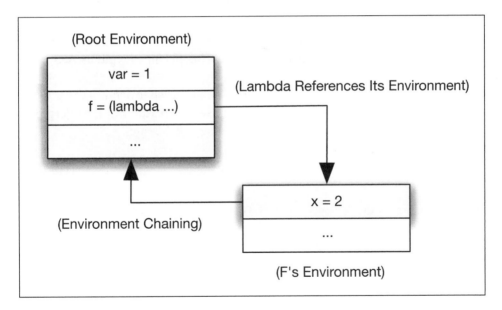

Figure 8-3. *An example of environment chaining*

> **Note** Ruby uses lexical scoping (with a few strange corner cases), as do most other modern languages. But it wasn't always that way. Lexical scoping didn't appear in Lisp until version 1.5, and it didn't become the default in any version of Lisp until Scheme. Sometimes good ideas take a while.

So given the need to support environment chaining, the constructor of your environment class probably should look something like this.

```
class Env
  def initialize(parent=nil, defaults={})
    @parent = parent
    @defs = defaults
  end
end
```

Each `Env` has a parent that is `nil` by default. Lookups and set operations will be chained to the parent. A new `Env` can also be passed a hash table to be used as its starting set of definitions. The `define` method is the easiest of the four I'll be providing, so let's start with it.

```
class Env
  def define(symbol, value)
    @defs[symbol] = value
    return value
  end
end
```

A call to `define` sets the definition for a given symbol. Actually, `define` could bind a value to any kind of object, not just a symbol. But you'll be sticking to symbols. At this point you're basically just wrapping the `@defs` hash table.

If you wanted, you could throw an exception if someone tried to define a variable that has already been defined in this scope, but I don't see any reason why the interpreter shouldn't allow the following code, so you can leave things as they are.

```
(define a 1)
(define a 2)
```

Now let's implement the `defined?` method. This will check to see if a symbol is defined in the environment.

```
class Env
  def defined?(symbol)
    return true  if @defs.has_key?(symbol)
    return false if @parent.nil?
    return @parent.defined?(symbol)
  end
end
```

If the binding is stored in the current environment's `@defs` hash, then the symbol is defined. If it's not and this environment doesn't have a parent, then it isn't defined. If, however, the symbol is not in the hash table, but the environment does have a parent, it asks the parent if the symbol is defined in its table and returns the answer. Here's some Ruby code to test what you've written so far:

```
e = Env.new
e.defined?(:var) ➤ false
e.define(:var, 1)
e.defined?(:var) ➤ true
```

Of course, you're going to want to know more than just whether a symbol has a value. You're also going to want to know what that value is!

```
class Env
  def lookup(symbol)
    return @defs[symbol] if @defs.has_key?(symbol)
    raise "No value for symbol #{symbol}" if @parent.nil?
    return @parent.lookup(symbol)
  end
end
```

The lookup function is patterned on the defined? method. However, instead of returning true or false, it returns the value or throws an exception. If it exists in the @defs hash, then return it. If it doesn't and the environment has no parent, throw an error. Otherwise, return the lookup from the parent Env. Here's an example in Ruby:

```
e = Env.new
e.define(:var, 1)
e.lookup(:var) ➤ 1
e.lookup(:var2) ➤ RuntimeError: No value for symbol var2
```

And last but not least, you'll need to be able to change the values stored in an environment.

```
class Env
  def set(symbol, value)
    if @defs.has_key?(symbol)
      @defs[symbol] = value
    elsif @parent.nil?
      raise "No definition of #{symbol} to set to #{value}"
    else
      @parent.set(symbol, value)
    end
  end
end
```

It's the same basic pattern again. If the binding already exists, change it; otherwise, try to change the value in the parent environment.

Understanding eval and apply

The archetypal design for a Lisp interpreter consists of two complementary functions (see Figure 8-4). These functions are named eval and apply. eval (which is short for evaluate) gets the values of expressions. apply calls functions. That's all there is to it, seriously.

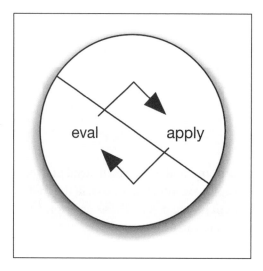

Figure 8-4. *The circular relationship between* eval *and* apply

eval

Let's think about eval first. I've talked about a few basic types already, like numbers and strings, as well as symbols and conses. Numbers and strings evaluate to themselves. Since the interpreter reuses Ruby's numbers and strings, all you need to do is add a lispeval method to each. Using Ruby's "monkeypatching" capability, it's easy to add this method to existing classes.

```
class Numeric
  def lispeval(env, forms)
    self
  end
end
```

```ruby
class String
  def lispeval(env, forms)
    self
  end
end
```

But at this point, it's worth wondering if you'll be stealing other Ruby types at some point. Instead of adding `lispeval` to each type you might want to use, just add a default `lispeval` method to `Object` that returns `self`. (You can delete the `lispeval` methods on `Numeric` and `String` now.)

```ruby
class Object
  def lispeval(env, forms)
    self
  end
end
```

Notice that the `lispeval` method takes two parameters that I've named `env` and `forms`. These aren't used in the default `lispeval` method.

```ruby
1.lispeval(nil, nil) ➤ 1
"foo".lispeval(nil, nil) ➤ 1
```

The evaluation method for the `Symbol` class is a little more interesting. In Lisp, unquoted symbols evaluate to the value stored in the environment under their name. This is where the `env` parameter to the `lispeval` method comes in.

```ruby
class Symbol
  def lispeval(env, forms)
    env.lookup(self)
  end
end
```

You take the environment passed into the `lispeval` method and look up the symbol that is being evaluated in it. This will return the value stored in the environment, if such a value exists; otherwise, it will throw an error. Let's play around with this in Ruby.

```ruby
e = Env.new
e.define(:a, 1)
:a.lispeval(e, nil) ➤ 1
:b.lispeval(e, nil) ➤ RuntimeError: No value for symbol b
```

You're astonishingly close to a working Lisp interpreter at this point. You've provided evaluation methods for three of the four literal values the interpreter offers (numbers, strings, and symbols). The last type that needs a `lispeval` method is cons.

Arbitrary cons expressions don't necessarily have a valid evaluation. However, there is a rule for evaluating cons structures that are valid lists. For example, the following cons list containing a + symbol and two numbers has a valid evaluation.

```
(+ 1 2)
```

The numbers will evaluate to themselves, the symbol + will evaluate to whatever is stored in the environment at the slot +. And last but not least, you will trigger the other half of the evaluator and attempt to "apply" the value returned from evaluating + to the values 1 and 2, which were the result of evaluating 1 and 2. By the time you've finished your work, the end result will hopefully be 3, but you're not quite there yet.

apply

In the classic "build your own" Lisp interpreter, `eval` and `apply` are written as functions that use the Lisp `cond` to decide what to do. This interpreter takes a slightly different approach and uses Ruby's class-based dispatch to let Ruby do the hard work of decision-making for you. For example, with `eval`, you can simply call `foo.lispeval(env, forms)`, and if foo is a number, you'll get the number back; but if foo is a cons, the cons will be evaluated using the rules for conses.

You're going to use the exact same model for `apply`. In fact, Ruby already has a built-in `apply` method for its own callable values like instances of `Proc` and `Method` classes. Ruby names the method `call` instead of `apply`, but the meaning is the same. The procedure is triggered, and the arguments to `call`/`apply` are used as its arguments.

You could define a `lispapply` method for the objects in your interpreter, but reusing the name `call` saves you some trouble. Here's an example of how this already works in Ruby:

```
a = proc{ "hello" }
a.call ➤ "hello"
b = proc{|x| x + 2}
b.call(3) ➤ 5
c = 3.method(:+)
c.call(1) ➤ 4
```

You can probably see how you're going to implement primitive functions in the interpreter. All you need to do is store Ruby `Proc` objects in the environment. Ruby `Proc` objects can also be defined with the `lambda` method instead of the `proc` method, a convention inherited from Lisp, actually.

First though, you need to go back and finish the `lispeval` method, now that you have an `apply` method (named `call`).

Talking About Special Forms

In order for you to finish the `lispeval` method for cons cells, I need to briefly talk about special forms. In Lisp, not all cons cells obey the standard rules of evaluation. A symbol in the first position of a list that causes that list to be evaluated abnormally is called a *special form.*

You'll be implementing special forms as functions whose arguments get passed in unevaluated and can choose whether to evaluate them or not. The previously mysterious `forms` parameter in the `lispeval` keeps track of these functions.

Finishing eval

So keeping the existence of special forms in mind, here's an implementation of `lispeval` for conses.

```
class Cons
  def lispeval(env, forms)
    return forms.lookup(car).call(env, forms, *cdr.arrayify) if forms.defined?(car)
    func = car.lispeval(env, forms)
    return func.call(*cdr.arrayify.map{|x| x.lispeval(env, forms) })
  end
end
```

You can ignore the first line of the function for now. It handles the special forms. You can see in the second line, though, that it evaluates the `car` of the current cons cell (the first item in the list) and assumes it's a function. The code then calls the function with the rest of the elements from the cons list evaluated.

Let's try out the evaluation function now:

```
env = Env.new(nil, {:+ => lambda{|x, y| x + y }})
Cons.new(:+, Cons.new(1, Cons.new(2, :nil))).lispeval(env, nil) ➤ 3
```

That's it. That's honest-to-goodness Lisp, right there, running. But it doesn't look very much like Lisp, does it? That's fixable, but first, in the preceding code I introduced a new method that I should talk about.

Using the Helper Functions Arrayify and Consify

Lisp uses cons-based lists, and Ruby uses the Array class. You'd like the two languages to interoperate as smoothly as possible. So I've added two methods, arrayify and consify. The consify method added to Object simply returns self. But if you call consify on an Array, it is converted into a cons list.

```
class Object
  def consify
    self
  end
end

class Array
  def consify
    map{|x| x.consify}.reverse.inject(:nil) {|cdr, car| Cons.new(car, cdr)}
  end
end
```

Arrayify goes the other direction. It also has a default method on Object that returns self. The arrayify method depends on the conslist? method, which simply checks to makes sure the entity in question is a valid list of cons cells that could be successfully transformed into an array. In all other cases, it leaves the object untransformed.

```
class Object
  def arrayify
    self
  end

  def conslist?
    false
  end
end

class Cons
  def arrayify
    return self unless conslist?
    return [car] + cdr.arrayify
  end

  def conslist?
    cdr.conslist?
  end
end
```

The processes are not necessarily reversible, though, because the Lisp nil symbol also represents an empty list. Without this additional definition, the method won't work.

```
class Symbol
  def arrayify
    self == :nil ? [] : self
  end

  def conslist?
    self == :nil
  end
end
```

That's what the arrayify and consify methods are all about. I didn't use the standard Ruby convention of to_a and to_cons because to methods in Ruby are expected to always make the conversion. They don't have this same behavior of converting some objects and leaving others alone.

■**Note** Why didn't I only add the arrayify method to the :nil symbol instance itself? In general, Ruby lets you add methods to specific object instances. Unfortunately, it doesn't let you add them to symbol instances. That's why you add the method to the symbol, and then check to see if the symbol is :nil.

Making It Look Like Lisp

Okay, back to the problem of making the user's code look more like Lisp. Luckily, there's a RubyGem available that can make your work a little easier. It's named sexp. That's short for *s-expression*, which is in turn short for *symbolic expression*. Symbolic expression is just a fancy term for the lists of symbols you've already been working with.

The sexp module provides a simple parser for strings of s-expressions. I've also added a call to the gem method to force the sexp gem to override files provided by other gems (the ParseTree gem also provides a file named sexp, which can conflict).

```
require 'rubygems'
gem 'sexp'
require 'sexp'

"1".parse_sexp ➤ 1.0
"foo".parse_sexp ➤ :foo
"\"foo\"".parse_sexp ➤ "foo"
"(+ 1 2)".parse_sexp ➤ [:+, 1.0, 2.0]
```

Oops. One problem: `parse_sexp` returns real arrays. Well, this makes sense for Ruby folks using the module, but not so much for us intrepid Lisp implementers. Luckily you already defined the `consify` compatibility method. You can tack on a call to `consify` after the calls to `parse_sexp`.

```
"(+ 1 2)".parse_sexp ➤ [:+, 1.0, 2.0]
"(+ 1 2)".parse_sexp.consify ➤ #<Cons:0x578aa0 @cdr=#<Cons:0x578b18 ➥
@cdr=#<Cons:0x578d0c @cdr=:nil, @car=2.0>, @car=1.0>, @car=:+>
```

The previous result is a little hard to read because Ruby's default printing of cons cells puts the `cdr` first, but if you flip things around in your head, this looks right. So where does this leave things?

```
env = Env.new(nil, {:+ => lambda{|x, y| x + y }})
"(+ 1 2)".parse_sexp.consify.lispeval(env, nil) ➤ 3.0
```

Oh yeah, that's more like it.

■**Note** The sexp library returns all numbers as `Float` values, so even numbers that go in as `Integer` values will return as `Float` values.

Choosing Your Primitive Functions

So what will the primitive functions be? The good news is you really only need to support a few operations to be considered Lisp.

> *One possible set of primitives might include CAR, CDR, and CONS for manipulation of S-expressions, READ and PRINT for the input/output of S-expressions and APPLY and EVAL for the guts of an interpreter. But then you might want to add LAMBDA for functions, EQ for equality, COND for conditionals, SET for assignment, and DEFUN for definitions. QUOTE might come in handy as well. If you add more specialized data types, such as integers, floats, arrays, characters, and structures, you'll need to add primitives to construct and access each.*

> —Lisp FAQ (www.cs.cmu.edu/Groups/AI/html/faqs/lang/lisp/part1/faq-doc-6.html)

You're going to get by with `cons`, `car`, `cdr`, `atom?`, `eq?`, `eval`, `quote`, `if`, `define`, `set`, and `lambda`, as well as some numeric functions. Of these, only `cons`, `car`, `cdr`, `atom?`, `eq?`, and `eval` are primitive functions. `quote`, `if`, `define`, `set`, and `lambda` are all special forms. I'll talk about how to add these in the section titled "But What About Special Forms?" Here's the default environment for your Lisp.

```
DEFAULTS = {
  :nil => :nil,
  :t => :t,
  :+ => lambda {|x, y| x + y },
  :- => lambda {|x, y| x - y },
  :* => lambda {|x, y| x * y },
  :/ => lambda {|x, y| x / y },
  :car => lambda {|x| x.car },
  :cdr => lambda {|x| x.cdr },
  :cons => lambda {|x, y| Cons.new(x, y) },
  :atom? => lambda {|x| x.kind_of?(Cons) ? :nil : :t},
  :eq? => lambda {|x, y| x.equal?(y) ? :t : :nil},
  :list => lambda {|*args| Cons.from_a(args)},
  :print => lambda {|*args| puts *args; :nil },
}
```

You'll notice the first two definitions aren't functions at all. When the symbols nil and t are looked up in the default environment, their value will be themselves. This is important for list termination literals, as well as true and false literals.

■**Note** Those familiar with Lisp will probably notice at this point that I'm using notation from both Scheme and more traditional Lisps. Scheme postfixes *predicate* functions (functions that return true or false) with a question mark. Common Lisp uses a postfixed letter "p" (like the function listp, which tests if something is a list). Of course, John McCarthy's original predicates atom and eq contained no distinguishing postfix. I'll be using Scheme question marks because I like the way they read. However, unlike Scheme, I won't be using #t to represent true and #f to represent false; I'll use the classical Lisp values t and nil.

The next four definitions are basic arithmetic. These aren't required to be a Lisp, but they're great for demos and test cases because the Lisp interpreter already understands numbers. You don't provide string operations, but who said life was fair?

■**Note** The primitive functions receive a standard argument list. If you didn't use the arrayify method and flatten the result into the parameter list, the primitives would receive a cons list and have to extract their own parameters.

The car, cdr, and cons functions are also provided. There should be no surprises here, considering you're using your own cons data structure.

atom? returns true if the value is not a list, and false otherwise. You can't just write `! x.kind_of?(Cons)` because you need to return :t or :nil, not Ruby's true and false. eq? tests address equality (whether two objects are actually the same object) and also returns Lisp truth values.

You might as well toss in the List constructor function list too, since the simple interpreter won't have the ability to write functions that accept a variable number of arguments on the Lisp side, a feature needed for the list function.

Creating an Interpreter Object

The Interpreter class doesn't actually do much. It's going to keep track of your root environment, and it's going to provide an eval method for evaluating Lisp code from Ruby, as well as a repl method (which stands for read-eval-print loop) that will let you interact with your Lisp interpreter on the command line.

```
FORMS = {}
class Interpreter
  def initialize(defaults=DEFAULTS, forms=FORMS)
    @env   = Env.new(nil, defaults)
    @forms = Env.new(nil, forms)
  end
end
```

I've defined DEFAULTS as stated in the preceding code, and I'll leave FORMS as an empty hash for now. They both get stored in the new interpreter unless the user specifies his or her own set of default bindings and special forms.

```
class Interpreter
  def eval(string)
    exps = "(#{string})".parse_sexp
    exps.map do |exp|
      exp.consify.lispeval(@env, @forms)
    end.last
  end
end
```

The eval method performs one little trick. It first wraps the code string in an extra set of parentheses. This means that if the user has specified multiple bare s-expressions in the string, you'll get both of them back from the parser, instead of just the first. This means you'll always get a list back from the sexp library. You'll evaluate each expression and then return the value of the last one.

You're also going to want a repl method. The classic REPL (read-eval-print loop) is defined with three chained functions. The read function returns an s-expression from the input. The eval function interprets that s-expression. The print function outputs the result. The whole process is then looped.

For a more classical REPL, you could have implemented each of these stages as a primitive function (eval is already there), and then defined repl to call each in turn. Instead, to take advantage of Ruby features like each_line and exception handling, you'll be implementing it as a single, monolithic Ruby method.

```ruby
class Interpreter
  def repl
    print "> "
    STDIN.each_line do |line|
      begin
        puts self.eval(line).to_sexp
      rescue StandardError => e
        puts "ERROR: #{e}"
      end
      print "> "
    end
  end
end
```

■**Caution** Because I use STDIN.each_line, s-expressions entered on the REPL will need to be on one line.

This repl uses a > prompt, reads input from STDIN, uses eval, and rescues any errors. It also calls the to_sexp method on the results before it prints them. The sexp library has provided to_sexp methods for symbols, arrays, numbers, and strings, but you'll want to add a to_sexp expression for your cons cells. If the cell is part of a list, you'll use standard list notation; otherwise you'll just print the cons cell.

```ruby
class Cons
  def to_sexp
    return "(cons #{car.to_sexp} #{cdr.to_sexp})" unless conslist?
    return "(#{arrayify.map{|x| x.to_sexp}.join(' ')})"
  end
end
```

You should now be able to execute the following code in Ruby:

```
lisp = Lisp.new
lisp.eval("(+ 1 2)")
```

You should also be able to call the `repl` method and have the following interaction:

```
> (+ 1 2)
3.0
```

But What About Special Forms?

Yeah, okay, but you can't do anything exciting yet. You can't define new functions, write conditional code, quote symbols without evaluating them, or even create and set variables. All of these things happen through the magic of special forms. And as you recall, you've left the special forms default hash empty.

Adding quote

Let's start by implementing `quote`, since it's probably the simplest of the special forms. You'll notice, the special forms don't look all that different from the primitive functions. But one obvious difference is that special forms receive the current environment and the special forms hash as parameters.

Just as important, though, the arguments to a special form are not evaluated. If the form wants them to be evaluated, it needs to call `lispeval` itself. This is one (of several) reasons that the env and forms are passed in.

```
FORMS = {
  :quote => lambda {|env, forms, exp| exp },
}
```

This definition is startling in its succinctness and power. The `quote` function's job is to prevent arguments from being evaluated. Since arguments to special forms aren't evaluated, all `quote` needs to do is return its argument as is.

```
(quote a) ➤ a
(quote (+ 2 3)) ➤ (+ 2 3)
(quote (quote 1)) ➤ (quote 1)
```

Adding define and set!

Variable definitions and how to set them are next. As a reminder, variable manipulation looks like this:

```
(define a 1)
a ➤ 1
(set! a (+ 1 2))
a ➤ 2
```

As you can see in the previous listing, the symbol name the value is stored under is not quoted. This means it is not evaluated. The second argument, however, is evaluated, allowing you to bind the evaluation of complex expressions. define and set! map almost directly onto the methods the Env class supports.

```
:define => lambda {|env, forms, sym, value|
  env.define(sym, value.lispeval(env, forms))
},
:set! => lambda {|env, forms, sym, value|
  env.set(sym, value.lispeval(env, forms))
},
```

You've got the preceding examples working now, so let's talk a little about conditional expressions.

Adding Conditional Expressions

McCarthy's original Lisp used a structure called cond. The cond form sometimes gets unwieldy, but it is very powerful.

```
(cond ((atom? a) (list 1))
      ((eq? a (quote b)) (list 1 2))
      (t (list 1 2 3)))
```

The value of the preceding code depends entirely on the value of a. The cond expression tries each clause. If the first half of the first clause is true and the value stored at a is an atom, the cond will evaluate to the list (1). If the second clause proves right and a equals the actual symbol b, then it will evaluate to (1 2). And if neither of these is true, the value t always evaluates to itself (which is not nil), so the cond will have the value (1 2 3).

Despite the history of cond, you'll be implementing the simpler if expression. if will give you the power you need and be slightly easier to implement.

```
(if (eq? 1 2) (+ 1 2) (- 3 2)) ➤ 1.0
(if (atom? (quote a))
    t
    nil) ➤ t
```

The first argument (the condition) is evaluated. If the condition evaluates to true, then the second argument is evaluated (the then clause), otherwise the third argument is evaluated (the else clause). As in Ruby, if returns a value that can be used in other expressions.

```
(cons (if t 0 1) nil) ➤ (0)
```

The implementation is pretty simple.

```
:if => lambda {|env, forms, cond, xthen, xelse|
  if cond.lispeval(env, forms) != :nil
    xthen.lispeval(env, forms)
  else
    xelse.lispeval(env, forms)
  end
},
```

You use Ruby's if expression to build Lisp's if special form. First the implementation evaluates the condition parameter, and if it evaluates to any value except the symbol :nil, which your Lisp considers false, it evaluates the then clause. If the condition evaluates to the symbol :nil, though, it evaluates the else clause. That's all it takes to add conditional statements to your interpreter.

Adding lambda

The use of the word "lambda" to refer to functions in Lisp is historical and dates back to the Lambda Calculus of Alonzo Church and Stephen Kleene. You can write Lisp lambda expressions like this:

```
(lambda () 1) ➤ (lambda () 1.0)
(lambda (x) (+ x 1)) ➤ (lambda (x) (+ x 1.0))
```

Lambda expressions are written starting with lambda, followed by a list of parameters, and then by an expression. When the lambda is invoked, the value of the evaluated expression will be returned. You'll allow the body of the lambda to contain several expressions.

The expressions will be evaluated sequentially and the evaluation of the last expression will be returned. In most cases, though, the body will consist of just one expression (it's more Lispy that way).

```
(define one (lambda () 1))
(one) ➤ 1.0
```

Lambda expressions are called/applied when they are the first value in a nonspecial form. They are typically called by name from the environment, or occasionally the value of a lambda expression is invoked immediately.

```
(define addone (lambda (x) (+ x 1)))
(addone 3) ➤ 4.0
((lambda () 1)) ➤ 1.0
((lambda (x) (+ x 1)) 3) ➤ 4.0
```

lambda is the most interesting of the special forms you'll be implementing. It's going to need to remember the names of its parameters and also the code that forms its body. But because lambdas are closures, they'll also need to capture the environment they were created in.

```
(define x 1)
(define increment (lambda () (set! x (+ x 1))))
x ➤ 1
(increment)
x ➤ 2
```

So what will the Lambda class look like in Ruby? Well, it will have a captured environment and a reference to the special forms mapping so that code inside the closure can be evaluated using lispeval. It will also have a list of parameter names and the expressions that will be evaluated when it is called.

```
class Lambda
  def initialize(env, forms, params, *code)
    @env    = env
    @forms  = forms
    @params = params.arrayify
    @code   = code
  end
end
```

The list of parameters is passed in as a cons list, but is turned into an array for ease of use. The code reference keeps its data as conses, though, because you'll need to call lispeval on them later.

What operations do lambdas support? Well, really just one—`apply`—which you've renamed to `call` as discussed previously.

```
class Lambda
  def call(*args)
    raise "Expected #{@params.size} arguments" unless args.size == @params.size
    newenv = Env.new(@env)
    @params.zip(args).each do |sym, value|
      newenv.define(sym, value)
    end
    @code.map{|c| c.lispeval(newenv, @forms) }.last
  end
end
```

The first thing it does is confirm that the same number of arguments were supplied to the call as the lambda has parameters.

The next step is to create a new environment for the call to take place in. Not all languages create the new environment at call time. In Squeak Smalltalk, blocks reuse their new context during successive calls. This means a block can see the values of its variables from past invocations. This makes for faster code, since each call does not need to create a new environment.

You could make your code behave this way by removing the creation of the new environment from the `call` method and adding it to the initializer. But this isn't really the way functions traditionally work in Lisp, so there's no need to tamper with things.

Now that the lambda has a new environment, it injects the arguments into the environment using the parameter names specified when the lambda was created.

```
@params.zip(args).each do |sym, value|
  newenv.define(sym, value)
end
```

As an interesting aside, Ruby gives its blocks new contexts, like your Lisp does. But even up until Ruby 1.8 (the latest released version at the time of this publication), blocks can reuse variables defined in the enclosing scope for their parameters, which can be very confusing. Matz (the creator of Ruby) has said he'd like to fix this in the future. The following code illustrates the problem:

```
a = 1
1.upto(5){|a| }
a ➤ 5
```

As you can see, despite doing no assignment at all, the value of a has been changed simply because it was reused as a block name. A more complicated example follows:

```
def foo
  x = 0
  return proc{ [proc{|x| }, proc{ x }] }.call
end
a, b = foo()
b.call ➤ 0
a.call(1)
b.call ➤ 1
```

Despite no assignment to x, it changes values when the first returned Proc instance is called. In the world of programming languages, this is very unusual. You could imitate this in your Lisp interpreter with the following snippet, but I don't know why you would want to.

```
@params.zip(args).each do |sym, value|
  if @env.defined?(sym)
    @env.set(sym, value)
  else
    @env.define(sym, value)
  end
end
```

Anyway, once you've got the environment all configured, it's time to actually evaluate the code.

```
@code.map{|c| c.lispeval(newenv, @forms) }.last
```

This evaluates each expression from the body of the function and returns the last one. Your lambdas are now callable!

```
l = Lambda.new(Env.new, Env.new, :nil, 1.0)
l.call ➤ 1.0
```

You're also going to want to provide a to_sexp method so that you can print lambdas on the REPL reasonably.

```
class Lambda
  def to_sexp
    "(lambda #{@params.to_sexp} #{@code.map{|x| x.to_sexp}.join(' ')})"
  end
end
```

You can demo to_sexp using the lambda defined in the previous example.

```
l.to_sexp ➤ (lambda () 1.0)
```

The only thing left is to hook this new class up to the lambda special form.

```
:lambda ➤ lambda {|env, forms, params, *code|
  Lambda.new(env, forms, params, *code)
},
```

With that last bit of wiring, you can now write pure Lisp functions in your interpreter.

```
(define addone (lambda (x) (+ x 1)))
(addone 3) ➤ 3.0
```

You have a working Lisp interpreter! Try running this:

```
Interpreter.new.repl
```

or this:

```
Interpreter.new.eval "(+ 1 2)"
```

You're part of the Lisp club now. You should probably consider buying a John McCarthy T-shirt (see Figure 8-5).

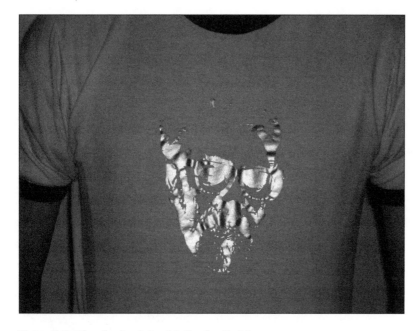

Figure 8-5. *The elusive John McCarthy T-shirt*

Saving the Environment

Now, if you've been following closely, you've noticed a problem with the closures. Most Lisps are relatively careful as to where they allow you to use define expressions. Because your Lisp interpreter lets you use define anywhere, you've created a problem for yourself. Consider the following code:

```
(define broken (lambda () b))
(broken) ➤ ERROR: No value for symbol b
(define b 3)
(broken) ➤ 3.0
```

This isn't really the expected behavior. A closure is only supposed to capture variables that exist when it was taken. There are a number of ways to solve this problem. Most of them are a little tricky, though. One way to get around this is to create a new environment for each line of code evaluated in the same scope using the previous line's environment as a parent. A naïve implementation of this method would be a major memory hog, but if you were smart about reusing environments that had no definitions in them, you could do a lot better.

The easiest solution, though, is probably just to remove define. It isn't a strictly necessary form, since you can build let expressions that will allow you to make bindings in a different way. (I'll talk about this more in the section titled "Implementing the let Macro.") But define sure does make coding at the top scope level easier.

Since trying to make define only available at the top scope would be complicated, you're going to take a third route. You'll leave define in (even with this funny behavior), but encourage people to use let expressions when inside nested scopes. Before you can define let, though, you're going to need to implement macros, one of the Lisp's coolest features.

Implementing Macros

If you need any more primitive functions, it's as simple as adding them to the DEFAULTS hash. And now that you have lambdas, you can add new functions from inside the interpreter. For example, defining the length function is as easy as this:

```
(define length (lambda (x) (if (eq? x nil) 0 (+ 1 (length (cdr x))))))

(length (list 1 2 3 4)) ➤ 4.0
(length ()) ➤ 0
```

If you need more special forms, you add them to the FORMS hash. But what if you want to define your own special forms inside the interpreter, using Lisp? User-defined special forms in Lisp are called *macros*. Macros are passed their arguments unevaluated, and the result of whatever transformations they apply to those arguments is evaluated once they are done.

Implementing the let Macro

I talked earlier about a `let` form that would help avoid using `define`. `let` looks like this in Lisp:

```
(let ((a (+ 1 3))
      (b (- 4 2)))
  (* a b))
```

First you define `a` to be 4, then `b` to be 2, then the value of the entire `let` expression is `a` times `b`. As you can see, `let` allows you to define multiple variables. A simpler version of `let` is named `let1`. `let1` only gives you one definition, but since `let1` can be nested when you need multiple definitions, it's just as powerful.

```
(let1 (a 5)
  (- a 1))
(let1 (a (+ 1 3))
  (let1 (b (- 4 2))
    (* a b)))
```

The cool thing about `let` and `let1` is that they can be implemented using lambdas. Here's a `let1` expression.

```
(let1 (a 4) (+ a 1))
```

Transformed into a lambda, the previous expression looks like this.

```
((lambda (a) (+ a 1)) 4)
```

You could implement this in your `FORMS` hash fairly easily by creating and calling a lambda object:

```
:let1 => lambda {|env, forms, binding, body|
  Lambda.new(env, forms, [binding.car], body).call(binding.cdr.car.lispeval(env, forms)
},
```

You could also build the Lisp code in Ruby and then evaluate it:

```
:let1 => lambda {|env, forms, binding, body|
  params = Cons.new(binding.car, :nil)
  func = Cons.new(:lambda, Cons.new(params, Cons.new(body, nil)))
  exp = Cons.new(func, Cons.new(binding.cdr.car, nil))
  exp.lispeval(env, forms)
},
```

But wouldn't it be better if you had a way to define special forms straight from Lisp code? That's what macros will let you do. Now, most Lisp implementations let you use some fancy syntax when defining macros. They often provide templating functionality as well. For example, in Common Lisp you could write it like the following, using the syntax and templating:

```
(defmacro let1 (binding body) `((lambda (,(car binding)) ,body) ➡
,(car (cdr binding))))
```

This means define a macro let1 that has binding and body arguments. The ` means *quasiquote* and does the templating. Quasiquotes act like regular quote (regular quote is also spelled ' in many Lisps, but we've ignored that convention so far—see Chapter 9 for more information). However, quasiquote will evaluate any expressions prefixed by , and include the result in the quasiquote. You can get by without fancy quasiquote templating, though, by using a ton of list and quote expressions.

```
(defmacro let1 (binding body) (list (list (quote lambda) (list (car binding)) body) ➡
(car (cdr binding))))
```

Your defmacro won't have a special syntax either, so you'll have to write it as a special binding between a name and a lambda. (It looks a lot like how you would define a function in your Lisp, except it defines a special form.)

```
(defmacro let1 (lambda (binding body) (list (list (quote lambda) ➡
(list (car binding)) body) (car (cdr binding)))))
```

This binds the macro expressed as a lambda expression to the special form let1. When a let1 form is encountered, your interpreter will call the lambda function passing in the two unevaluated arguments. It will build a list that contains a lambda and the value of the variable, so when the whole expression is evaluated, the code inside the lambda will have a parameter with the variable name and the given value.

Okay, but how do you implement `defmacro`? Well, it needs to be a special form instead of a primitive function. This is because it uses the name of the macro unevaluated, but it also needs access to the `forms` object so it can insert a new special form for the macro.

```
:defmacro => lambda {|env, forms, name, exp|
  func = exp.lispeval(env, forms)
  forms.define(name, lambda{|env2, forms2, *rest| ➥
func.call(*rest).lispeval(env, forms) })
  name
},
```

The first thing the `defmacro` special form does is to evaluate its second argument to get a lambda expression it will use to perform the actual transformation. You then add a Ruby `Proc` object into the forms object. This `Proc` object invokes the lambda expression using the environment and forms defined at the time the macro was added.

You can now define your `let1` macro form in pure Lisp inside your interpreter. You can also add other macros like the following `unless` macro:

```
(defmacro unless (lambda (cond then else) (list (quote if) cond else then)))
```

Everything just works.

It Just Ain't Lisp Without eval

One of Lisp's coolest features is its programmer accessible `eval` function. Ruby and most other dynamic languages provide `eval` functions today, but Lisp blazed the trail.

`eval` takes Lisp code as data, and then evaluates the result. Indeed, the story goes that the first implementation of Lisp came about when Steve Russell realized that the Lisp `eval` function could be implemented in a lower-level language, thus creating a Lisp interpreter. This is basically what you've been doing, although it might not be accurate to describe Ruby as a lower-level language.

Anyway, `eval` has been a part of Lisp from the beginning. You don't technically need to provide an `eval` function, since it is quite possible to build one within your interpreter. However, since you've already done the work, you might as well make yours available to code running inside the interpreter. This is accomplished easily enough.

I wish I could make `eval` a primitive function instead of a special form. Unfortunately, while you don't need any of its arguments unevaluated (Lisp code passed to `eval` is expected as data), you do need access to an environment and special forms map. If you were willing to always use the default bindings, you could create a new environment and special forms using the standard values. But `eval` is more interesting when it has access to all the definitions your normal code has access to. You can define `eval` as a special form with behavior like this:

```
:eval => lambda {|env, forms, *code|
  code.map{|c| c.lispeval(env, forms)}.map{|c| c.lispeval(env, forms) }.last
},
```

I've intentionally written the preceding definition so it can handle multiple expressions. These expressions in the code array are each evaluated using the environment and special forms dictionary at the point of definition. This evaluation brings them to the state they would be at if `eval` had been defined as a regular primitive function instead of a special form with unevaluated arguments.

Then you evaluate them again. This second evaluation does the dirty work and allows arbitrary s-expressions from inside the interpreter to be executed:

```
(eval (quote (+ 1 2))) ➤ 3.0
```

Just as important, because you use the current environment, the following is also possible:

```
(let1 (a 1) (eval (quote (+ a 2))))
```

Now it really feels like Lisp.

Adding Lexical Macros

One thing you may have noticed at this point is that a macro defined anywhere affects all code run after it. You never create a new `forms` environment.

```
(define a (lambda () (defmacro myquote (lambda (thing) (list (quote quote) thing))) ➥
(myquote b)))
(myquote b) ➤  ERROR: No value for symbol myquote
(a) ➤ b
(myquote b) ➤ b
```

When `a` is run, the `myquote` macro suddenly becomes usable everywhere. It will also overwrite any macros named `myquote` that already existed and were defined elsewhere.

You could avoid this situation with a setup called *lexical macros*. Lexical macros work just like your lexical closures. You create a new `forms` environment object for new scopes. Within this scope, the macro exists, but elsewhere it won't bother anything else. What's really cool is that you can change your macros to work this way with two lines of code (see the bold code in the definition that follows this one). The original `call` method for the `Lambda` class looked like this:

```
class Lambda
  def call(*args)
    raise "Expected #{@params.size} arguments" unless args.size == @params.size
    newenv = Env.new(@env)
    @params.zip(args).each do |sym, value|
      newenv.define(sym, value)
    end
    @code.map{|c| c.lispeval(newenv, @forms) }.last
  end
end
```

To implement lexical macros, you'll add a line that creates a new `forms` environment, and then evaluate the function body using that new `forms` environment.

```
class Lambda
  def call(*args)
    raise "Expected #{@params.size} arguments" unless args.size == @params.size
    newenv = Env.new(@env)
    newforms = Env.new(@forms)
    @params.zip(args).each do |sym, value|
      newenv.define(sym, value)
    end
    @code.map{|c| c.lispeval(newenv, newforms) }.last
  end
end
```

Let's try rerunning that previous example in the modified interpreter.

```
(define a (lambda () (defmacro myquote (lambda (thing) (list (quote quote) thing)))
(myquote b)))
(myquote b) ➤ ERROR: No value for symbol myquote
(a) ➤ b
(myquote b) ➤ ERROR: No value for symbol myquote
```

This time around, the `myquote` macro is only available inside the function it was defined in. Unfortunately, this technique suffers from the same scoping issues as the closures. A `defmacro` defined in the following code is a closure, but in the same scope, will affect the closure.

```
(define example (lambda () (define closure (lambda () (myquote b)))
                           (defmacro myquote (lambda (thing) (list (quote ➥
quote) thing)))
                           closure))
((example)) ➤ b
```

Even though the `myquote` macro is defined after the closure, the closure is affected by it. The techniques I talked about early on, like creating new chained environments after each successive expression, would solve this problem if you extended them to do the same thing for forms as for the environment. But as before, that would add some complexity to the interpreter. Instead, you can steal a construct that other Lisps have, named `letmacro`. Just as `let1` allowed you to define local bindings, `letmacro` lets you define a local macro. Unfortunately, you can't just use the old trick of transforming `let1` into a lambda expression. Thankfully, it's not too hard to just implement `letmacro` in Ruby.

```
:letmacro => lambda{|env, forms, binding, body|
  name = binding.car
  func = binding.cdr.car.lispeval(env, forms)
  newforms = Env.new(forms)
  newforms.define(name, lambda{|env2, forms2, *rest| func.call(*rest).lispeval(env, ➥
forms)})
  body.lispeval(env, newforms)
},
```

The name of the macro is the first part of the bindings pair, and the function that will implement the macro is available when you evaluate the second part of the pair. You create a new `forms` environment and register a lambda expression to the transformation, then evaluate the body with the new `forms` environment. This gives you `letmacro`:

```
(letmacro (myquote (lambda (thing) (list (quote quote) thing))) (myquote b))
(myquote b) ➤ ERROR: No value for symbol myquote
```

That's all there is to lexical macros.

Interoperating with Ruby

Okay, so you provided some primitive functions to manipulate numbers, but you didn't provide your users any functions to manipulate strings. And you don't have an easy way to add objects like files or network sockets to the interpreter.

You could add primitives for each string operation and for creating objects with names like `substring` or `newfile`. But that would be a lot of work. Let's aim higher.

Opening a Window to Ruby

Since all Ruby objects are already valid values in the interpreter, let's provide a window into the Ruby world. You'll define it as a special form so the names of the Ruby objects don't need to be quoted.

```
:ruby => lambda {|env, forms, name|
  Kernel.const_get(name)
},
```

You can use this to retrieve constants (like classes) from the Ruby base namespace.

```
(ruby Integer) ➤ Integer
```

Without the ability to send messages to these objects, they aren't very useful.

Sending Messages

You'll need a good convention for message sends. You could name the function something like send, but if you're going to be typing it over and over again, a one-character symbol might be a better name. Let's name the method !.

```
(! object message param1 param2)
```

You can implement the message send primitive extremely easily. You'll also make it a special form so the message name doesn't need to be quoted.

```
:"!" => lambda {|env, forms, object, message, *params|
  object.lispeval(env, forms).send(message, *params.map{|p| p.lispeval(env, forms)})
},
```

First it evaluates the object and all of the parameters, then it calls the Ruby send method to trigger the appropriate method on the object. This enables you to write the following:

```
(define f (! (ruby File) open "lisp.rb"))
(define lines (! f readlines))
(! f close)
```

Unfortunately, if you try to interact with lines, you hit a problem.

```
(car lines) ➤ ERROR: undefined method `car' for #<Array:0x50a5a0>
```

The Ruby method has quite unsurprisingly returned an array. Most types are shared between Ruby and your Lisp interpreter, but on the Lisp side, it's better to interact with conses rather than arrays. You can modify your ! special form to use the consify method defined earlier.

```
:"!" => lambda {|env, forms, object, message, *params|
    object.lispeval(env, forms).send(message, *params.map{|p| ➡
p.lispeval(env, forms)}).consify
},
```

However, you probably also want the reverse as well. Ruby doesn't know what to do with cons lists, so it should probably receive arrays from the Lisp code. You'll use arrayify here:

```
:"!" => lambda {|env, forms, object, message, *params|
    object.lispeval(env, forms).send(message, *params.map{|p| ➡
p.lispeval(env, forms).arrayify }).consify
},
```

Now the Lisp interpreter can interact with Ruby when it needs to. New primitive functions and values are easy to add. In fact, you could rewrite a lot of the primitive functions in pure Lisp at this point if you wanted using the ! method.

Making Lisp Lambda Work in Ruby

What if you want to pass Lisp lambdas into Ruby code? This would be a pretty cool feature, but adding it is a little complicated. How come? Unlike most other languages with closures, Ruby doesn't pass blocks in a standard argument slot. Ruby has a special slot for passing a single block. Even worse, there's no way to tell if a given method expects a block or not. This makes the decision to coerce a Lisp lambda into a block difficult.

Still, the following heuristic is probably good enough. If the last argument to a method call is a lambda, try passing it in the block slot. In order to do this, though, you'll need a to_proc method for the Lambda class.

```
class Lambda
  def to_proc
    return lambda{|*args| self.call(*args) }
  end
end
```

The to_proc method just builds a Proc wrapper. Even though your Lambdas support the call method, Ruby will only accept a proper Proc object in the block slot. Even if Ruby was more flexible, you'd still probably be better off creating a real Proc in case other code depended on methods besides call.

With to_proc defined, you can begin to look at modifying your ! function:

```
:"!" => lambda {|env, forms, object, message, *params|
  evaled_params = params.map{|p| p.lispeval(env, forms).arrayify }
  proc = nil
  proc = evaled_params.pop if evaled_params.last.kind_of?(Lambda)
  object.lispeval(env, forms).send(message, *evaled_params, &proc).consify
},
```

The previous code relies on two idiosyncrasies of Ruby. First of all, anything passed as the last argument of a method call and prefixed with a & calls to_proc on the object and then inserts it into the block slot. Obviously, you could call to_proc yourself, but it's convenient that Ruby will do it for you.

The other idiosyncrasy you rely on is that Ruby allows one other non-Proc value in the block slot. A nil value in the slot means there is no block. Between the two of these, you've got a system that works both when the method is and isn't expecting a block. Another option would have been to use a different invocation function, perhaps double exclamation points (!!), when you want to pass a block. I suspect the smarter, first approach is easier to use. You can see the results in the following code.

```
(define f (! (ruby File) open "datafile"))
(! f each (lambda (line) (print line)))
(! f close)
```

It works like a charm.

Summary

In this chapter, you implemented the basic Lisp data types, implemented the eval/apply cycle, looked at primitive functions and special forms, and even touched on Lisp integration with Ruby. At this point you have the keys to the kingdom.

Ever wanted to add a new feature to Lisp? Ever wanted to build your own programming language? You really can do anything. Especially if you don't obsess over writing everything in C. If you use a higher-level language like Ruby, you'll get it done sooner and you'll have more fun doing it. Here's your chance to do something that no one's ever done before.

LISP BASICS

This section is meant to be read before the rest of the chapter if you're not familiar with Lisp. I definitely recommend reading *Structure and Interpretation of Computer Programs* if you're interested in learning Lisp. *The Little Schemer, Fourth Edition*, by Daniel P. Friedman and Matthias Felleisen (MIT, 1995) is also a fascinating book and definitely worth picking up at the library.

Lisp can seem strange at first, but it's governed by a few basic rules. At its most basic, Lisp syntax consists of lists and symbols. Most Lisp implementations also support other literal values, including numbers and strings (see Table 8-1).

Table 8-1. *Example Symbolic Expressions*

Expression	Example
Symbol	foo
Symbol	nil
Symbol	t
Empty List	()
Empty List	nil
List	(foo t)
Number	2
String	"a string"

This syntax of symbols and lists is called *symbolic expressions*, or *s-expressions*. These s-expressions are not only Lisp code, but also Lisp data structures, too. When you enter an s-expression into a Lisp implementation, it is converted into data, and then that data is treated as code and evaluated. Evaluating a symbol like foo looks it up in the current environment. So you can give values (including functions) symbolic names in the same way you might use variables in other languages.

Evaluating a list like (foo 1) means calling the function named foo on the value 1. What if foo is not a function? Well, your Lisp implementation will probably complain. Here's an example that will hopefully make things clearer:

```
(+ 1 2) ➤ 3.0
```

When the + symbol is evaluated, it is looked up in the current environment. It turns out that it corresponds to a function that adds numbers together, so the evaluation of (+ 1 2) is 3.

It's important to realize though that the arguments are evaluated as well, before the function named + is called. Literals like numbers or strings evaluate to themselves. The symbols t and nil also evaluate to themselves. t is used to represent true values, and nil is used for many purposes.

The standard rules of evaluation hold for arguments, so if the symbol a is associated with the value 4, the following expression is valid.

```
(+ a 3) ➤ 7.0
```

And the following compound expression is also evaluated like you might think:

```
(+ 4 (- 5 2)) ➤ 7.0
```

Now what if you want to use the value of a symbol or a list, instead of having the Lisp implementation evaluate them? Well, there's a special Lisp function named quote that prevents its parameter from being evaluated.

```
(quote foo) ➤ foo
(quote (these (symbols will not) be evaluated)) ➤ (these (symbols will not) be ➥
evaluated)
(quote (+ 1 2)) ➤ (+ 1 2)
```

quote and other expressions that don't obey standard evaluation rules are called *special forms*. That's all there is to basic Lisp syntax.

■**Note** Most Lisps provide a shorthand for quote written as '. You'll use the simpler full-named version.

You'll probably also want to know about cons cells and list structure before you begin though. A *cons cell* is conceptually just a pair of values. A new cons cell, often just called a *cons*, is created with the function of the same name.

```
(cons "a" "b") ➤ (cons "a" "b")
(cons "a" (cons "b" "c")) ➤ (cons "a" (cons "b" "c"))
```

Cons cells can be used independently and often are. But they also form the backbone of Lisp's list data structure. A list is a sequence of cons cells terminated by the symbol nil.

```
(cons "a" (cons "b" (cons "c" nil))) ➤ ("a" "b" "c")
```

Note that unlike the previous examples, the result is not expressed as a chain of cons. It could have been printed as (cons "a" (cons "b" (cons "c" nil))), but the shorthand in the preceding code is typically used because it's more concise. This is the shorthand you're using anytime you input code into your Lisp implementation. So your addition of 1 and 2 from before is actually represented like this:

```
(cons + (cons 1 (cons 2 nil)))
```

What if you want to retrieve the values you stashed inside a cons cell? Well, you've got two functions to do that, one for each value in the cell. The first item in the cons is called the car and the second is called the cdr. These names are historical as well, and there's a brief discussion of their origin in the section titled "Building Cons Cells" in the main part of this chapter.

```
(car (cons 1 2)) ➤ 1.0
(cdr (cons 1 2)) ➤ 2.0
(car (cdr (cons 1 (cons 2 3)))) ➤ 2.0
```

So when you want to generate lists without using cons cells, the quote expression works well provided you don't want the arguments evaluated. If you do, though, the list function is useful.

```
(list 1 2 3) ➤ (1.0 2.0 3.0)
(list (+ 0 1) 2 3) ➤ (1.0 2.0 3.0)
(car (list 1 2 3)) ➤ 1.0
(car (cdr (cdr (list 1 2 3)))) ➤ 3.0
```

That's the secret of cons cells. The only other thing you need to know about before diving in is *lambda* expressions. The word "lambda" means function in Lisp convention. The word lambda is historical and reflects Lisp's close relationship with Church's Lambda Calculus. Lambdas are written like this using the lambda special form:

```
(lambda (parameter1 parameter2) (body))
```

A more concrete example looks like this:

```
(lambda (a) (+ 1 a))
```

This defines a function that takes one parameter named a and adds 1 to the value of a. You would call the function like this:

```
((lambda (a) (+ 1 a)) 2) ➤ 3.0
```

lambda is a special form, like quote, so the parameter list and the function body aren't evaluated when the function is created. If you want to name the function and keep it around for later, you'll use a define expression. define expressions can be used to associate values with symbols in the current environment.

```
(define a 1)
a ➤ 1.0
(define addone (lambda (a) (+ a 1)))
(addone 2) ➤ 3.0
(addone a) ➤ 2.0
```

define is also a special form. The symbol name the value is assigned to doesn't need to be quoted, and it is not evaluated. The last thing you'll need to know before you can get on with the chapter is *scoping*.

Lambda expressions can reference variables besides their parameters and the temporary variables they define inside themselves. The rules for which variables they can reference are called scoping. It's not required that a lambda expression be able to access variables outside its own body, but in practice almost all Lisps provide this ability. Equally important, with the exception of Emacs Lisp, almost all Lisps have settled on a form of scoping called *lexical scoping*. What does lexical scoping mean? It means that lambda can reference bindings that exist inside scopes that the code also exists in. (This should be familiar from Ruby.) Have a look at this example:

```
(define a 1)
(define adda (lambda (x) (+ x a)))
(adda 3) ➤ 4.0
(set! a 2)
(adda 4) ➤ 6.0
```

The a expression used inside the adda lambda refers to the a defined in the same scope as the adda function itself. And when you change that value for a, the value the lambda sees changes as well. This makes the lambda expression a *closure*. It "closes" on the values it can see when it is defined. I'll talk a bit more about scoping in the rest of the chapter, so if that didn't quite click, don't worry.

It's time to dive in and write your own Lisp implementation. Ready? Then pull a "choose your own adventure," and flip back to the beginning of the chapter.

CHAPTER 9

■ ■ ■

Parsing in Ruby

There are a few fields in computer science that are generally regarded as "experts only." Judging from the structure of most undergraduate computer science curriculums, operating systems and programming language implementation (especially compilers) are probably two of the most deeply revered.

I won't try to pretend that operating systems are easy. Anything that touches hardware has a way of becoming a real pain in the neck. But while advanced compilers and programming language work can sometimes be just as daunting, as you've seen in the last chapter, it's easy to dip your toe into the world of programming languages. In fact, the biggest barrier to entry is simply the breadth of knowledge required for a full implementation. But the good news is that a lot of the required expertise can be learned incrementally. Equally important, a lot of that knowledge is useful on its own!

This chapter is dedicated to talking about parsing. Parsing is a central part of programming language implementation, but it's also a wonderfully useful skill for all sorts of projects. So what is *parsing*? The Oxford English Dictionary defines its meaning in computing as "to analyze (a string) into syntactic components, esp. to test conformability to a grammar." In other words, to recognize when text satisfies certain structural rules. In practice, though, most uses of parsing also convert the structured text into data structures. Compilers definitely do this, but so does almost any code that reads a data file. Everything from "parsing XML" to opening a Word document uses some parsing. Typically, though, when you hear someone speaking of parsing, they're talking about using a formal grammar.

In this chapter, you'll use grammars along with a technique known as *recursive descent parsing* to build parsers with a "parser combinator" library. If that sounded complicated, just hang on. It's not! I'll mostly focus on parsing from the perspective of programming languages, but everything is directly relevant to parsing data files as well.

By the end of the chapter, you'll be seeing situations everywhere where a good parser would make your code better, whether you're writing compilers, games, or even business logic. And as a bonus, you'll look at the process of test-driven development, a technique you can use to dramatically increase your confidence in the correctness of your code.

Parsing with Ruby

I think one of the reasons parsing has a reputation for being somewhat esoteric is that there is some theory involved. But you only need to know a little bit to open up a lot of interesting applications. Let's start by talking about grammars.

Understanding Grammars

A grammar formally encodes the rules of a language. Grammars are somewhat abstract concepts, and there are many ways to express them. One common notation is Extended Backus-Naur Form (EBNF). You can think of EBNF as a series of rules to describe "what comes next." Consider this example:

```
Food = Soup | Sandwich
Soup = Meat " " SoupType
Meat = "Chicken" | "Turkey"
SoupType = "Noodle" | "Chili"
Sandwich = Meat " on " Bread {" with " Cheese}
Bread = "Wheat" | "Rye"
Cheese = ("Cheddar" | "Swiss") "Cheese"
```

Given that Food is the start rule, you know that any particular sentence or string satisfying this grammar will follow either the Soup or Sandwich rules. So the equal sign means "composed of," while the vertical bar means "this or that."

So a Soup consists of Meat followed by a space, followed by a SoupType, like this:

```
Food ➤ Soup
Soup ➤ Meat " " SoupType
Meat " " SoupType ➤ "Turkey" " " SoupType
"Turkey" " " SoupType ➤ "Turkey" " " "Noodle"
```

That's an example of how you use a grammar to generate a valid string. But how about checking to see if a string is valid for a grammar? It's basically the reverse!

```
"Turkey Noodle" ➤ Meat " " SoupType
Meat " " SoupType ➤ Soup
Soup ➤ Food
```

Many parsing systems are built to be able to accept grammars in notations very similar to this. Probably the most famous system is YACC. Short for Yet Another Compiler Compiler, YACC translates grammars similar to this one into the C code for a parser.

Ruby has its own library based on a similar principle. It is named Racc and is also very cool. You won't be using Racc in this chapter (since its separate grammar syntax and dependence on a native code core make it a little complicated). Instead, you're going to be using the excellent RParsec library.

Recursive Descent Parsing

What makes a parser a recursive descent parser? Well, to start with, it must be made of recursive components. And it must also be a kind of parser known as *top-down* (hence the *descent*). You're familiar with the term "recursive," but what does top-down mean?

A top-down parser uses its knowledge about the acceptable states of the grammar to keep track of which possible rules might have been applied to produce the input. And of course, if you stray into a state that couldn't possibly be produced from the grammar, you know immediately that the input is not a production of that grammar.

Recursive descent parsers can be further subdivided over whether they can always tell which production rule a particular portion of the input belongs to, or if they sometimes have to guess and then later change their mind. Changing their mind is called *backtracking*. Backtracking is powerful, but it comes with a performance and complexity cost. There are a lot of ways you can write recursive descent parsers. As long as you have functions and basic data types, you can always manually construct a recursive descent parser.

But parser combinators make life even easier! Parser combinators can be easily assembled to form larger components. A parser combinator library is a toolkit that provides useful basic components that you can build your own parser components (and ultimately a complete parser) on top of. All of the common match types, like "sequences," "alternatives," "optionals," and "repeats," are there. And the best of all? Because parser combinator frameworks are usually written with combinators as first-class values directly in your language, there's no need for special grammar files. This also makes it easy to dynamically generate and manipulate them for really powerful effects.

Probably the most famous parser combinator library is called Parsec. Implemented in Haskell, it's drawn a lot of alternative geek and academic press. Parsec has spawned a number of ports, including JParsec and, the tool you'll be using, RParsec!

RParsec

So what does code using a parser combinator library look like in Ruby? It looks something like this:

```
require 'rubygems'
require 'rparsec'

include Parsers
```

```
Space = string(" ")
With = string("with")
On = string("on")

Swiss = string("Swiss")
Cheddar = string("Cheddar")
Rye = string("Rye")
Wheat = string("Wheat")
Chili = string("Chili")
Noodle = string("Noodle")
Chicken = string("Chicken")
Turkey = string("Turkey")

Cheese = alt(Cheddar, Swiss)
Bread = alt(Wheat, Rye)

SoupType = alt(Noodle, Chili)
Meat = alt(Chicken, Turkey)

RepeatCheese = sequence(Space, With, Space, Cheese).many

Sandwich = sequence(Meat, Space, On, Space, Bread, RepeatCheese)
Soup = sequence(Meat, Space, SoupType)

Food = alt(Soup, Sandwich) << eof
```

It's a little overwhelming, but I've tried to divide it into sections for easier reading. The first few combinators are created with the `string` method. This method returns a parser that matches the exact string passed in. In fact, the combinator itself is an instance of class `AreParser`, a parser that matches only when the head of the input is identical to one of its stored values. The method `string` is just a convenience method you can mix into your current namespace (with that `include` line) that will create an instance you can use.

You can try it out for yourself like this:

```
Food.parse("Chicken Noodle")
Food.parse("Turkey Chili")
Food.parse("Turkey on Rye")
Food.parse("Chicken on Wheat with Cheddar")
Food.parse("Chicken on Wheat with Cheddar with Swiss")

Food.parse("This will fail!")
```

Parsing S-Expressions

In the previous chapter, you used the sexp RubyGem to turn Lisp code into s-expressions. Want to see how it works? In fact, the sexp gem is implemented using parser combinators!

Revisiting S-Expressions

Here's a quick reminder of what s-expressions look like. Numbers and string literals are parsed in much the same way as Ruby would parse them. Bare words are interpreted as symbols, and lists consist of any of these values delimited by spaces inside parentheses. They look like this:

```
(define ignore (lambda (x) 4.0))
```

Parsing Integers

You can create a module named SExpressionParser to contain all your combinator objects. Start with the simplest rule, the rule that turns strings into Integers.

```
require 'rubygems'
require 'rparsec'

module SExpressionParser
  extend Parsers

  Integer = integer.map{|x| x.to_i }
end
```

As you can see, you'll need to require the rparsec gem and then extend the Parsers module. This makes all of the convenience methods from Parsers available. These methods will help you instantiate all the prebuilt parser components you need to build your Parser. The module has everything from simple parsers that match exact text to intelligent parsers like integer that know the rules for parsing numbers.

The preceding integer method is actually creating an instance of the RegexpParser using the following regular expression /\d+(?!\w)/, which, if you know regular expressions, matches a series of digits not immediately followed by any standard word characters.

But what does the map call do at the end? It transforms the text matched by the parser into something new. Well, sort of. What you're seeing there is a little more complex. The code is actually not doing the transformation when map is called. Instead it's returning a new parser object. This parser is just like the parser that map was called on, except that it knows how to do the transform when the parser is finally called.

It helps to keep in mind that none of the parser code you're writing is imperative. It's declarative, so most methods you can call on parser combinators actually return a new `Parser` instance.

■**Caution** For such an excellent library, RParsec plays very fast and loose with namespaces. Its parser classes are installed directly into the root namespace. As a library author, try not to do this.

Unit Test Everything

Complete parsers are notoriously complicated pieces of code. You'd be crazy to write a parser without a serious test suite to compare your final product against. Unfortunately, some parsing techniques make unit testing difficult because their correct behavior depends on a complete set of rules. One bug can cause errors to surface in multiple locations. One of the great features of parser combinators is that each rule can always be considered in isolation, so testing is easy!

So with no more excuses, it's time to see if it works. As always, the best way to find out is to write a test! You'll be using `Test::Unit` and keeping your unit tests in separate files (if you called the first file `sexp.rb`, perhaps call this one `test_sexp.rb`). At its simplest, a `Test::Unit` test suite consists of at least one subclass of `Test::Unit::TestCase`. Any method declared on this object will be executed when the file is run. `TestCase` provides a number of easy-to-use assertion methods as you can see in the following code.

For complicated test suites, each test can have its own class and can make use of methods to initialize special data structures, and so on. But for these purposes, one method per test will be fine.

```
require 'test/unit'
require 'sexp'

class SExpressionParserTest < Test::Unit::TestCase
  include SExpressionParser

  def test_int
    assert_equal(45, Integer.parse('45'))
  end

  def test_int_fail
    assert_raises(ParserException) { Integer.parse('not an integer') }
  end
end
```

By including SExpressionParser in your SExpressionParserTest module, you get direct access to the values defined inside the module. This saves you from extra typing! And when you refer to Integer inside the test_int method, you're really referring to the SExpressionParser::Integer class, not the core Ruby Integer class (what you'd get if you typed 7.class). Running this file should tell you that two tests succeed. Notice how you wrote a test for both success and failure. It won't be uncommon to have even more test cases for complicated rules.

From now on, I'll be writing the code for the tests and parsing interleaved. It shouldn't be hard to figure out which file the code belongs to (the parser or the test suite) because the test methods will all start with "test." I also won't be using fully qualified module and class syntax (where every method is clearly placed inside an open module or class) because this would add significantly to the length of the code with very little real value.

■**Note** For the rest of your SExpressionParser you'll be using a style of programming known as *test-driven development*. You'll write tests for each unit of code before you even start writing the code. This process can produce amazingly reliable software because you define the behavior of the code (via the tests) before you've even written it. This approach doesn't work everywhere. If you're exploring a new problem domain and constantly rewriting code, test-driven development can make you want to pull your hair out (and slow you down to a crawl). But for a well-defined problem domain, like parsing, it's very effective.

Parsing Floats

Following the decision to use test-driven development, here are some tests for your unwritten Float parser.

```
def test_float
  assert_equal(4.5, Float.parse('4.5'))
end

def test_float_fail
  assert_raises(ParserException) { Float.parse('not a float') }
end
```

And here's the code that does the actual parsing.

```
Float = number.map{|x| x.to_f }
```

Unsurprisingly, it looks a lot like the integer example. The rule is constructed from a prebuilt parser type.

Deciding Between Different Number Types

You'd like the next rule (Number) to accept either an Integer or a Float, depending on the presence of a decimal point.

```
def test_number
  assert_equal(4.5.class, Number.parse('4.5').class)
  assert_equal(45.class, Number.parse('45').class)
end
```

See how you can pass either type of number into Number and get the right type back? This is actually a little tricky to do. Since you've already seen the alt parser in use, you might as well start there.

```
Number = alt(Integer, Float)
```

You'd like this to match either an Integer or a Float, but you've got a little problem. Let's run the tests.

A failure! Why? Your Float is being parsed as an Integer. Unless you force a parser to require the end of a string, it can always leave whatever input it doesn't want unconsumed. So your Integer combinator is matching the leading 4 of 4.5 and leaving .5 for the next parser to accept or deny.

Unfortunately, reversing the order doesn't help! Because you've defined float using number, it can also match integers (not just floats). One solution might be to only use number and return a different value type (integer or float), depending on the presence of a decimal point. I like having two distinct combinators, though, and you can make this work.

```
Number = longest(Integer, Float)
```

The longest parser always chooses the parser that consumes the most input. So, it will select Integer unless it could also match as a Float and consume more characters. This solves the problem.

So what else will you need to parse for s-expressions? How about symbols?

Parsing Symbols with Regular Expressions

As you will recall, Lisp symbols are just bare words.

```
def test_symbol_simple
  assert_equal(:foo, Symbol.parse('foo'))
end
```

```
def test_symbol_tricky
  assert_equal(:+, Symbol.parse('+'))
end

def test_number_letter_number
  assert_equal(:'4w4', Symbol.parse('4w4'))
end

def test_symbol_no_leading_numbers
  assert_raises(ParserException) { Symbol.parse('4word') }
end

def test_symbol_fail
  assert_raises(ParserException) { Symbol.parse('4') }
end
```

You can start from the Parsers module's word method. Out of the box, it handles a string of letters.

```
Symbol = word.map {|x| x.to_sym }
```

But this only gets you past some of the tests. If you're going to use this parser for Lisp code, you'll need to be able to handle symbols like + and make-array. You'll have to match more than just letters. There's no easy prebuilt combinator for this, so you'll have to put one together. You could define an exact match using the string method for each additional character you want, and then put together an alt parser that accepts both regular letters and any of your symbols. Then you could use repeat to collect a series of them. But wow, does that sound painful.

Instead, just use the regular expression parser. Here's a first attempt:

```
Symbol = regexp(/\w+/).map{|x| x.to_sym }
```

Unfortunately, \w means a word character that is either a letter or a number! It's not a problem for your symbols to contain numbers, but you'd like them to contain at least one alphabetic character or a symbol (otherwise, they'd be parsed as numbers). You can rewrite it like this:

```
Symbol = regexp(/[\w]*[A-Za-z][\w]*/).map{|s| s.to_sym }
```

But you're going to need to add special characters manually if you want them. And it's worth noting that you should take care when using nonalphanumeric characters inside regular expressions. Many of these characters have special meanings there. Although, interestingly, many of these special meanings are ignored inside character groups (the brackets that describe acceptable matches).

So while + and * normally need to be escaped, you only need to worry about - and / inside the character group.

```
Symbol = regexp(/[\w+\-*\/]*[A-Za-z+\-*\/][\w+\-*\/]*/).map{|s| s.to_sym }
```

Of course, you'd like to add more special characters beyond just basic math operators. It's quickly going to get painful to maintain three separate lists in the two character groups. So, take advantage of Ruby's string interpolation and avoid repeating yourself.

```
Special = '+\-*/'
Symbol = regexp(/[\w#{Special}]*[A-Za-z#{Special}][\w#{Special}]*/)➥
.map{|s| s.to_sym }
```

That's a big win in terms of maintenance and readability. But you can probably do a little bit better! You can use the Regexp.escape class method to do your backslash escaping for you. This will actually escape all of the normal dangerous characters, even the ones that are safe inside character classes. But since this is still valid, you can rewrite the preceding code like this:

```
Special = Regexp.escape('+-*/=<>?!@#$%^&:~')
Symbol = regexp(/[\w#{Special}]*[A-Za-z#{Special}][\w#{Special}]*/)➥
.map{|s| s.to_sym }
```

Notice how you didn't need a backslash before the minus or any of the other symbols you added. This is because the call to Regexp.escape does the work for you. All your tests from before should pass. You should also add a test that exercises all of the newly added special characters.

Parsing Values

You'll add a few more of these literals (so far you have numbers and symbols) in a minute. But let's first collect the ones you've defined so far using an alt combinator. The tests should make sure that Value accepts both numbers and symbols.

```
def test_value
  assert_equal(:x, Value.parse('x'))
  assert_equal(7, Value.parse('7'))
end

def test_value_on_numbers
  assert_equal(:'4w4', Value.parse('4w4'))
end
```

And here's the rule itself:

```
Value = alt(Symbol, Number)
```

`Symbol` is listed first because substrings of valid symbols can look like numbers. However, because of the constraint that `Symbol` must include at least one alphabetic character, if it doesn't find one, the `Number` definition can take over.

This is a good start to your s-expression parser, but now it's time to think about lists.

Parsing Lists and Discarding Return Values

You can begin by writing a parser to handle a series of `Value` matches. They will be separated by plain old whitespace, since that's how s-expression lists work.

There's a cool prebuilt `Parser` method to help you out here. It's called `separated` and takes a parameter that matches the separation between the repeated type. This may sound odd, but it is quite common, even in the English language. When you make a list in a sentence, you separate each item with a comma and a space.

You can use this in combination with the built-in `whitespaces` parser (which accepts one or more characters of whitespace) to match your sequence. Here's the test code:

```
def test_values
  assert_equal([:x, 1], Values.parse('x 1'))
end
```

And here's the implementation:

```
Values = Value.separated(whitespaces)
```

Just like `map`, `separated` actually returns a new parser that gets assigned to the `Values` constant.

You've almost got lists! All you need to do is wrap the `Values` class in parentheses.

```
def test_list_empty
  assert_equal([], List.parse('()'))
end

def test_list_of_symbols
  assert_equal([:x, :y, :z], List.parse('(x y z)'))
end

def test_list_of_lists
  assert_equal([[:x], [:y, :z]], List.parse('((x) (y z))'))
end
```

You want to test not only a simple list of symbols, but also the empty list and nested lists. To get the first of these tests starting to pass, you'll need to define a `List` combinator.

```
List = char('(') >> lazy{Values} << char(')')
```

The `char` combinator simply takes a single character (the `string` combinator would have worked fine as well). But what do the `>>` and `<<` operators mean?

To start with, you could have avoided using the shift and unshift operators by using a `sequence` combinator instead. `sequence` parsers must match each combinator in order. By default, a `sequence` returns the last matched item as the result. In this case, that would be a closing parenthesis. Not very useful.

However, if you call `sequence` with a block, all of the matched items are passed in as parameters and the return value of the block is used as the parser return value. So to use `sequence` in the previous code, you'd have written this.

```
List = sequence(char('('), lazy{Values}, char(')')){|lparen, values, rparen| ➥
values }
```

In other words, you'd throw away the results of the parentheses matching and only keep the list of `Values`.

You're doing the exact same thing with the `>>` and `<<` operators. Each of these operators produces a new parser that must match the combined parsers in the right order. However, the parser produced by `<<` returns the result of the first merged parser. The parser produced by `>>` returns the result of the second merged parser. You can think of these as "use the next guy's result" or "use my result."

So, your list definition using the two operators throws out the parentheses and returns only the `Values` result. This leaves one last question. What does the `lazy` method do? And why have you wrapped `Values` inside a block?

Using the Lazy Combinator

The reason that `Values` is wrapped inside the `lazy` combinator and a code block becomes clear when you think about what you'll need to do to support nested lists. Have a look at the code as a whole:

```
module SExpressionParser
  extend Parsers

  Integer = integer.map{|x| x.to_i }
  Float = number.map{|x| x.to_f }
```

```
  Number = alt(Float, Integer)
  Special = Regexp.escape('+-*/_=<>?!@#$%^&:.~')
  Symbol = regexp(/[A-Za-z#{Special}][\w#{Special}]*/).map{|s| s.to_sym }
  List = char('(') >> lazy{Values} << char(')')
  Value = alt(List, Number, Symbol)
  Values = Value.separated(whitespaces)
end
```

You need List to be a Value, but you also need Lists to be made up of Values. Ruby won't let you write Values in the list definition, however, because you haven't defined Values yet! The problem arises because the definition is recursive, and you're using Ruby constants. You can get around this by forging one of the connections lazily. The lazy method does just this and ensures the Values constant won't be looked up until call time.

You could have accomplished something similar by wrapping each definition in a method instead of storing them in constants. Method bodies are always lazy, so this problem couldn't arise. But then, you'd also be wastefully creating new parser objects for every parse attempt. There are reasons you might want to do that; but this parser's needs are much simpler, so constants will be fine.

Parsing Your First S-Expressions to the End of File Marker

You're going add a few more niceties in a minute, but for all intents and purposes, you have a working s-expression parser now. Congratulations! Let's just add a final line to the module.

```
Parser = Values << eof
```

With this you've created a main Parser object. All real parses should go through this object. You can even wrap this in a module level parse method for convenience.

```
def self.parse(text)
  Parser.parse(text)
end
```

The eof is a combinator that demands that all input must have already been consumed for a particular input string to be considered validly parsed. Here's the result!

```
SExpressionParser.parse("(+ 1 (- 5 3))") ➤ [:+, 1, [:-, 5, 3]]
```

Right on! Let's go ahead and add some other common features.

Quoting in Lisp

Almost all Lisps allow you to prefix a value with a single quote to prevent it from being evaluated. Under the hood, this is sometimes translated into an application of the `quote` special form.

```
def test_quoted
  assert_equal([:quote, :foo], Quoted.parse("'foo"))
end

def test_quoted_double
  assert_equal([:quote, [:quote, :foo]], Quoted.parse("''foo"))
end

def test_quoted_complicated
  assert_equal([:quote, [:foo, [:quote, :baz]]], Quoted.parse("'(foo 'baz)"))
end
```

The tests start with the simple test of a quoted symbol. Then they test a twice-quoted symbol. And finally they try quoting a list containing a symbol and a quoted symbol. In every case, you expect the quotes to get translated into applications of the `quote` form.

Here's how you make it happen. You need to match the single quote character using `char` and then throw away its return value using `>>`. Since `Quoted` will be a `Value`, but also uses `Value`, you'll need to use `lazy` again. And the matched result must be enclosed in the special `quote` form. (Well, actually, it's only a call if the result is fed into a Lisp interpreter; otherwise, it's just items in a list.)

```
Quoted = char("'") >> lazy{Value}.map{|value| [:quote, value] }
```

And to make it properly a `Value`, you add the following:

```
Value = alt(Quoted, List, Number, Symbol)
```

Now the only thing you're missing is proper string handling.

Parsing String Literals

S-expression strings are enclosed inside double quotes, but they can also contain back-slash escaped characters. These escapes let you write another double quote without ending the string, as well as represent newlines, tabs, and so on.

■**Caution** You'll be using the special Ruby %q{} quote operator to avoid the confusion of writing s-expression strings contained in quotes inside Ruby strings enclosed by quotes.

```
def test_string
  assert_equal('foo bar', String.parse(%q{"foo bar"}))
end

def test_string_escape
  assert_equal('a', String.parse(%q{"\a"}))
end

def test_string_escape_quote
  assert_equal(%q{"}, String.parse(%q{"\""}))
end
```

As you see, even the quote marks themselves can be difficult to decipher. In the first test, you're parsing a %q{} quoted Ruby string that contains an s-expression string built with double quotes. It is then compared against an answer written with single quotes instead of %q{} (because regular quotes are more readable when the string doesn't actually contain quote marks).

In the second test, you can see escaping working, although for a character with no special meaning. Since a has no special meaning, you'll just pass it through, just as you do with the escaped double quote mark in the third test. After you've got this working, you can look into adding translations for \n and \t.

Here's a first attempt at implementing strings:

```
Escape = (string('\\') >> any)
Quote = string("'")
NotQuote = not_string("'")
String = (Quote >> (Escape|NotQuote).many << Quote).map do |charseq|
  charseq.map{|charnum| charnum.chr }.to_s
end
```

Any other character is allowed to follow an Escape. They are consumed together as a unit, with the backlash being thrown away. When you add tab and newline handling, you can do it here easily with a map block.

Since you'll be using it twice, you'll define a Quote constant for the parser that handles a double quote mark. You'll also define a parser that handles everything except a quote mark.

The `String` definition itself is then remarkably simple. A `Quote` is followed a sequence of many things that are `NotQuotes` or are `Escapes`, and is finally terminated by another `Quote`. You use the `>>` and `<<` operators again to throw out matched data you have no interest in. And you define the repetition using the `many` method, which by default accepts 0 or more matches for the parser.

This now leaves you with the chore of putting the string back together. The `many` method returns an array by default. The matched text is returned as character numbers, so you need to translate each character number into a string containing that character and then use `to_s` to smush them together.

All the tests are passing now, but I find this code a little messy.

Abstracting String Parsing

What if you rewrote string parsing as a method in `Parsers` that produced a parser using the specified quotation symbol and escape symbol? This would also be a good time to add escape translations like I talked about.

Consider this helper method:

```
module Parsers
  def stringer(opener, closer=nil, translate={})
    closer = opener if closer.nil?
    escape = (string('\\') >> any).map do |charnum|
      escaped = charnum.chr
      translate[escaped] || escaped
    end
    open  = string(opener)
    close = string(closer)
    other = not_string(closer).map{|charnum| charnum.chr }
    string = (open >> (escape|other).many << close).map {|strings| strings.to_s }
  end
end
```

The method `stringer` works almost identically to the previous example. The two changes you've made involve the separation of `opener` and `closer` quote marks, as well as an escape translation mechanism. Allowing different open and closing quote marks adds a little flexibility without much cost. This would let you support something like Ruby-style word lists.

■**Tip** Ruby word lists are written `%w{one two three}` and translated into `["one", "two", "three"]`. They are opened with `%w{` and closed with `}`, and the result is split on whitespace.

The stringer method also allows you to omit a closing quote mark, since many string systems use the same character for both opening and closing. The translation happens in a map statement on the escape. If a translation is found, it is used instead of the original character; but if no translation is found, the original is simply returned. Because the translations are done on actual strings, it makes sense to move the character number to character conversion a little earlier in the process (up into the definition of escape and other).

You can replace the previous multipart String definition using this code:

```
String = stringer(%q{"})
```

Or if you'd like to add some translations, you'd do this:

```
String = stringer(%q{"}, %q{"}, "n" => "\n", "t" => "\t")
```

Now you just have to make String a proper Value.

```
Value = alt(Quoted, List, String, Number, Symbol)
```

You've implemented a complete s-expression parser!

Putting It to Work

You've been unit testing the parser all along, so you should feel pretty confident that it actually works. Let's just add a system test now and call it done.

■**Note** While unit tests are supposed to verify one single component in a software system, system tests are intended to exercise the software as a whole.

Usually you'd want a few system tests, but this one does a pretty good job of exercising the whole parser system.

```
def test_system
  assert_equal([[:*], [:quote, [:a3e, :b, :c]], :b, "a\nstring", [:add, 4, 5.5]],➡
Parser.parse("(*) '(a3e b c) b \"a\\nstring\" (add 4 5.5)"))
end
```

And with that, you're done with s-expressions.

Parsing List Comprehensions

Before I even talk about what list comprehensions are, I'd like to start by saying that they're not a very good fit for Ruby. I'll discuss why in a minute, as soon as I've talked about the list comprehension basics.

A *list comprehension* is a special syntactic structure that is used to transform and select values from lists. List comprehensions can be found in languages like Python, Haskell, Erlang, and even in newer versions of C#.

It's not that I have anything against transforming and selecting values from arrays, per se. But Ruby has such a concise syntax for anonymous closures that adding list comprehensions to the core Ruby language would increase syntactic complexity with no real benefit.

Compare the following Python and Ruby code. Here's the Python:

```
results1 = [thing.transform() for thing in things]
results2 = [thing.transform() for thing in things if thing.valid()]
```

Here's the Ruby:

```
results1 = things.map{|thing| thing.transform }
results2 = things.select{|thing| thing.valid? }.map{|thing| thing.transform }
```

As you can see, the Ruby is a little shorter in the `transform`-only case, and a little longer in the `select`/`transform` case. Both are very readable and do the same thing.

The uncomfortable question the Python example forces me to ask myself is, why do only `transform` and `select` get their own special syntax? Ruby's more general usage of concise, anonymous closures ends up being more flexible.

With that said, a lot of people really like list comprehensions, so wouldn't it be cool if you could support them in Ruby? Even better, what if you could support them as a simple add-on? Not to mention, list comprehensions need special syntax, and that means parsing! This is a perfect project to tackle next, since it will require more sophisticated parsing.

Just a warning, though: this will be a somewhat complex example. I'll try to limit the scope by ignoring a lot of the full Ruby syntax. I won't deal with blocks, classes, or most control structures. But even with those restrictions, you're going to need to allow method calls plus literals like numbers and strings at the very least. And in the middle of all this, you'll learn a little parsing theory as well. Ready?

Making a Plan

You can actually reuse quite a bit of your s-expression parser here. The `Integer` and `Float` combinators stay the same. Single- and double-quoted strings can be defined in one line using the `stringer` helper.

Symbols are a little different in Ruby—they have a leading colon (:)—but you'll want to keep around a notion similar to Lisp symbols. You'll parse these unprefixed words with the Word combinator instead. These words will be used for method and variables names.

■**Caution** Ruby has slightly stricter rules about variable names than I will be using.

The tricky bit will be putting it all together (well, that and method calls). Method calls are going to be surprisingly complicated, but you'll learn some pretty important lessons about recursive descent parsers in the process.

You're also going to use an abstract syntax tree (AST). An AST is an interconnected tree of objects representing the programming language structures. This tree can then be used in any number of ways. It could be interpreted like Ruby's own internal AST, compiled into native code, analyzed for assertions, or optimized via restructuring. You'll interpret the AST in order to run the list comprehension.

Creating Abstract Syntax Tree Nodes

By default, your nodes will have no behavior associated with them. They just need slots to hold their children. You can add methods to them later, if you want, using Ruby's open class mechanism.

Instead of creating a new class for each, you'll take advantage of Ruby's built-in Struct class. Structs provide a straightforward way to declare classes with slots. Here's a simple example:

```
Struct.new("Example", :one, :two)
example = Struct::Example.new(1, 2)
example.one ➤ 1
example.two ➤ 2
```

This isn't quite what you want, though. To start with, you probably don't want your nodes living inside of Struct's namespace. You also probably want a common base class, in case you need to add any features to all of the nodes. Turns out you get all this just by subclassing Struct.

```
module ListComp
  class AST < Struct; end
  AST.new("Symbol", :value)
  AST.new("Integer", :value)
  AST.new("Float", :value)
  AST.new("String", :value)
```

```
    AST.new("Variable", :name)
    AST.new("Call", :target, :method_name, :args)
    AST.new("Comprehension", :transform, :name, :source, :conditional)
end
```

The AST should give you basic idea what you'll need to handle in the parser.

Reusing Combinators from the Last Parser

You should put all of your code under a `ListComp` module, including both the AST and the parser combinators. To keep them out of everyone's hair, you'll put the parser combinators in a separate `Parsers` submodule. Unfortunately, if you're not careful, you'll "shadow" RParsec's `Parsers` module with that name and prevent yourself from reaching the real one to extend it. You can solve this by saving a reference to `Parsers` in a constant named `ParsersAlias`.

```
require 'rubygems'
require 'rparsec'

module ListComp
  ParsersAlias = Parsers
  module Parsers
    extend ParsersAlias

    _ = whitespaces
    Special = Regexp.escape('+-*/_=<>?!@#$%^&:~')
    Word = regexp(/[A-Za-z#{Special}][\w#{Special}]*/).map{|s| s.to_sym }
    Symbol = string(":") >> Word.map{|x| AST::Symbol.new(x) }
    Integer = integer.map{|x| AST::Integer.new(x.to_i) }
    Float = number.map{|x| AST::Float.new(x.to_f) }
    Number = longest(Integer, Float)
    String = stringer('"').map{|x| AST::String.new(x) }
    String1 = stringer("'").map{|x| AST::String.new(x) }
    String2 = stringer('"', '"', "n" => "\n", "t" => "\t").map{|x| ➥
AST::String.new(x) }
    Variable = Word.map{|x| AST::Variable.new(x) }
    Literal = alt(Symbol, Number, String1, String2, Variable)
  end
end
```

You can basically reuse your tests from the last section, so I won't take up space on them here. Do notice, however, I made a super short alias for `whitespaces` named with an underscore. This reads pretty well, as you'll see later.

Parsing the List Comprehension Syntax

To add in the syntax support for "`for`" and "`in`", you'll need to provide some structure.

```
Expr = Literal

For = string("for")
In = string("in")
If = string("if")

Conditional = If >> _ >> Expr
Iteration = sequence(Expr, _, For, _, Word, _, In, _, Expr) do
  |transform, w1, f, w2, name, w3, i, w4, source|
  AST::Comprehension.new(transform, name, source)
end
CompBody = sequence(Iteration, (_ >> Conditional).optional) do |comp, cond|
  comp.conditional = cond
  comp
end
Comp = char("[") >> CompBody << char("]") << eof
```

You assign `Literal` to `Expr` for now. Later you'll have to add in method calls and change this definition, but it works for now. `For`, `In`, and `If` all match the strings of the same name. `Conditional`'s job is to parse the optional `if` statement at the end of the comprehensions.

See how the underscore makes it more readable than writing `whitespaces` in all of those places?

The `Iteration` section represents the main looping part of the comprehension. Separating it out like this makes it easier to test. As you can see from the block, you ignore many of the parser's matches. You can't use the `>>` and `<<` operators this time because you want more than one of the values, but you can use a block instead to throw out all the matches except the transformation, the name, and the source.

The `CompBody` is then responsible for knitting the `Iteration` and the optional `Conditional` together. If no `Conditional` was found, `cond` is `nil`. Either way, you just set the conditional on the `AST::Comprehension` object and return it. Any methods on the `Comprension` node will need to support this potentially `nil` `Conditional`.

And last but not least, you put `Comprehension` inside brackets and require it to be followed by the end of the string.

If you intended to use the component as part of a larger parser for a whole programming language, you'd leave out the `eof`. But since each string you parse is only supposed to contain one list comprehension and nothing else, adding it here is the right thing.

Testing Your Partial Implementation

Here are some tests to try it out:

```
def test_conditional
  assert_equal(AST::Integer.new(1), Conditional.parse("if 1"))
end

def test_iteration
  transform = AST::Variable.new(:thing)
  name = :thing
  source = AST::Variable.new(:things)
  answer = AST::Comprehension.new(transform, name, source)
  assert_equal(answer, Iteration.parse("thing for thing in things"))
end
```

Here you can see both the Conditional and the Iteration parser combinators working. And here's the test that proves the whole thing works together!

```
def test_comp_simple
  transform = AST::Variable.new(:thing)
  name = :thing
  source = AST::Variable.new(:things)
  cond = AST::Variable.new(:thing)
  answer = AST::Comprehension.new(transform, name, source, cond)
  assert_equal(answer, Comp.parse("[thing for thing in things if thing]"))
end
```

Notice that the names the parser expects are raw symbols, not AST types. This is because these names aren't part of the syntax tree. They are only information about which slot to inject the iterated variable into.

Even though getting back an AST::Comprehension won't do you a lot of good until you implement some way to evaluate it, let's stick with parsing for the moment and add method calls to the mini-language you used inside your list comprehensions.

Parsing Method Calls with Dot

This is about to get interesting. Let's try simplifying the example as much as possible. For the moment, forget about list comprehensions. Instead, picture an imaginary language named Dot. This language's only features are number literals and postfix, unargumented, method calls. Here's an example:

```
4.inc.recip
```

You can imagine the preceding line evaluating to 1/5 (the reciprocal of the result of four incremented by one). You might be tempted to try to parse the language like this:

```ruby
require 'rubygems'
require 'rparsec'

module Dot
  extend Parsers

  class AST < Struct; end
  AST.new("Integer", :value)
  AST.new("Call", :target, :name)

  Dot = string(".")
  Word = word
  Integer = integer.map{|x| AST::Integer.new(x) }
  Call = sequence(lazy{Expr}, Dot, Word){|expr, dot, name| ➥
AST::Call.new(expr, name) }
  Expr = alt(Call, Integer)
  Parser = Expr << eof
end
```

Go ahead and give this code a shot!

```ruby
Dot::Parser.parse("4.inc.recip")
```

You should be almost immediately greeted by a message like this: "stack level too deep (SystemStackError)." What's going on?

Recursive descent parsers parse input from left to right. Unfortunately, you've created a situation with a left recursive loop. Left recursion causes recursive descent parsers to infinitely loop. An Expr can start with a Call, and a Call starts with an Expr. Reordering the elements in Expr's alt won't help either. Putting Integer first just causes it to be consumed, and then an error is thrown about the extra input (because you require eof).

Eliminating Left Recursion

Luckily, there's a rule for translating left recursive grammars into non-left-recursive grammars. The basic idea is that you start with a grammar like the following (this is essentially the grammar from the previous code written in a simpler EBNF-style notation).

```
Call = Expr "." Word
Expr = Call | Integer
```

You then translate it into something that looks like this:

```
Call = "." Word CallChain
CallChain = Call | Empty
Expr = Integer CallChain
```

In the preceding example, `Empty` is a special parser that always matches and consumes no input. The previous code has factored out the common parts of the grammar to the left side. So now you look for the actual values you know can start off one of these call chains (in this case, only an `Integer`), and then you allow as many calls as desired to chain off that. The previous example uses right recursion, but you could have written it using `repeat` as well (to hide the details under the hood).

```
CallChain = "." Word
Expr = Integer CallChain*
```

What do these look like in Ruby code? Here's the recursive version:

```
Empty = string("").map{|x| nil }
Call = sequence(Dot, Word, lazy{CallChain})
CallChain = alt(Call, Empty)
Expr = sequence(Integer, CallChain)
```

And here's the slightly shorter version that uses `many`:

```
CallChain = sequence(Dot, Word).many
Expr = sequence(Integer, CallChain)
```

But you've got a problem. The original recursive version you wrote made it really easy to build up your AST. But your new version is more complicated. Putting together any sort of node after a `Call` match is tricky because the `Call` doesn't have access to the target the method is being invoked on. You can work around this in the recursive case by returning `proc` objects that will produce the appropriate node type later when called with the missing target.

```
Empty = string("").map{|x| nil }
Call = sequence(Dot, Word, lazy{CallChain}) do |dot, method_name, chain|
  proc do |target|
    call = AST::Call.new(target, method_name)
    return call if chain.nil?
    chain[call]
  end
end
```

```
CallChain = alt(Call, Empty)
Expr = sequence(Integer, CallChain) do |expr, chain|
  return expr if chain.nil?
  chain[expr]
end
```

Cool, huh? But it's complicated. It's probably best to use the repeat version instead. While still not as nice as the first way you tried to write it, this version will help simplify building the AST.

```
CallChain = sequence(Dot, Word).many
Expr = sequence(Integer, CallChain) do |expr, chain|
  chain.inject(expr){|chain, name| AST::Call.new(chain, name.to_sym) }
end
```

Because many returns a list, you can just use inject to left fold the list! And if the call chain is empty, then expr is just returned. The feasibility of this technique depends on how many important matches the chain contains.

Method Calls in List Comprehensions

With this new understanding about how to avoid left recursion, let's add method calls into the list comprehension syntax. You can worry about argument lists in a minute. For now, start with the no-argument list methods from the previous section.

Here's the unit test:

```
def test_method_call
  answer = AST::Call.new(AST::Call.new(AST::Integer.new(1), :baz), :grr)
  result = Expr.parse("1.baz.grr")
  assert_equal(answer, result)
end
```

And here is the code to make it happen:

```
Literal = alt(Symbol, Number, String1, String2, Variable)
Dot = string(".")
CallChain = sequence(Dot, Word).many
Expr = sequence(Literal, CallChain) do |expr, chain|
  chain.inject(expr){|target, name| AST::Call.new(target, name) }
end
```

Okay, so you'd like to add argument lists as well, though. Start by writing a test case to show what they look like. Let's replace the old test.

```ruby
def test_method_call
  args = [AST::Integer.new(2), AST::Integer.new(3)]
  answer = AST::Call.new(AST::Call.new(AST::Integer.new(1), :baz, []), :grr, args)
  result = Expr.parse("1.baz().grr(2, 3)")
  assert_equal(answer, result)
end
```

And then you can implement it. Notice how the number of definitions increased (though the grammar is still quite manageable).

```ruby
Literal = alt(Symbol, Number, String1, String2, Variable)
Dot = string(".")
Comma = string(",")
Delim = _.optional >> Comma << _.optional
LParen = string("(")
RParen = string(")")
ArgList = LParen >> lazy{Expr}.separated(Delim) << RParen
Call = sequence(Dot, Word, ArgList){|dot, name, args| [name, args] }
CallChain = Call.many
Expr = sequence(Literal, CallChain) do |expr, chain|
  chain.inject(expr){|target, name| AST::Call.new(target, name[0], name[1]) }
end
```

You've added several more simple parsers like Comma, LParen, RParen, and even Delim (which is just a comma surrounded by optional whitespace). You use them to build an ArgList enclosed in parentheses and separated by commas.

You've also broken the definition of Call out of CallChain. Adding ArgList to the sequence means you'll need a translation block to preserve both the method name and the method args (return them as a pair). Separating Call makes this easier.

Lastly, you've changed the code that builds Call nodes to use both the method name and the argument list. And with that, the parser is done!

Running the Comprehensions

All that's left now is the behavioral code to make the list comprehensions run. Because you'll be adding the methods via Ruby's open classes, you can put this code in a separate file if you choose so that you could potentially have multiple behavior implementations.

In this case, you could pull in the `asteval.rb` for the simple execution model, or perhaps `bytecode.rb` for a version that compiled down to byte code for one of the next-generation Ruby virtual machines.

```
require 'listcomp'
require 'listcomp/asteval'
```

For now, though, you'll put them in the same file (`listcomp.rb`).

Just as in your Lisp interpreter, you'll add an eval method to each AST node type. And like your Lisp interpreter, you'll pass an environment into each. Because of the odd way in which Struct subclasses are stored inside their parent, you'll have to nest the definitions of each AST subclass inside the AST class. But you'll also provide a default eval method that simply calls and returns the value method (just an accessor for the value instance variable).

```
class AST
  def eval(env)
    value
  end
end
```

In this default case, you totally ignore the passed-in environment. Not so in the evaluation of the AST::Variable node.

```
class AST
  class Variable
    def eval(env)
      env[name]
    end
  end
end
```

Evaluating a Variable node type retrieves its value from the environment and returns it.

The Call evaluation looks a lot like the Lisp apply code.

```
class Call
  def eval(env)
    target.eval(env).send(method_name, *args.map{|a| a.eval(env) })
  end
end
```

You evaluate both the target and the arguments, and then use `send` to actually invoke the method. All that's left is the `Comprehension` node itself (well, that and some glue, as you'll see in a minute).

```ruby
class Comprehension
  def eval(env)
    list = source.eval(env)
    unless conditional.nil?
        list = list.select do |value|
          env[name] = value
          conditional.eval(env)
      end
    end
    list.map do |value|
      env[name] = value
      transform.eval(env)
    end
  end
end
```

The source you'll be iterating over is first evaluated in the environment. If the comprehension has a conditional statement, `eval` uses a `select` call to filter the list. You bind each list item into the given name (one at a time) and evaluate the conditional to determine if the element should remain. Then `eval` uses `map` to transform the list. Again, each of its components is bound into the environment with the designated name. The transformation is then evaluated once for each binding and the result is returned. You can try it out right now!

```ruby
ListComp::Parsers::Comp.parse("[n.+(1) for n in s]").eval({:s => [1, 2, 3]})
➤ [2, 3, 4]
```

Wow, is that cumbersome! Let's add a little glue to make the whole thing nicer.

Adding Some Convenience

The biggest win will come from wrapping up the parser and evaluating code inside a helper method.

```ruby
def list_comp(text, env)
  ListComp::Parsers::Comp.parse(text).eval(env)
end
```

```ruby
list_comp("[n.+(1) for n in s]", {:s => [1, 2, 3]})
```

As you can see, this helps, but passing in the environment is still painful. You can make this a little easier with the help of Ruby bindings.

Abusing Ruby Bindings

Ruby ships with a class named `Binding`. It represents a Ruby environment (which contains variables and constants). You can create one at any time using the `binding` kernel method. By default the objects aren't terribly useful, except that you can evaluate code in the context they were created. This is typically used when you want to explicitly restrict the environment code runs in when you call Ruby's native `eval` method.

However, the members of the Ruby Extensions project have cleverly extended the `Binding` class for you. If you install the gem `extensions`, you can make use of their extra methods. You'll need them for the next section.

One member, Tom Sawyer, has used `eval` to implement a series of methods that let you easily look inside `Binding` objects. You can use this to convert `Binding` objects into hash tables that your `eval` method can understand. Consider this new `list_comp` definition:

```ruby
def list_comp(text, b)
  env = {}
  b.local_variables.each{|var| env[var.to_sym] = b[var] }
  ListComp::Parsers::Comp.parse(text).eval(env)
end
```

The `list_comp` method would be called like this:

```ruby
s = [1, 2, 3]
list_comp("[n.+(1) for n in s]", binding)
```

There's actually an even more interesting extension to `Binding` that actually allows you to look at the values defined in the caller's environment. This is perfect, since it would let the `list_comp` method peek outside of its own scope and use the values defined in the scope it was called.

Unfortunately, since Ruby 1.8.5, this extension no longer works. The Ruby community may eventually get this functionality back via one of several projects that involved manipulating Ruby internals from within Ruby, but I won't sidetrack you by diving into those. Suffice it to say that if you are running Ruby 1.8.4 or before, you could write the following:

```ruby
require 'extensions/binding'

def list_comp(text)
  ast = ListComp::Parsers::Comp.parse(text)
```

```
  Binding.of_caller do |rubyenv|
    env = {}
    rubyenv.local_variables.each{|var| env[var.to_sym] = rubyenv[var] }
    ast.eval(env)
  end
end
```

This code uses `Binding.of_caller` to grab the environment that called the method. Because of the way it's written, `of_caller` is used with a block (you can read about why on the Ruby Extensions web site). You then copy all the variables out of the captured Ruby environment into a hash that you'll use as your environment. And then you `eval` the AST! This would let you completely omit the call to bindings.

```
list_comp("[n.+(1) for n in s]")
```

If you were using this regularly, you might consider removing the brackets around the comprehension because they aren't really required. And for a complete solution, you'd probably also want to add array and hash literals and maybe cache the results of previous parse attempts. Infix operators like + might not be bad either. But I'll leave those up to you! If you get that far, you'll have made a good start on your very own complete Ruby parser.

Best of luck!

Summary

In this chapter, you covered the basics of parsing using the RParsec parser combinator library. You worked with grammars and learned about what it means to be a top-down parser and a recursive descent parser. Then you dove in and implemented a full s-expression parser that handled all the basic literal types, plus extras like quoting. In the process, you built a relatively generic combinator for parsing quoted strings. Then you moved on to parsing list comprehensions and learned about what's required to parse Ruby method calls and how to avoid using left recursion. Your parser built an executable abstract syntax tree using the helpful Ruby `Struct` class. All along the way you used test-driven development to help you write reliable and accurate code.

If you're looking for more information about parsing and Ruby, the following web pages (the documentation for RParsec and Racc) may be of use to you:

```
http://docs.codehaus.org/display/JPARSEC/rparsec+overview
http://i.loveruby.net/en/projects/racc/
```

Additionally, most good compiler books dedicate a portion of their pages to parsing. *Principles of Compiler Design* by Alfred V. Aho and Jeffrey D. Ullman (Addison-Wesley, 1977), affectionately nicknamed "the Dragon book," has been a standby for years, although a newer text, *Compilers: Principles, Techniques, and Tools* (Addison-Wesley, 2006, 2nd Edition) has been released by the same authors as well. Andrew W. Appel also has several compilers books available for a variety of languages (although not Ruby).

I hope this chapter has shed some light into the dark magic of parsers. In the end, they really aren't that hard. You've focused mostly on parsing programming languages (because they're fun!). But keep your eyes out for places where parsers can make your life easier. Parsers are everywhere!

Index

Numbers and symbols

& (bitwise and), 204
^ (bitwise exclusive or), 204
| (bitwise or), 204
[] method
    and []= methods, 64
    in Pattern class, 33
---/*--* (on/off) characters, in Pattern
        class, 29
= (equal sign)
    extending notes with, 33
    meaning in grammars, 262
== method, for testing, 103–104
+ (plus) symbol, 232
* prefix operator, 134–135
` (quasiquote), in Lisp, 249
%q quote operator, parsing literal strings
        with, 275–276
<< (shift operator), moving bytes with, 15

A

"A Genetic Algorithm Tutorial" paper, web
        site address, 221
@@permutations_cache class variable,
        memoizing code, 106–107
@at callbacks hash table, initializing, 56
@base variable, in Pattern class, 30
@choosen_rep, 178–179
@load_time variable, 43
@terrain Matrix, populating, 125–127
@units Matrix, 124–125
Abelson, Harold, 224
abstract syntax tree (AST)
    creating nodes, 279–280
    interpreting to run list comprehensions,
        279
accessors, required by Terrain and Unit
        instances, 124–125
aconnect command-line utility, ALSA, 22

Action class, taking actions with, 136–139
Action subclasses, implementing, 137–139
add method, 169–170
    inserting objects into animations with,
        56–57
add_unit method, BasePlayer class, 140
Advanced Linux Sound Architecture
        [ALSA] for Linux, 9
Aho, Alfred V., 291
algorithmic iterations, running, 200–201
algorithms, for exploring large solution
        spaces, 197
alias keyword, 78
all_positions method, 127
    finding moves with, 135
ALSA, interfacing with, 19–22
amount helper, implementation, 102
Animation class, 55–57
animation loop, settings in, 58
Animation objects, managing and
        tracking time increments with, 56
animations
    code skeleton for, 78
    putting together, 83–86
    rendering, 57–58
    spicing them up, 86–91
    writing message for, 80
    your first GridDrawer, 78–82
animations, 91
animator, converting pictures to
        animations with, 55–66
ant colony optimization, 197
Appel, Andrew W., 291
application bundle, Cocoa applications
        distributed as, 161
ApplicationGameDelegate, 161
applications and windows, 157–158
apply method, 232–233
arithmetic definitions, in Lisp default
        environment, 237

Array class
   building Matrix class with, 122–124
   calling consify on, 234
arrayify method, 233–235
arrays, in Ruby, 121
at method, 59
audio tracks, adding to iMovie
         animations, 84

■B

backtracking, 263
bang
   as regularly scheduled action, 22
   callback, 40
   counter master kept by Monitor, 42
BasePlayer class
   adding functionality of, 140–142
   command line interface for, 139–140
Binding class, shipped with Ruby, 289–290
binding kernel method, capturing current
         bindings with, 62
Binding objects, 62–63
Binding.of_caller, using, 289–290
bit strings
   implementing, 203–207
   using integers as, 203–204
Bite action, implementing, 137–139
BitInt class
   subclassing, 209–210
   wrapping return values, 210–211
bits_to_int, calling, 205–206
bitwise and (&), 204
bitwise exclusive or (^), 204
bitwise or (|), 204
BIT_SIZE, setting, 209–210
blocks, registering as callbacks, 58–60
bpm method, 40
brute force algorithm, 96–97

■C

C module, defining inside LiveMIDI class,
         13
call method
   in Ruby, 232–233
   invoking to perform actions, 136
callbacks, registering and running, 58–60
car function, 224–225

cartography 101, 124–125
cdr function, 224–225
cells, 195. *See also* views, controls, and
         cells
Centipede game, making drawing
         mechanism work as, 87–90
chaining, environments, 227–230
change making simulation, 211–216
change method, change_making
         operation performed by, 98–99
change simulation
   adding a coin, 112
   coin systems, 114–115
   Customer class, 100–110
   determining change carried around,
         111
   going shopping for, 93–95
   hash problems, 107–109
   making change, 95–99
   memoization, 106–107
   optimal coins, 113–114
   pay! method, 109–110
   replacing a coin, 111–112
   wizard money, 116–117
change.rb, creating, 94–95
ChangeGenome class, 214
ChangeMaker class, 98–99
ChangeSimulator, 110
   adding a coin, 112
   adjusting for wizard money, 116–117
   beyond four coin systems, 115
   coin systems, 114–115
   determining optimal coins, 113–114
   four coin system, 114–115
   getting the price list, 111
   initializing, 110
   replacing a coin, 111–112
   simulating 10K purchases, 111
   telling number of purchases to run for,
         110
ChannelManager class, 47–49
Choice class, 134
Choice objects, rep method, 177
ChoiceBar class, 169–171
choices, making, 177–179
choices? method, 141
choose_all method, building, 141–142

choose_all_or_done method, 141–142, 149

choose_or_done method, 141–142, 149–150

chromosomal crossover, in sexual reproduction, 204

ChucK, 7, 40

class eval, adding definitions with, 72

class method, defining directional methods with, 71–72

clear method, 169

clear_units method, BasePlayer class, 140

clicked method, 170

CLIPlayer class, writing, 143–144

close method
  CoreMIDI for OS X, 18
  defining, 14
  writing ALSA, 20

C.mIDIPacketListAdd, using, 18–19

cmusic, 7

Cocoa application. *See also* RubyCocoa
  odd way to do things, 161–162
  packaging it up, 192–194

Cocoa Application Kit, 153

CocoaPlayer class
  as subclass of BasePlayer class, 159
  changing initialize method, 164–165
  creating, 163
  defining convenience method in, 180
  DinoCocoaPlayer subclass, 173–174
  mouseDown method for, 182–183
  TBSView initialization by, 182

CocoaTBS#initialize method, changing to use ChoiceBar, 171

coin list, encoding in genome, 211–212

coin system solver, writing generic, 114

coin systems, simulating with Ruby, 93–118

ColorTile class, 173
  coding ImageTile to replace, 185–186

combinators. *See also* parser combinators
  reusing, 280.

command-line player, writing, 143–144

comparison method, for cube objects, 79

Compilers, Principles, Techniques, and Tools, 291

composing music, 29–36

conditional expressions, adding, 241–242

cons cells, 258–259
  building, 224–226

Cons class, building in Ruby, 225–226

cons function, cons cells created with, 224

consify method, 235

const_set method, declaring BIT_SIZE with, 210

Contents of Address of Register, 225

Contents of Decrement of Register, 225

controls. *See* views, controls, and cells

CoreFoundation string, taken by MIDIClientCreate function, 16–17

CoreMIDI for OS X, 9
  interfacing with, 16–19

create_button_bar method, 167–168

create_menu method, 194

create_messages method, building message box with, 166

create_window method, sizing window with, 175

crossover method, playing with, 204–205

crossover modeling, 205–206

crossover_when method, 206–207

Ctrl+C, stopping program with, 154

Cube class, 73

cubes
  drawing, 65–78
  giving depth to, 86–87
  making visible every four beats, 90

Customer class, 100–110
  creating new American, 103
  creating new customer in, 101
  giving and receiving coins, 105

CUTE_TERRAIN_SHORTEN_Y, 188–190

CUTE_TILE_OFFSET_Y, 190

■D

Danc, PlanetCute tileset by, 184

data bytes, MIDI, 10–11

data types, choosing Lisp, 224

deferred execution, 74–76
  adding to GridDrawer, 76–77

define and set! special forms, variable manipulation with, 241

define expression, 259–260

define method, for Env class, 228–230

define method method, 72

defined? method, implementing, 228–230
defmacro, syntax for, 249
defmacro?, implementing, 250
def_draw method, parameters, 72
delegate library, using, 209
delegation, using when subclassing
        Interger class, 209
denoms method, defining helper methods
        for, 213
die method, 130–131
DinoCocoaPlayer class, 173–174
    adding extra padding, 191–192
    adding image-based tilesets to, 186
    creating present_TYPE_choice methods
        in, 180–181
    fixing mouse down handling, 191
DinoWars game class, 150–151
directional methods, 69–71
dispatch method, Timer class, 23–24
DL::Importable, 13
DL.sizeof method, 14
domain-specific languages (DSLs). *See*
        DSLs
DONE Choice, 134
done method, 146
done? method, 146
do_choose method, 140–141
    implementing, 177–179
    making choices with, 179
Dragon book, 291
draw method, 73, 128
    drawing map with, 172–176
    populating Location objects with, 176
Drawer class, 172–173
    passed into each Location, 174–175
drawing mechanism, 87–90
drawRect, writing, 175–176
draw_all method, redrawing displays
        with, 146
DRY (don't repeat yourself), 71
DSLs (domain specific languages), 67–68.
        See also external DSLs; internal
        DSLs
DumbComputer class, coding simple,
        142–143
dup, calling on value stored in cache, 107
duration parameter, for play method, 27

duration prefixes, changing parser to use,
        35–36
dynamic linking library, provided by
        Ruby, 9
dynamic programming, 99–100

■ E
each method, 95
encodings
    choosing, 212–214
    thinking about, 203–207
end_choice method, 179
Enumerable module
    adding min_by method to, 97–98
    defining random method in, 200
    defining rest method in, 32–33
Env class, constructor supporting
        chaining, 228
env parameter, lispeval method, 231
environments
    chaining, 227–230
    changing values stored in, 229–230
    saving, 247
    saving values in, 226–230
eof combinator, 273
equal sign (=)
    extending notes with, 33
    meaning in grammars, 262
ERB (embedded Ruby templating
        language), 60–61
error checking, 101–106
eval function, 230–232
    defining as a special form, 251
    in Lisp, 250–251
eval method, 62–63
evolution, simulating, 198–206
execution, deferring, 74–76
extend keyword, in Ruby, 13
Extended Backus-Naur Form (EBNF),
        262–263
extern method, calling, 13
external DSLs, 67

■ F
Felleisen, Mathias, 257
File.unlink, removing intermediate SVG
        files with, 62

fill attribute, 53
fitness method, 200
fittest method, 200
Float parser, tests for, 267
forest tile, implementing, 188
forms parameter, lispeval method, 231
Fowler, Chad, 2
Fowler, Martin, 67
frame id method, 58
frame method, getting and printing
        current frame with, 59
free function, 14
free= accessor, 15
freeze, calling on value stored in
        cache, 107
Friedman, Danial P., 257
from_gray method, 218–219

G

<g> tag, 65–66
galleons currency system, used by
        wizards, 116
Game class, controlling game with,
        144–150
garbage collector, Objective-C, 155
gem method, adding, 235–236
General MIDI standard, 15
generate method, 136–137
Generator class, example, 74–76
Genetic Algorithm class
    adding block for value computation,
        221
    implementing, 199–200
genetic algorithms, 197–221
    adding improvements, 216–221
    experimenting with Gray code, 217–219
    implementing, 199–200
    initial population needed for, 198–199
    letting parents live on, 216–217
    roulette selection, 219–221
genome, 200
    dealing with invalid, 216
    designing to test algorithm, 201–202
    encoding coin list in, 211–212
    remembering winning solutions,
        202–203
    requirements, 201–202

grammars, understanding, 262–263
Gray code, experimenting with, 217–219
greedy algorithm, 95–99
GridDrawer
    adding deferred execution to, 76–77
    defining def draw class method on,
        71–72
    helper methods, 77–78
    implementing, 69–71
    initializer for, 73
    subclassing into LetterDrawer, 80–81
GridDrawer.new block, internal DSL
        example written in, 68–69

H

Hackers, Heroes of the Computer
        Revolution, 7
"Hacking Perl in Nightclubs" article, 22, 40
Hakoiri-Musume RubyCocoa example,
        Makefile based on, 192–194
handle_events method, 160
hash, problems with, 107–109
hash keys, duplicating before storing
        objects, 107–109
hash method, 107–109
Hash.new([]) method, caution about
        using, 56
health points, counter for, 129–130
Hello World application
    RubyCocoa style, 154
    written in Objective-C, 156
helper functions, using arrayify and
        consify, 233–235
helper methods, for GridDrawer, 77–78
hex color notation, 53
highlight, setting Location instance's,
        180–181
hill climbing algorithms, 197
homoiconic syntax, in Lisp, 223
href attribute (hypertext reference), 55
Hunt, Andy, 2

I

tag, embedding images in SVG
        with, 55
image tiles, using, 184–191

ImageMagick utility
    converting SVG to JPEG files with, 62
    putting animations together with, 83
    web site for, 62
images, embedding in SVG, 55
ImageTile class
    coding to replace ColorTile, 185–186
    creating new initializer for, 193–194
    eliminating padding in, 188
iMovie, putting animations together with,
    83–84
Impromptu, 7, 40
include keyword, in Ruby, 13
Info.plist.tmpl, filling with APPNAME, 193
initAt method, 170
initialization phase, genetic algorithms,
    198
initialize method, 166
    Genetic Algorithm class, 199–200
    getting button bar up and running, 168
    helper methods for, 199–200
    Map class, 126
    writing ALSA, 20
inject_with_index method, 205
installing, RubyCocoa, 153–154
instance_eval, evaluating code with, 40
instrument method, adding new, 46
Integer class, 208–211
Integer method, 265–266
Integer#to_s, specifying output base with,
    206
integers, parsing, 265–266. *See also* Ruby
    integers
internal DSLs, 67, 91
Interpreter class, creating, 238–240
interval, as time between bangs, 22
irb (interactive Ruby environment), 4
iterations, running, 200–201

■J–K

JParsec, 263
JPGVideo, putting animations together
    with, 85

knuts, used by wizards, 116

■L

Lambda class, 252
lambda expressions, 259–260
lambda special forms, adding, 242–246
last convenience method, saving
    rendering time with, 79–80
lazy combinator, using, 272–273
left recursion, eliminating, 283–285
let macro, implementing, 248–250
LetterDrawer, initializing, 81–82
Levy, Stephen, 7
lexical macros, adding, 251–253
lexical scoping, 227
libraries, for making music, 7
Lisp
    basics of, 256–260
    choosing your data types, 224
    default environment for, 237
    FAQ about primitives, 236
    implementing in Ruby, 223–260
    learning, 224
    making code look like it, 235–236
    quoting in, 274
Lisp lambda, making it work in Ruby,
    255–256
Lisp symbols, parsing with regular
    expressions, 268–270
lispapply method, defining, 232–233
lispeval method
    adding to existing classes, 230–232
    implementation of for conses, 233
List combinator, defining, 272
list comprehensions
    making a plan, 278–279
    method calls in, 285–286
    parsing, 278–290
    running, 286–288
list function, using in Lisp, 259
lists, parsing and discarding return values,
    271
list_comp method, 289
Little Schemer, The, 257
live coding, 39–49
    adding proxy class, 45
    examples, 44

reusing instance across reloads, 45
  using text editor for, 40
LiveMIDI class, defining C module in,
    12–13
load method, 42–43
Location class, 172, 190–191
Location instance, setting highlight for,
    180
Location objects, populating, 176
LocationOccupiedError exception, 125
log2 method, web site for information, 206
longest parser, 268
lookup function, 229
loosely coupled, 120

■M

macros
  adding lexical, 253
  implementing, 247–250
main.m Objective-C file
  binary stub provided by, 192–193
  changing to run Ruby code, 192
make choice method, 178
Make!, building DinoWar.app with,
    193–194
Manhattan distance, calculating, 127
Map, representing, 128–129
Map class
  adding helper methods to, 127
  building, 122–124
map method, current objects returned
    by, 145
Map#place method, 130
maps
  adding to game instance, 145–146
  drawing, 172–176
  highlighting locations, 180–181
maps with matrices, implementing,
    122–124
Matrix class, building, 122–124
Matrix instances, creating and inserting
    Terrain types, 126–127
Matsumoto, Yukihiro (Matz), 58
McCarthy, John, 223
McLean, Alex, 40

memoization, using in change method,
    99–100
memory allocation (malloc), 14
MergedTile class, 187
message method, 15
  CoreMIDI for OS X, 18–19
  implementing, 143
  needed for operating systems, 12
  updating to send messages, 166–167
  writing ALSA, 20–21
messages
  displaying, 166
  sending, 254–255
message_all(text) method, 146
metaprogramming, 71–72
method calls
  in list comprehensions, 285–286
  parsing with dot, 282–283
metronome
  creating Timer for, 26
  duration parameter, 27
  fixing time drift, 26
  implementing, 25
  writing the play method, 26–28
Metronome class, rewriting methods for,
    27–28
MIDI, 8–9
  interfaces for, 9–12
  talking C and making noise, 9–22
  using keyboard for tepo tap, 34–35
min_by method
  adding, 97–98
  for selecting best coins to use, 105–106
  implementating, 97–98
mkdir method, 57
modified? method, 43
Monitor class, on_bang method called
    by, 42
mouseDown method, for CocoaPlayer,
    182–183
mouseDown(event) method,
    implementing on TBSView, 182
move method, 131–132
move to and move by methods, 65
move_choices method, finding moves
    with, 135

multi-argument methods, 156–157
music
    composing, 29–36
    playing, 33–34
    saving, 36
Musical Instrument Digital Interface
        (MIDI). *See* MIDI
mutation, using, 208–211
myquote macro, in modified interrpreter,
        252–253

∎N
name method, 133
navigation methods, using when drawing,
        69–71
near_positions method, 127
next_map method, indexes advanced
        by, 145
next_player method, indexes advanced
        by, 145
NilClass class, 129
no-argumet methods, 156
node types, drawing images with, 53–55
NoMIDIDestination exception, CoreMIDI
        for OS X, 18
north method, 69
note number, 8
NSApplication, 161
NSButtonCells, 162
    creating a row of, 167–168
NSCell, 162
NSControls, 162
NSImage, loading image with, 186
NSTextView, 166
NSViews, 162
NSWindow, moving creation of to own
        method, 163–164
number method, implementing, 102
number types, deciding between, 268

∎O
object class, 73
Objective-C
    calling from Ruby, 156–157
    learning basics of, 155–156

opening a window and connecting to,
        154–155
    runtime, 153
on_bang method, called by Monitor class,
        42
on_click method, handling clicks with,
        181–183
open method, needed for operating
        systems, 12

∎P
pack method, CoreMIDI for OSX, 19
packet list structure, CoreMIDI for OSX,
        18–19
padding frames, used by ImageMagick, 83
parse method, in Pattern class, 30, 32–33
Parsec parser combinator library, 263
parser, putting to work, 277
parser combinators, library code example,
        263–265
Parsers module, starting from word
        method, 269
ParsersAlias constant, saving a reference
        to Parsers in, 280
parse_sexp, 235–236
parsing
    abstracting string parsing, 276–277
    list comprehensions, 278–290
    lists and discarding return values, 271
    method calls with dot, 282–283
    string literals, 274–276
    values, 270–271
Pattern class, making usable, 30–33
patterns
    breaking into individual characters, 30
    taking further, 35–36
pay! method, 104–106, 110
permuations_of_size method,
        implementing, 113–114
permutations method, adding to
        Enumerable module, 104–105
place method, adding units with, 124–125
PlanetCute tileset
    prototyping games with, 184–191
    web site address, 184
play method, writing metronomes, 26–28

Player class, managing callbacks with, 40–42

player method, current objects returned by, 145

Player objects, loaded in @players, 42

players
adding to a game instance, 145–146
coding simple, 142–143
passing into a game instance, 160
proving you have one, 159–160

point crossovers, implementing, 207

pointers, using in Ruby, 13–15

points attribute, for polygons, 54

polygons, drawing, 54

Portland Ruby Brigade (PDX.rb), 2

Practical Common Lisp, 224

Practical Ruby Projects, introduction, 1–5

present_choice method, 178–179

present_TYPE_choice methods, 178
code for, 183–184
creating, 180–181

"pretty print" module, dumping terrain and units with, 143

price file, reading, 95

prices.txt, list of purchases in, 94

primitive functions, choosing, 236–238

Principles of Compiler Design, 291

program change, 9

Programming Ruby, The Pragmatic Programmer's Guide, 2

proxy class, adding to improve readability, 45

Python code vs. Ruby code, 278

■**Q**

quasiquote (`), in Lisp, 249

quote special form, implementing, 240

quoting, in Lisp, 274

■**R**

Racc, web site address for, 290

random method, defining in Enumerable module, 200

raw API, provided by ALSA, 19

recombination phase, genetic algorithms, 198

recursive descent parsing, 263

Regexp.escape class method, 270

registration methods, code for, 59

regular expressions, parsing symbols with, 268–270

render method, 64–65
rendering frames with, 61–62

renewRows_columns method, 169

rep method, 133, 136
for Matrix class, 128
making choices with, 177–179

reproduce method, 201
choosing an encoding with, 212–214

rep_mapping method, 144

rescue modifier
for mkdir method, 57
used by sum method, 103

rest method, 178
adding to Enumerable module, 104–105
use on Array instance, 32

roulette method, 220–221

roulette selection, implementating, 219–221

Rowlings, J. K., 116–117

rparsec RubyGem, 265

RParsec tool, 263–265
web site address for, 290

Ruby
animating, 51–91
calling Objective-C from, 156–157
community, 2
genetic algorithms in, 197–221
implementing Lisp in, 223–260
interoperating with, 253–256
making Lisp lambda work in, 255–256
opening a window to, 254
parsing with, 262–265
reasons to use, 1–2
setting up, 3–4
web site address for, 3

Ruby bindings, abusing, 289–290

Ruby code vs. Python code, 278

Ruby DL, 9–10

Ruby Extension project, methods provided by, 63

Ruby integers, exploring features of, 203–207

Ruby library, manually adding lines to, 154

RubyCocoa, 153–195
   adding a view, 163–165
   basics of, 153–158
   ChoiceBar, 169–171
   creating row of NSButtonCells, 167–167
   development tools, 195
   displaying messages, 166–167
   drawing the map, 172–176
   handling clicks in, 181–183
   highlighting map locations, 180–181
   installing, 153–154
   making choices, 177–179
   odd way to do things, 161–162
   opening a window, 154–155
   packaging your application, 192–194
   selecting units from map, 180–183
   understanding views, controls, and
      cells, 162
   using image tiles, 184–191
RubyGems
   symbolic expression (sexp), 235–236
   web site address for, 4
run loop, putting together, 43–44
run method, 146–147, 200–201
   calling, 57–58
   that runs forever, 44

■S

s-expressions, parsing, 265–277
Samson, Peter, 7
save method, for writing out MIDI file, 39
Sawyer, Tom, 289
scalable vector graphics (SVG)
   basics, 52
   embedding images in, 55
   node types, 53–55
   rendering the frames, 61–62
   shapes, 52–55
   specification web site, 53
   viewing and debugging images, 56
   W3C drawing standard, 51–55
   wrapping with objects, 64–65
Scheme dialect
   Common Lisp and, 224
   postfixes, 237
seconds_to_delta method, 38–39
Seibel, Peter, 224

selection phase, genetic algorithms, 198
separated prebuilt Parser method, 271
sequencer API, provided by ALSA, 19
sequences, in Pattern class, 31–32
setup method, 169–171
sexp (symbolic expression), 235–236
sexp library, numbers returned by, 236
SExpressionParser module, creating,
      265–266
Shallit, Jeffery, 117
shapes, rectangle defined with SVG, 52–55
Shoot and FirstAid actions, implementing,
      137–139
shortname, calling on Dinosaur class, 133
SimpleSynth application, 16
Simula-67, designed for simulation, 93
simulated annealing algorithms, 197
sleep interval, Timer class, 24
sleep method, implementing, 75–76
Sleeper class, adding to GridDrawer, 76–77
SongPlayer class, using with FileMIDI, 39
songs, playing, 33–34
sort method, 97
SortedSVG container, creating, 78–82
sort_by method, 97
source code, for book, 4
spaceship operator, for cube objects, 79
special forms, 233–235
   using, 240–247
sprintf method, 58
start_choice method, 179
STDIN.each_line, using on REPL, 239
step callback, 59–60
step method, 58, 200
   modifying to let parents live on,
      216–217
string literals, parsing, 274–276
string parsing, abstracting, 276–277
stroke attribute, 53
stroke-width attribute, 53
Struct namespace, subclassing, 279–280
*Structure and Interpretation of Computer
      Programs*, 224, 257
sum method, 102–103
SuperCollider, 7
Sussman, Gerald, 224

SVG (scalable vector graphics). *See* scalable vector graphics (SVG)
<svg>/</svg> tags, 52
SVG wrapper, drawing a cube with, 65–66
SVGObject subclasses, 65
SVGObjects class, creating thin wrapper to represent, 64–65
symbolic expression (sexp), 235–236, 257–258
symbols
  parsing with regular expressions, 268–270
  refresher in Ruby, 224
system test, exercising parser with, 277

■T

TBSView
  adding, 164
  mouseDown(event) method on, 182
Template variable, in ERB, 60–61
tempo tap, using, 34–35
termination phase, genetic algorithms, 199
Terrain class, building, 122
test-driven development
  testing partial implementation, 282
  using for SExpressionParser, 267
The Little Schemer, 257
Thomas, Dave, 2
time, keeping in Ruby, 23–24
time drift, fixing metronomes, 26
Timer, creating for metronome, 26–27
Timer class, 23–24
Timer instances, sharing, 28–29
timers, avoiding too many, 28–29
TiMidity program, connecting ALSA client to, 21–22
TOPLAP, web site address for, 39
to_s method, 103–104, 206
turn method, 147–148
turn-based strategy games
  building a player, 158–161
  building the world around us, 121–129
  building using RubyCocoa, 158–179
  cartography 101, 124–125
  choices interaction in, 120

  choosing among actions, 135
  finding possible moves, 135
  Game class for controlling game, 144–150
  how players interact with, 120
  implementation, 121
  interactions in, 120
  making choices, 133–135
  meeting your heroes, 129–133
  players, 139–142
  putting it all together, 150–151
  representing a map, 128–129
  representing units, 133
  in Ruby, 119–152
  simple computer player, 142–143
  starting the terrain, 122
  strategy for building, 119–121
  stubbing out undefined classes, 132
  taking action, 136–139
  universal skeleton, 129–132
  where terrains come from, 125–127
  writing command-line player, 143–144

■U

Ullman, Jeffrey D., 291
undefined classes, stubbing out, 132
uniform_crossover method, 204–207
Unit class
  adding features for making choices, 133–135
  choosing among actions, 135
  creating player's characters and dinosaurs, 129–133
  finding possible moves, 135
  name and health counter, 129–132
units
  determining friends or enemies, 131
  in turn-based strategy games, 120
  keeping track of turns, 131
  programming for injuries to, 130
  representing, 133
unit_choices method, BasePlayer class, 140
unpack method, 213–214
user-defined special forms, in Lisp, 247

■V

variable keyword arguments, emulating in method call, 72
view, adding, 163–165
views, controls, and cells, understanding, 162

■W

web site addresses
"A Genetic Algorithm Tutorial" paper, 221
DarwinPorts tool, 153
ImageMagick utility, 62
Lisp FAQs, 236
log2 method information, 206
Perl, 22
PlanetCute tileset, 184
Racc, 290
RParsec tool, 290
Ruby, 3
RubyGems, 4
RubyCocoa, 153
RubyCocoa resources, 195
Ruby simulation information, 118
SimpleSynth application, 16
SVG specification, 53
TOPLAP, 39
weighted_ranges method, 220
Whitley, Darrell, 221
windows, applications and, 157–158
within? method, 127
wizard money, 116–117

■XYZ

XLink namespace, 52

forums.apress.com
FOR PROFESSIONALS BY PROFESSIONALS™

JOIN THE APRESS FORUMS AND BE PART OF OUR COMMUNITY. You'll find discussions that cover topics of interest to IT professionals, programmers, and enthusiasts just like you. If you post a query to one of our forums, you can expect that some of the best minds in the business—especially Apress authors, who all write with *The Expert's Voice™*—will chime in to help you. Why not aim to become one of our most valuable participants (MVPs) and win cool stuff? Here's a sampling of what you'll find:

DATABASES
Data drives everything.

Share information, exchange ideas, and discuss any database programming or administration issues.

INTERNET TECHNOLOGIES AND NETWORKING
Try living without plumbing (and eventually IPv6).

Talk about networking topics including protocols, design, administration, wireless, wired, storage, backup, certifications, trends, and new technologies.

JAVA
We've come a long way from the old Oak tree.

Hang out and discuss Java in whatever flavor you choose: J2SE, J2EE, J2ME, Jakarta, and so on.

MAC OS X
All about the Zen of OS X.

OS X is both the present and the future for Mac apps. Make suggestions, offer up ideas, or boast about your new hardware.

OPEN SOURCE
Source code is good; understanding (open) source is better.

Discuss open source technologies and related topics such as PHP, MySQL, Linux, Perl, Apache, Python, and more.

PROGRAMMING/BUSINESS
Unfortunately, it is.

Talk about the Apress line of books that cover software methodology, best practices, and how programmers interact with the "suits."

WEB DEVELOPMENT/DESIGN
Ugly doesn't cut it anymore, and CGI is absurd.

Help is in sight for your site. Find design solutions for your projects and get ideas for building an interactive Web site.

SECURITY
Lots of bad guys out there—the good guys need help.

Discuss computer and network security issues here. Just don't let anyone else know the answers!

TECHNOLOGY IN ACTION
Cool things. Fun things.

It's after hours. It's time to play. Whether you're into LEGO® MINDSTORMS™ or turning an old PC into a DVR, this is where technology turns into fun.

WINDOWS
No defenestration here.

Ask questions about all aspects of Windows programming, get help on Microsoft technologies covered in Apress books, or provide feedback on any Apress Windows book.

HOW TO PARTICIPATE:
Go to the Apress Forums site at **http://forums.apress.com/**.
Click the New User link.

You Need the Companion eBook

Your purchase of this book entitles you to buy the companion PDF-version eBook for only $10. Take the weightless companion with you anywhere.

We believe this Apress title will prove so indispensable that you'll want to carry it with you everywhere, which is why we are offering the companion eBook (in PDF format) for $10 to customers who purchase this book now. Convenient and fully searchable, the PDF version of any content-rich, page-heavy Apress book makes a valuable addition to your programming library. You can easily find and copy code—or perform examples by quickly toggling between instructions and the application. Even simultaneously tackling a donut, diet soda, and complex code becomes simplified with hands-free eBooks!

Once you purchase your book, getting the $10 companion eBook is simple:

❶ Visit **www.apress.com/promo/tendollars/**.

❷ Complete a basic registration form to receive a randomly generated question about this title.

❸ Answer the question correctly in 60 seconds, and you will receive a promotional code to redeem for the $10.00 eBook.

2855 Telegraph Avenue • Suite 600 • Berkeley, CA 94705

eBookshop

Offer valid through 6/10/08.